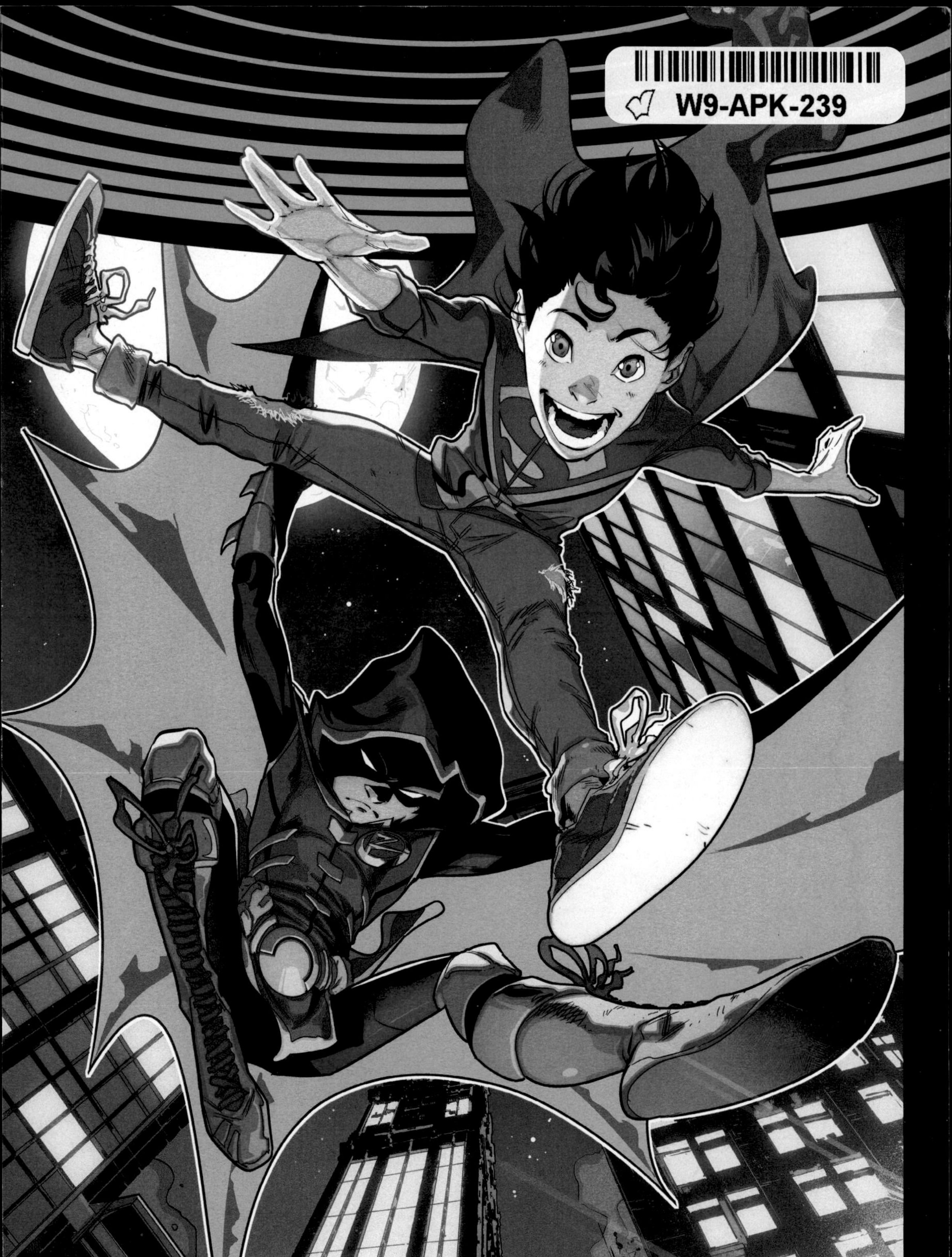

SUPER SONS

VOL.2 PLANET OF THE CAPES

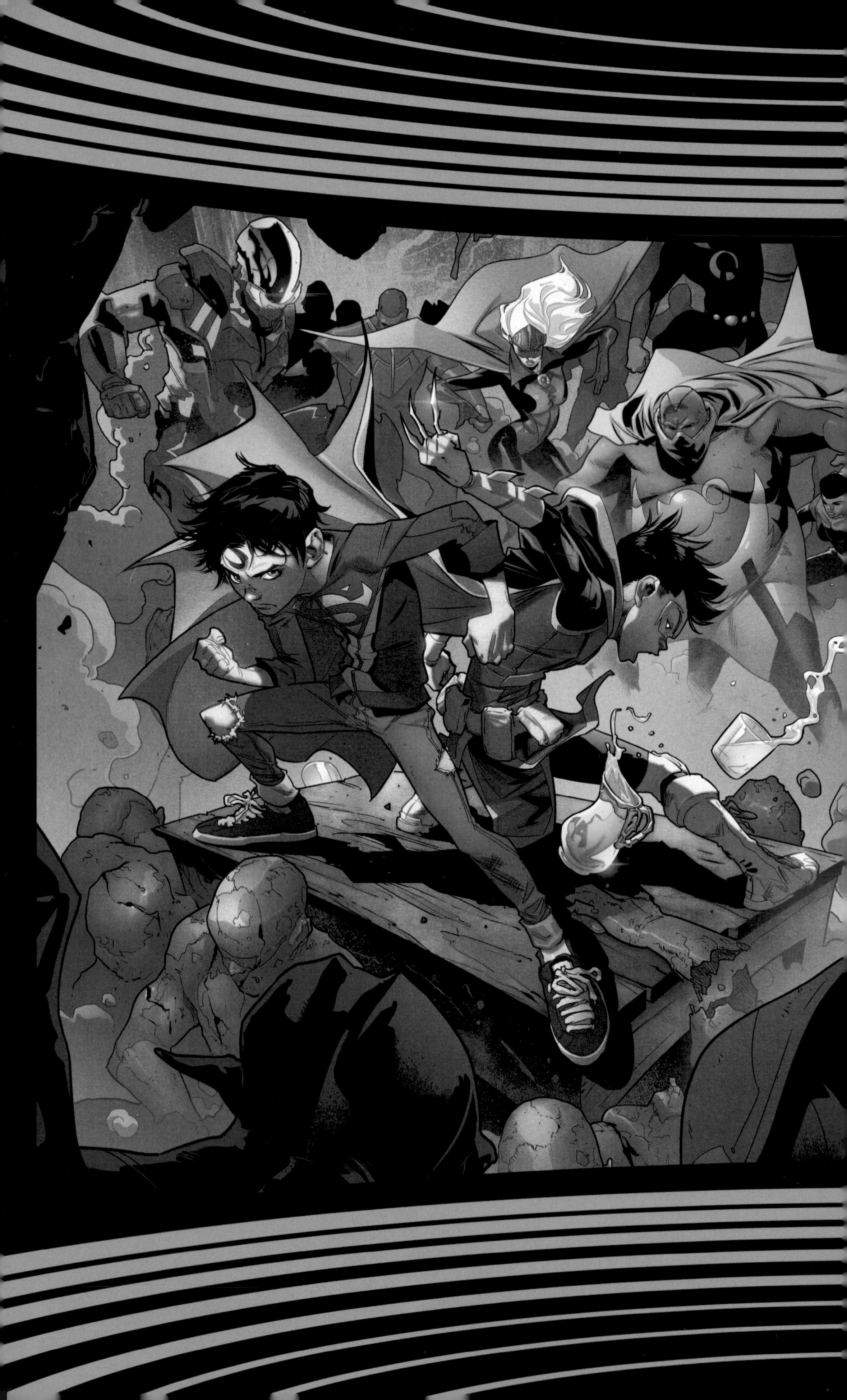

SUPER SONS
VOL.2 PLANET OF THE CAPES

PETER J. TOMASI
writer

JORGE JIMENEZ
CARMINE DI GIANDOMENICO * JOSÉ LUÍS * SCOTT HANNA
artists

ALEJANDRO SANCHEZ
IVAN PLASCENCIA * HI-FI
colorists

ROB LEIGH
ALW'S DAVE
letterers

JORGE JIMENEZ & ALEJANDRO SANCHEZ
series and collection cover artists

SUPERMAN created by **JERRY SIEGEL** and **JOE SHUSTER**
By special arrangement with the **JERRY SIEGEL** family
SUPERBOY created by **JERRY SIEGEL**
By special arrangement with the **JERRY SIEGEL** family

PAUL KAMINSKI EDDIE BERGANZA Editors - Original Series * **ANDREA SHEA** Associate Editor - Original Series
JEB WOODARD Group Editor - Collected Editions * **ALEX GALER** Editor - Collected Edition
STEVE COOK Design Director - Books * **MONIQUE NARBONETA** Publication Design

BOB HARRAS Senior VP - Editor-in-Chief, DC Comics
PAT McCALLUM Executive Editor, DC Comics

DIANE NELSON President * **DAN DiDIO** Publisher * **JIM LEE** Publisher * **GEOFF JOHNS** President & Chief Creative Officer
AMIT DESAI Executive VP - Business & Marketing Strategy, Direct to Consumer & Global Franchise Management
SAM ADES Senior VP & General Manager, Digital Services * **BOBBIE CHASE** VP & Executive Editor, Young Reader & Talent Development
MARK CHIARELLO Senior VP - Art, Design & Collected Editions * **JOHN CUNNINGHAM** Senior VP - Sales & Trade Marketing
ANNE DePIES Senior VP - Business Strategy, Finance & Administration * **DON FALLETTI** VP - Manufacturing Operations
LAWRENCE GANEM VP - Editorial Administration & Talent Relations * **ALISON GILL** Senior VP - Manufacturing & Operations
HANK KANALZ Senior VP - Editorial Strategy & Administration * **JAY KOGAN** VP - Legal Affairs * **JACK MAHAN** VP - Business Affairs
NICK J. NAPOLITANO VP - Manufacturing Administration * **EDDIE SCANNELL** VP - Consumer Marketing
COURTNEY SIMMONS Senior VP - Publicity & Communications * **JIM (SKI) SOKOLOWSKI** VP - Comic Book Specialty Sales & Trade Marketing
NANCY SPEARS VP - Mass, Book, Digital Sales & Trade Marketing * **MICHELE R. WELLS** VP - Content Strategy

SUPER SONS VOL. 2: PLANET OF THE CAPES

DC Comics, 2900 West Alameda Ave., Burbank, CA 91505
Printed by LSC Communications, Kendallville, IN, USA. 2/2/18. First Printing.
ISBN: 978-1-4012-7846-5

Library of Congress Cataloging-in-Publication Data is available.

PEFC Certified
Printed on paper from sustainably managed forests, controlled sources
PEFC
PEFC/29-31-337
www.pefc.org

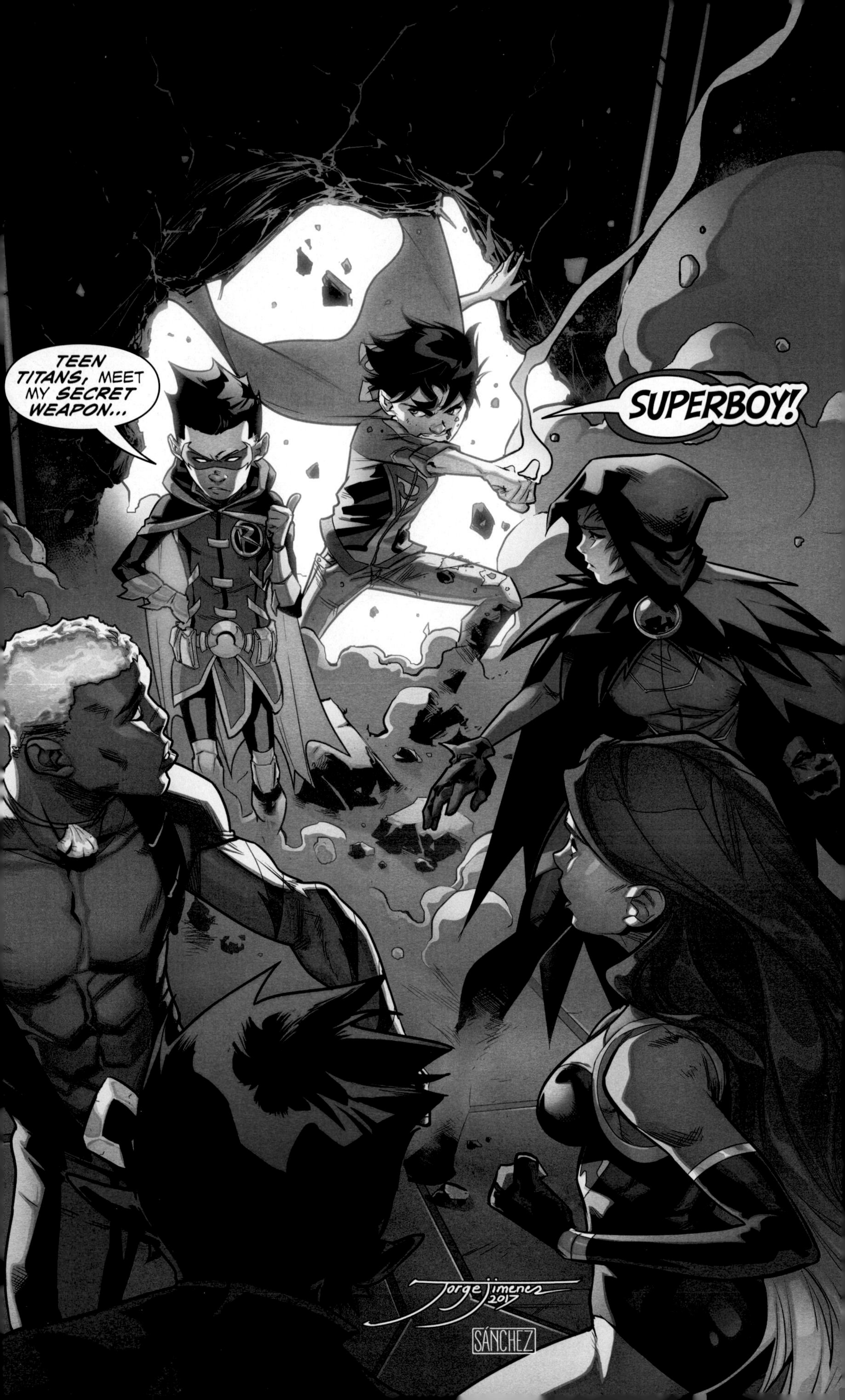
TEEN TITANS, MEET MY SECRET WEAPON...
SUPERBOY!
Jorge Jimenez 2017
SÁNCHEZ

The mud of a dead Multiverse.

Crafted and shaped into quasi-life by my slowly decaying hands.

Hands that, until now, had only known arthritic failure time and again.

This earthen gift from the other, counter-_me_...this is my _rebirth,_ a new life's work.

When my time passes, I will never be remembered.

But my new life's work...?

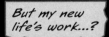

They will never be _forgotten._

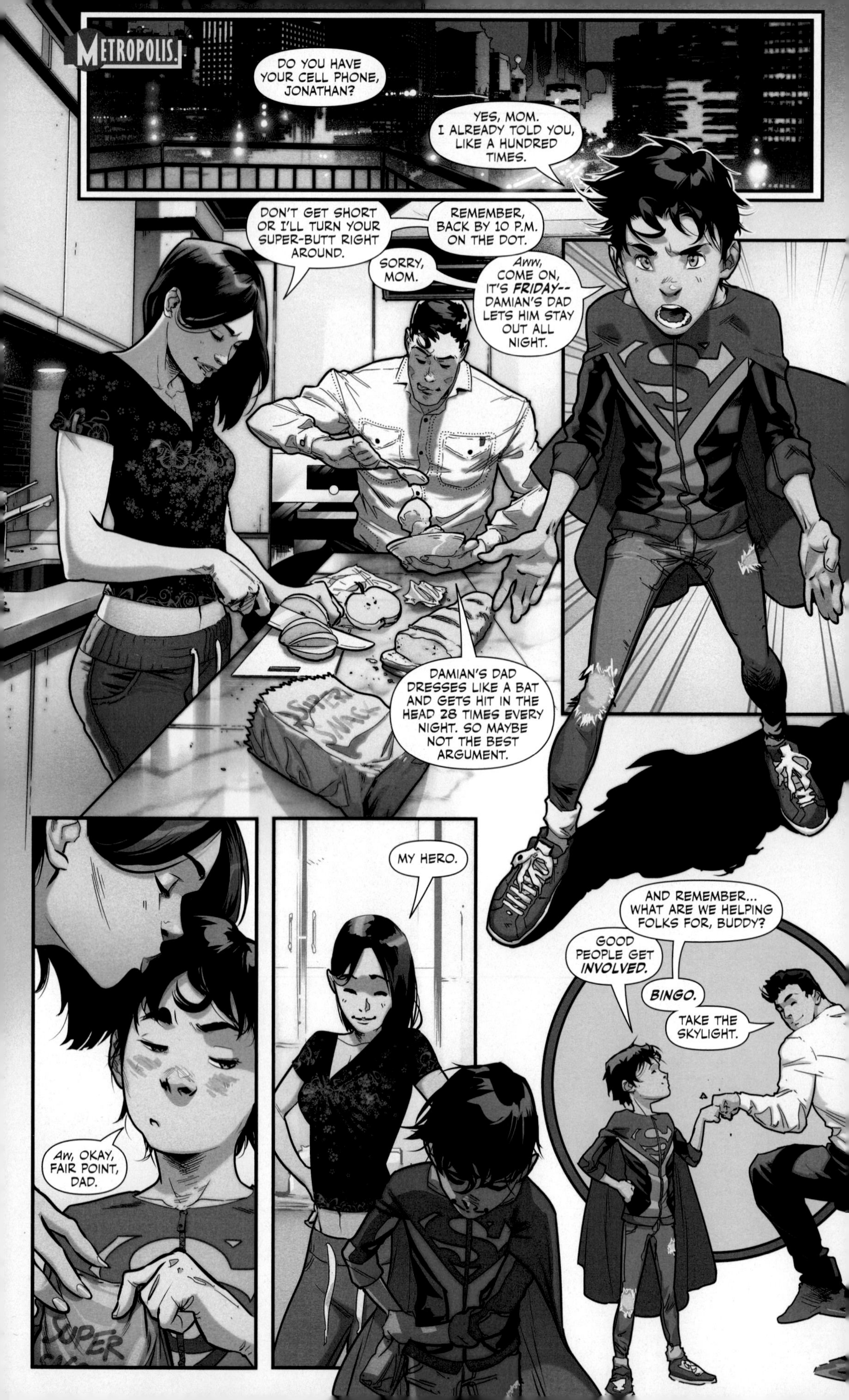
METROPOLIS.
DO YOU HAVE YOUR CELL PHONE, JONATHAN?
YES, MOM. I ALREADY TOLD YOU, LIKE A HUNDRED TIMES.
DON'T GET SHORT OR I'LL TURN YOUR SUPER-BUTT RIGHT AROUND.
REMEMBER, BACK BY 10 P.M. ON THE DOT.
SORRY, MOM.
AWW, COME ON, IT'S FRIDAY-- DAMIAN'S DAD LETS HIM STAY OUT ALL NIGHT.
DAMIAN'S DAD DRESSES LIKE A BAT AND GETS HIT IN THE HEAD 28 TIMES EVERY NIGHT. SO MAYBE NOT THE BEST ARGUMENT.
AW, OKAY, FAIR POINT, DAD.
MY HERO.
AND REMEMBER... WHAT ARE WE HELPING FOLKS FOR, BUDDY?
GOOD PEOPLE GET INVOLVED.
BINGO.
TAKE THE SKYLIGHT.

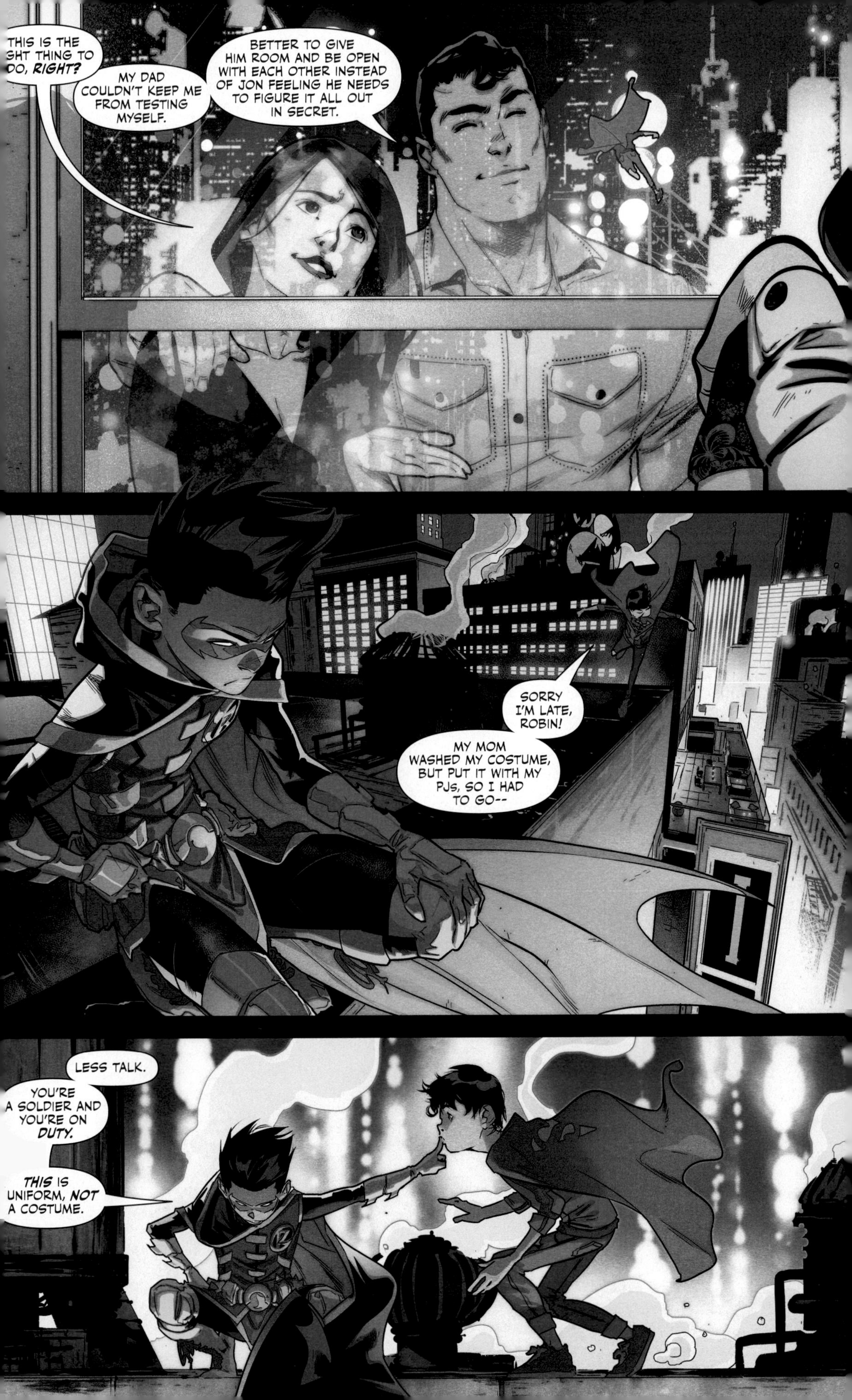

THIS IS THE
GHT THING TO
DO, RIGHT?
MY DAD COULDN'T KEEP ME FROM TESTING MYSELF.
BETTER TO GIVE HIM ROOM AND BE OPEN WITH EACH OTHER INSTEAD OF JON FEELING HE NEEDS TO FIGURE IT ALL OUT IN SECRET.
SORRY I'M LATE, ROBIN!
MY MOM WASHED MY COSTUME, BUT PUT IT WITH MY PJs, SO I HAD TO GO--
LESS TALK.
YOU'RE A SOLDIER AND YOU'RE ON DUTY.
THIS IS UNIFORM, NOT A COSTUME.

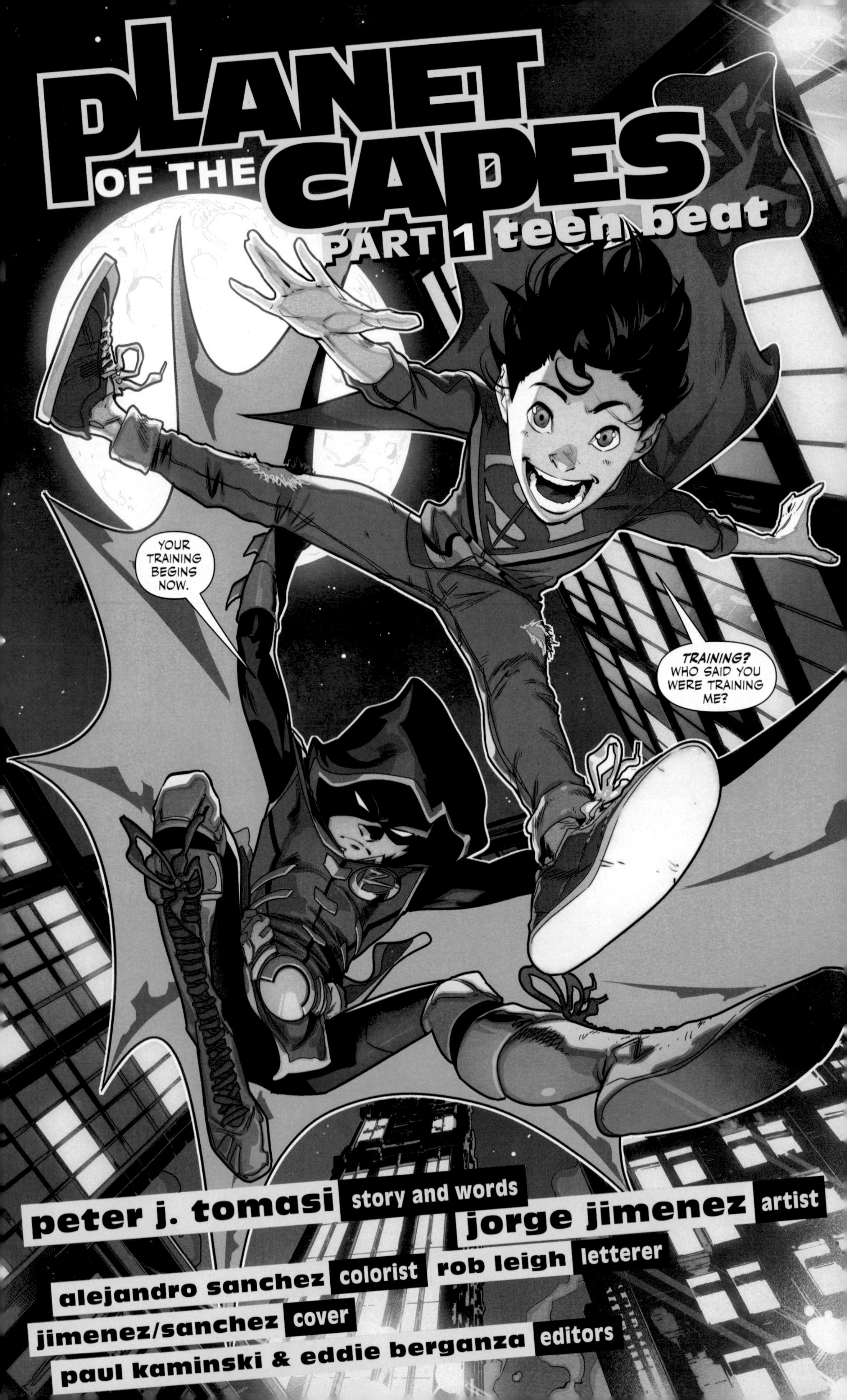
PLANET OF THE CAPES
PART 1 teen beat
YOUR TRAINING BEGINS NOW.
TRAINING? WHO SAID YOU WERE TRAINING ME?
peter j. tomasi story and words
jorge jimenez artist
alejandro sanchez colorist
rob leigh letterer
jimenez/sanchez cover
paul kaminski & eddie berganza editors

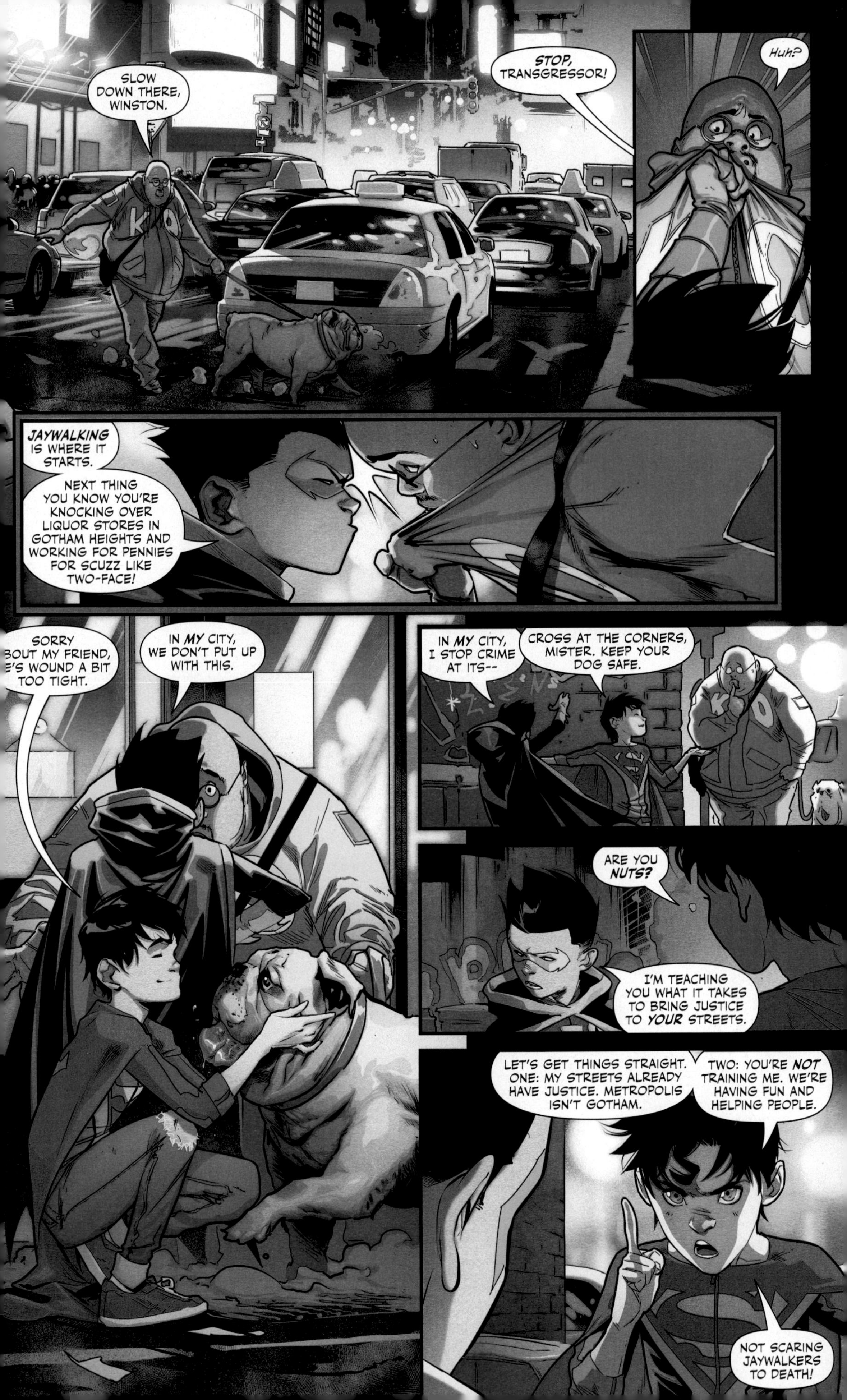
SLOW DOWN THERE, WINSTON.
STOP, TRANSGRESSOR!
Huh?
JAYWALKING IS WHERE IT STARTS.
NEXT THING YOU KNOW YOU'RE KNOCKING OVER LIQUOR STORES IN GOTHAM HEIGHTS AND WORKING FOR PENNIES FOR SCUZZ LIKE TWO-FACE!
SORRY BOUT MY FRIEND, E'S WOUND A BIT TOO TIGHT.
IN MY CITY, WE DON'T PUT UP WITH THIS.
IN MY CITY, I STOP CRIME AT ITS--
CROSS AT THE CORNERS, MISTER. KEEP YOUR DOG SAFE.
ARE YOU NUTS?
I'M TEACHING YOU WHAT IT TAKES TO BRING JUSTICE TO YOUR STREETS.
LET'S GET THINGS STRAIGHT. ONE: MY STREETS ALREADY HAVE JUSTICE. METROPOLIS ISN'T GOTHAM.
TWO: YOU'RE NOT TRAINING ME. WE'RE HAVING FUN AND HELPING PEOPLE.
NOT SCARING JAYWALKERS TO DEATH!

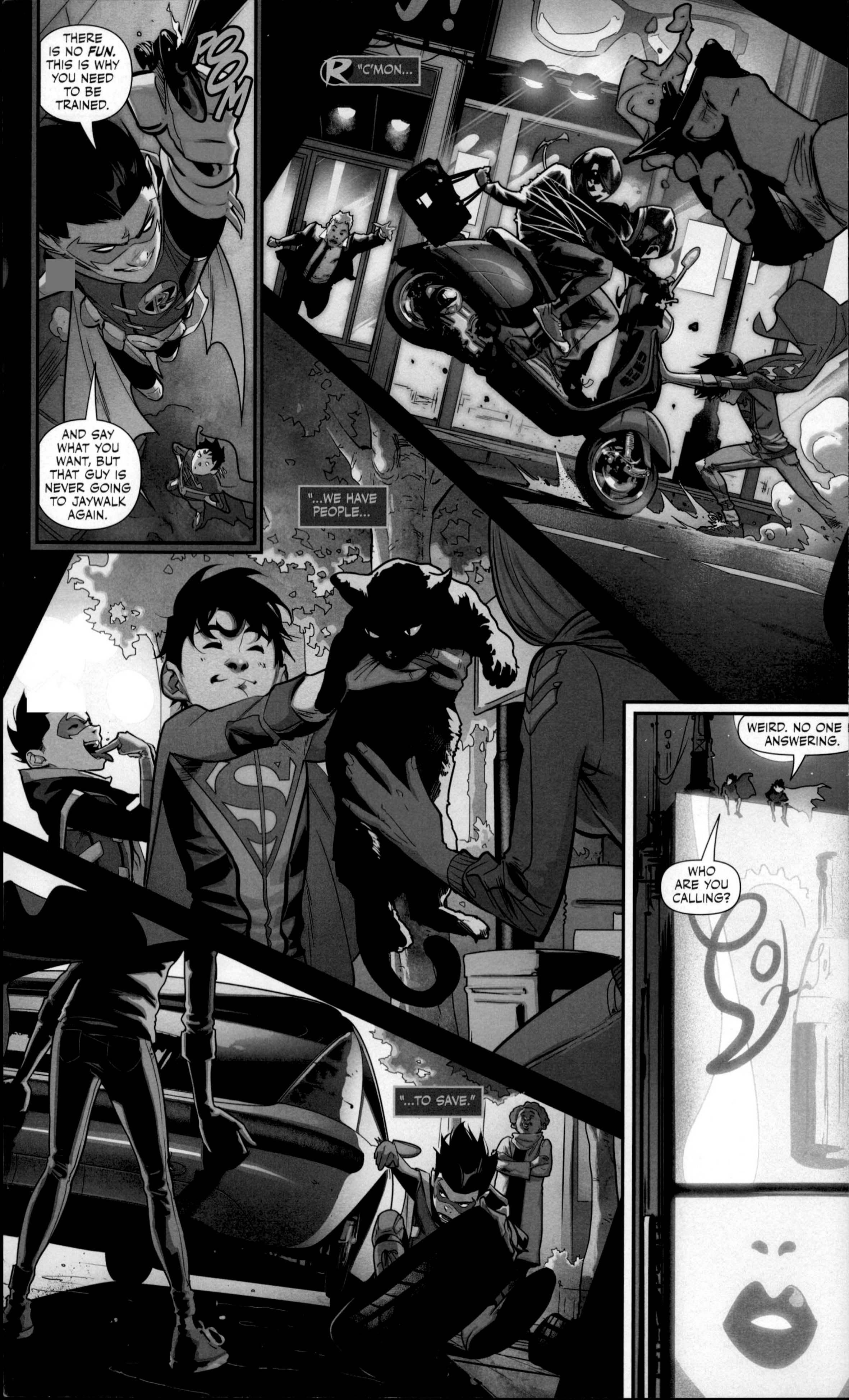
THERE IS NO FUN. THIS IS WHY YOU NEED TO BE TRAINED.
FOOM
AND SAY WHAT YOU WANT, BUT THAT GUY IS NEVER GOING TO JAYWALK AGAIN.
"C'MON...
"...WE HAVE PEOPLE...
"...TO SAVE."
WEIRD. NO ONE ANSWERING.
WHO ARE YOU CALLING?

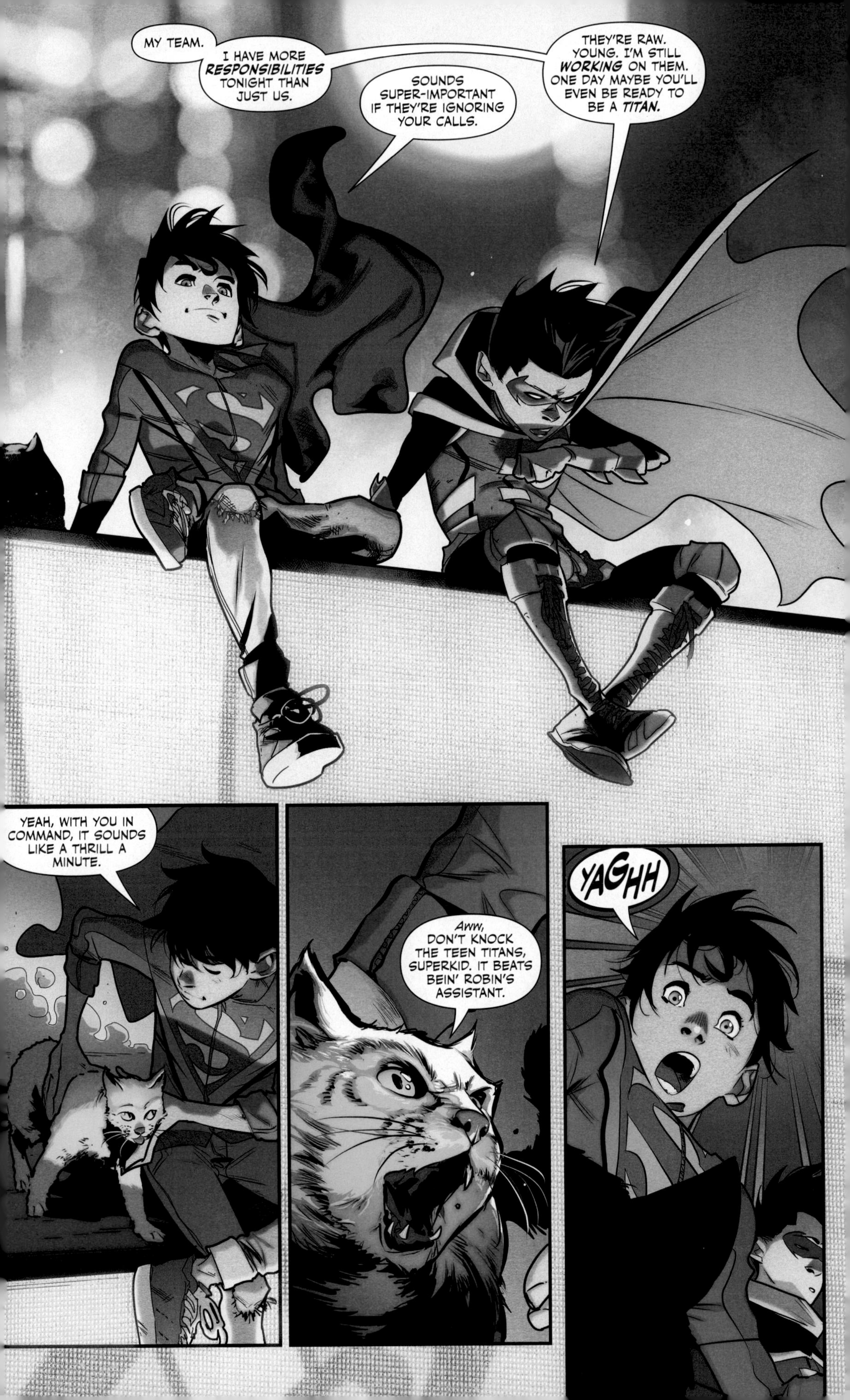
MY TEAM.
I HAVE MORE *RESPONSIBILITIES* TONIGHT THAN JUST US.
SOUNDS SUPER-IMPORTANT IF THEY'RE IGNORING YOUR CALLS.
THEY'RE RAW. YOUNG. I'M STILL *WORKING* ON THEM. ONE DAY MAYBE YOU'LL EVEN BE READY TO BE A *TITAN.*
YEAH, WITH YOU IN COMMAND, IT SOUNDS LIKE A THRILL A MINUTE.
AWW, DON'T KNOCK THE TEEN TITANS, SUPERKID. IT BEATS BEIN' ROBIN'S ASSISTANT.
YAGHH

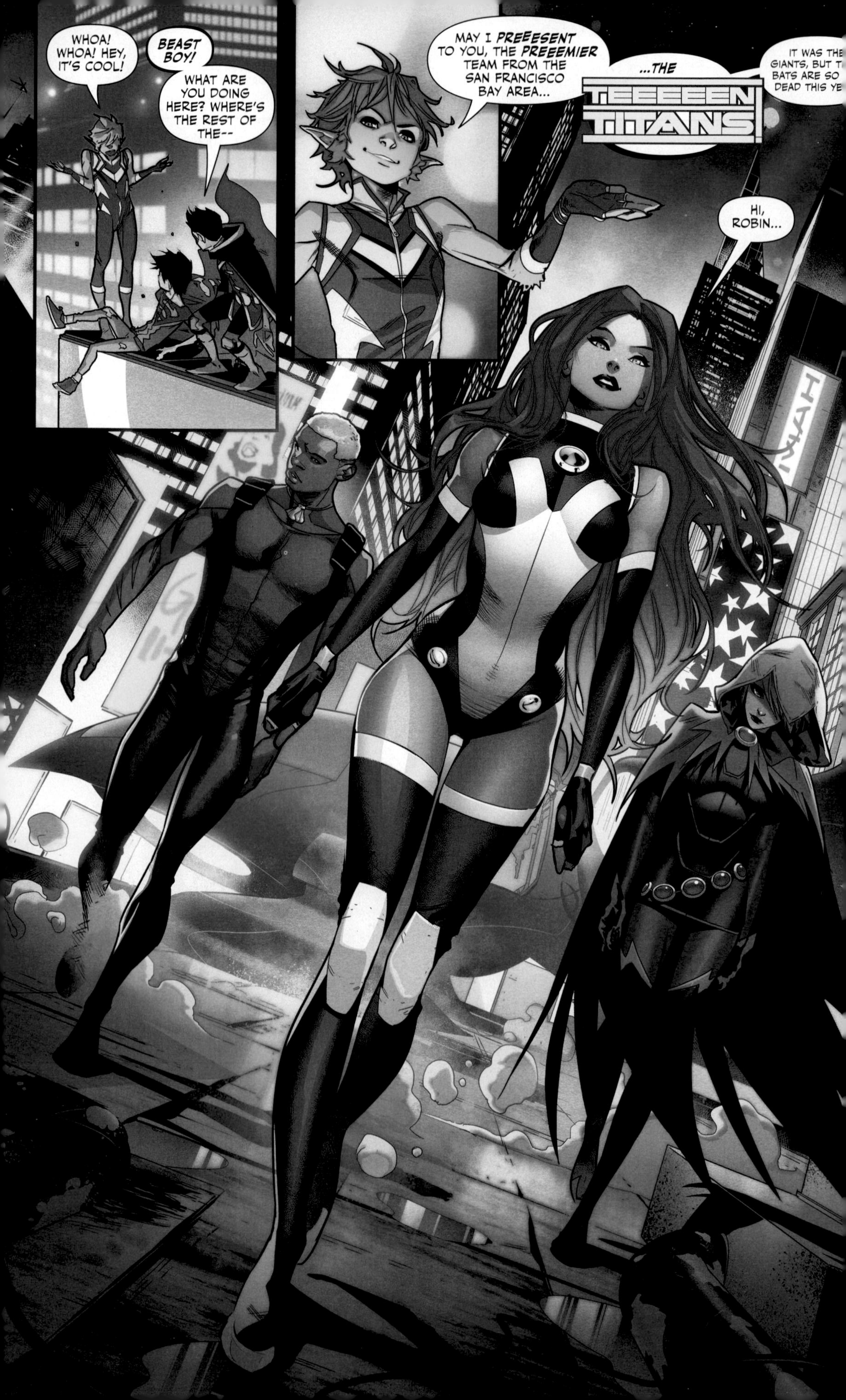
WHOA! WHOA! HEY, IT'S COOL!
BEAST BOY!
WHAT ARE YOU DOING HERE? WHERE'S THE REST OF THE--
MAY I PREEESENT TO YOU, THE PREEEMIER TEAM FROM THE SAN FRANCISCO BAY AREA...
...THE TEEEEEN TITANS!
IT WAS THE GIANTS, BUT T BATS ARE SO DEAD THIS YE
HI, ROBIN...

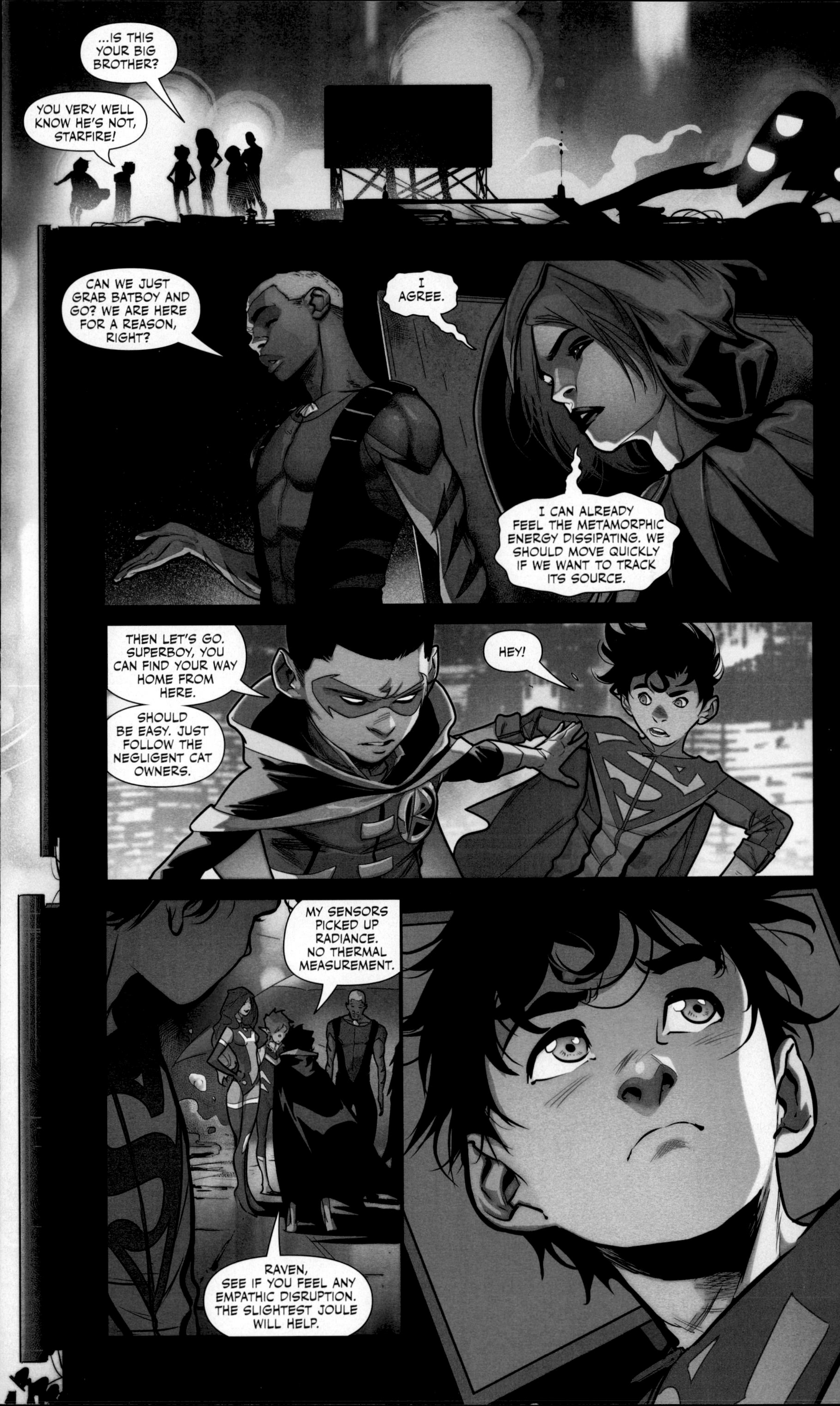

...IS THIS YOUR BIG BROTHER?
YOU VERY WELL KNOW HE'S NOT, STARFIRE!
CAN WE JUST GRAB BATBOY AND GO? WE ARE HERE FOR A REASON, RIGHT?
I AGREE.
I CAN ALREADY FEEL THE METAMORPHIC ENERGY DISSIPATING. WE SHOULD MOVE QUICKLY IF WE WANT TO TRACK ITS SOURCE.
THEN LET'S GO. SUPERBOY, YOU CAN FIND YOUR WAY HOME FROM HERE.
SHOULD BE EASY. JUST FOLLOW THE NEGLIGENT CAT OWNERS.
HEY!
MY SENSORS PICKED UP RADIANCE. NO THERMAL MEASUREMENT.
RAVEN, SEE IF YOU FEEL ANY EMPATHIC DISRUPTION. THE SLIGHTEST JOULE WILL HELP.

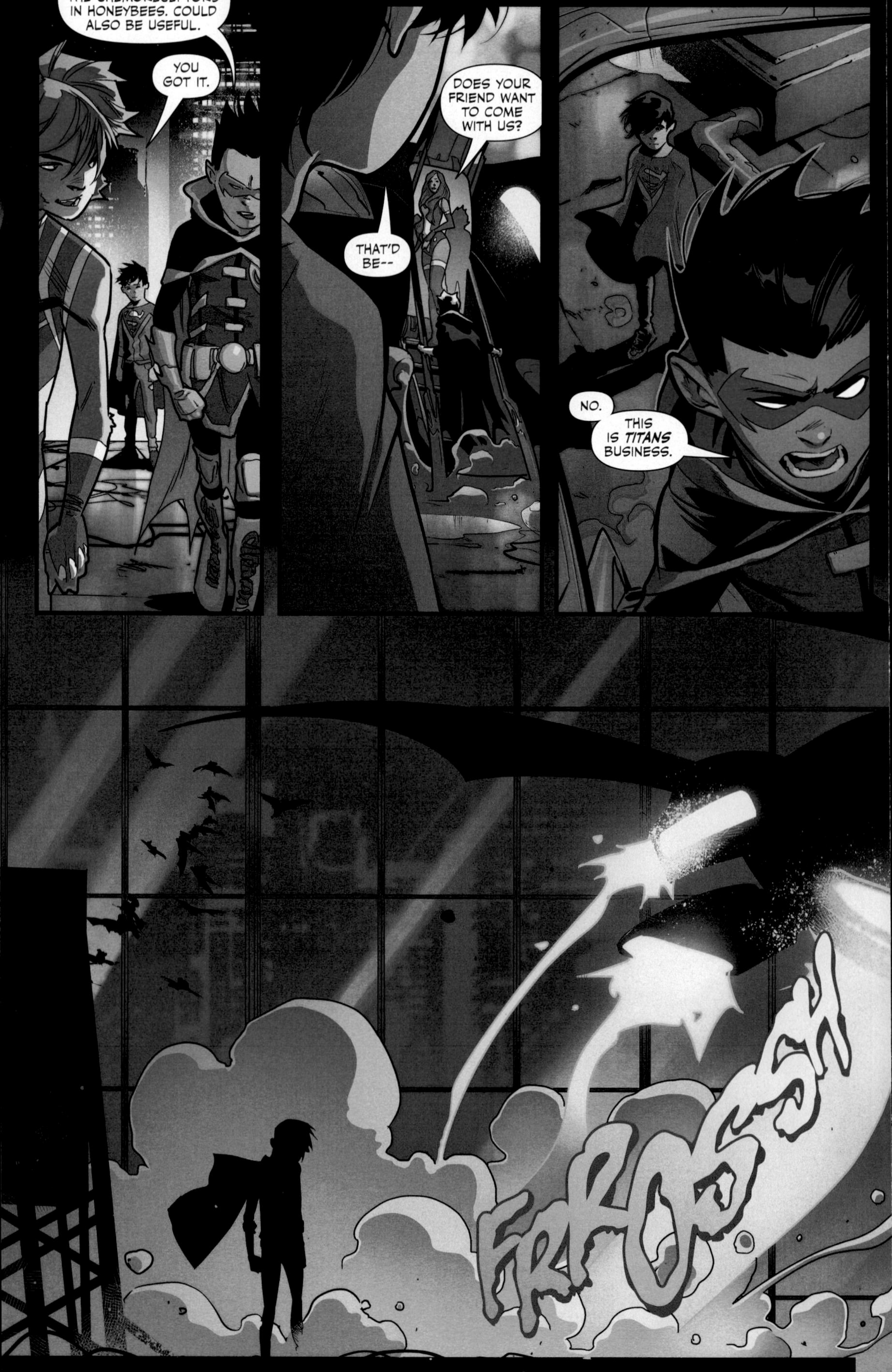
BEAST BOY, I TOLD YOU ABOUT THE CHEMORECEPTORS IN HONEYBEES. COULD ALSO BE USEFUL.
YOU GOT IT.
DOES YOUR FRIEND WANT TO COME WITH US?
THAT'D BE--
NO.
THIS IS *TITANS* BUSINESS.
FRROSSSH

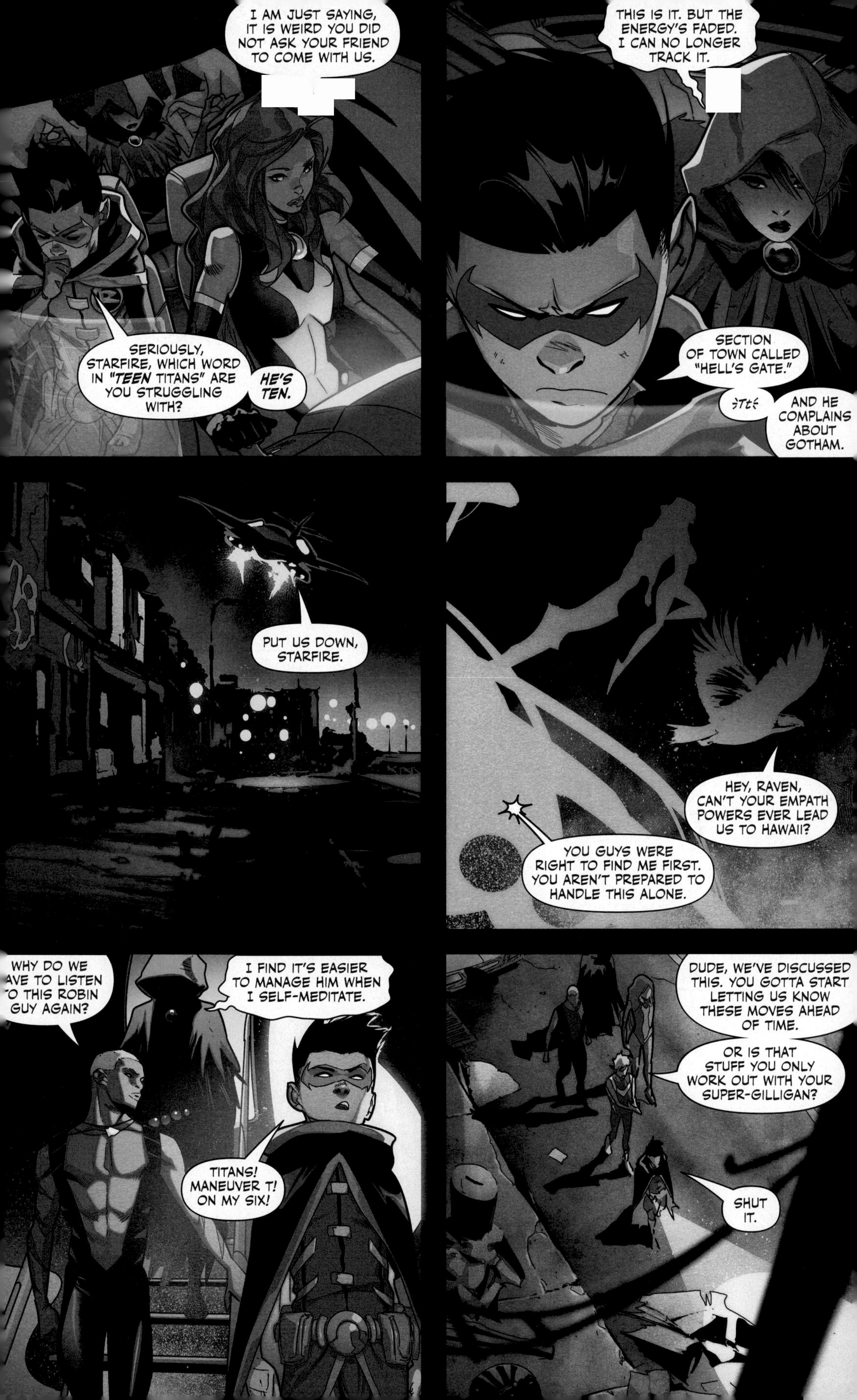
I AM JUST SAYING, IT IS WEIRD YOU DID NOT ASK YOUR FRIEND TO COME WITH US.
SERIOUSLY, STARFIRE, WHICH WORD IN "TEEN TITANS" ARE YOU STRUGGLING WITH?
HE'S TEN.
THIS IS IT. BUT THE ENERGY'S FADED. I CAN NO LONGER TRACK IT.
SECTION OF TOWN CALLED "HELL'S GATE."
AND HE COMPLAINS ABOUT GOTHAM.
PUT US DOWN, STARFIRE.
HEY, RAVEN, CAN'T YOUR EMPATH POWERS EVER LEAD US TO HAWAII?
YOU GUYS WERE RIGHT TO FIND ME FIRST. YOU AREN'T PREPARED TO HANDLE THIS ALONE.
WHY DO WE AVE TO LISTEN O THIS ROBIN GUY AGAIN?
I FIND IT'S EASIER TO MANAGE HIM WHEN I SELF-MEDITATE.
TITANS! MANEUVER T! ON MY SIX!
DUDE, WE'VE DISCUSSED THIS. YOU GOTTA START LETTING US KNOW THESE MOVES AHEAD OF TIME.
OR IS THAT STUFF YOU ONLY WORK OUT WITH YOUR SUPER-GILLIGAN?
SHUT IT.

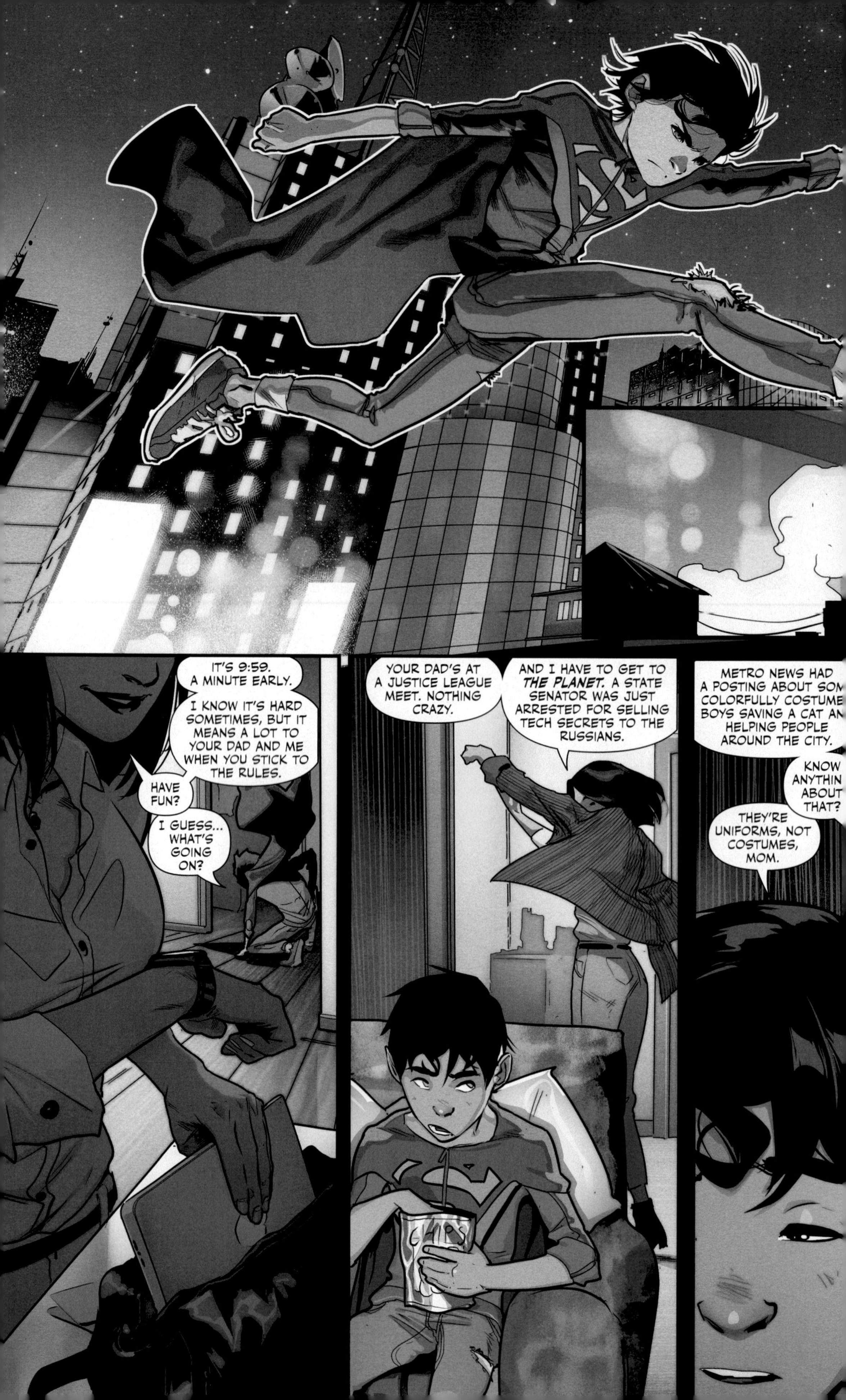
IT'S 9:59. A MINUTE EARLY.
I KNOW IT'S HARD SOMETIMES, BUT IT MEANS A LOT TO YOUR DAD AND ME WHEN YOU STICK TO THE RULES.
HAVE FUN?
I GUESS... WHAT'S GOING ON?
YOUR DAD'S AT A JUSTICE LEAGUE MEET. NOTHING CRAZY.
AND I HAVE TO GET TO *THE PLANET.* A STATE SENATOR WAS JUST ARRESTED FOR SELLING TECH SECRETS TO THE RUSSIANS.
METRO NEWS HAD A POSTING ABOUT SOM COLORFULLY COSTUME BOYS SAVING A CAT AN HELPING PEOPLE AROUND THE CITY.
KNOW ANYTHIN ABOUT THAT?
THEY'RE UNIFORMS, NOT COSTUMES, MOM.

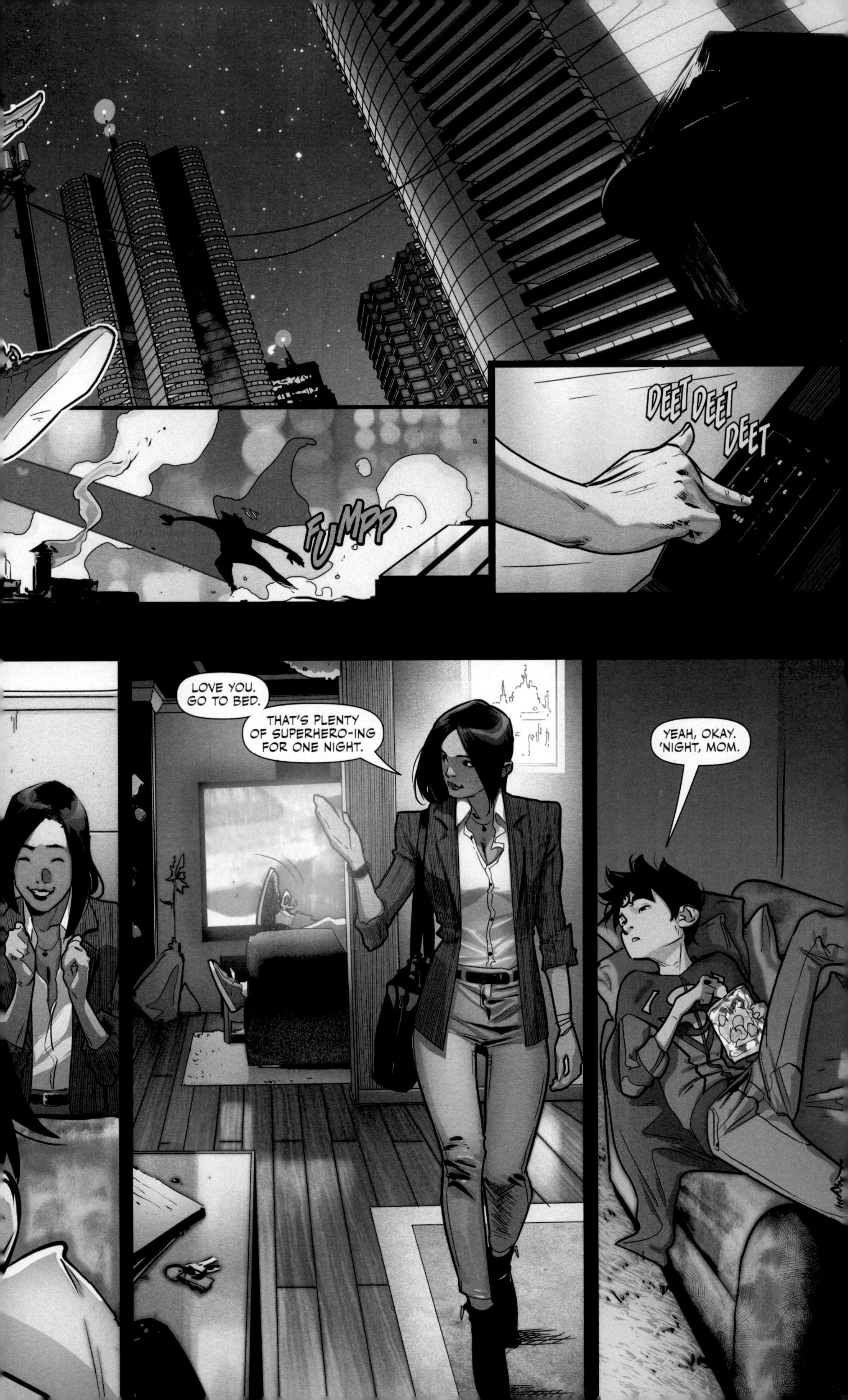
FUMPP
DEET DEET DEET
LOVE YOU. GO TO BED.
THAT'S PLENTY OF SUPERHERO-ING FOR ONE NIGHT.
YEAH, OKAY. 'NIGHT, MOM.

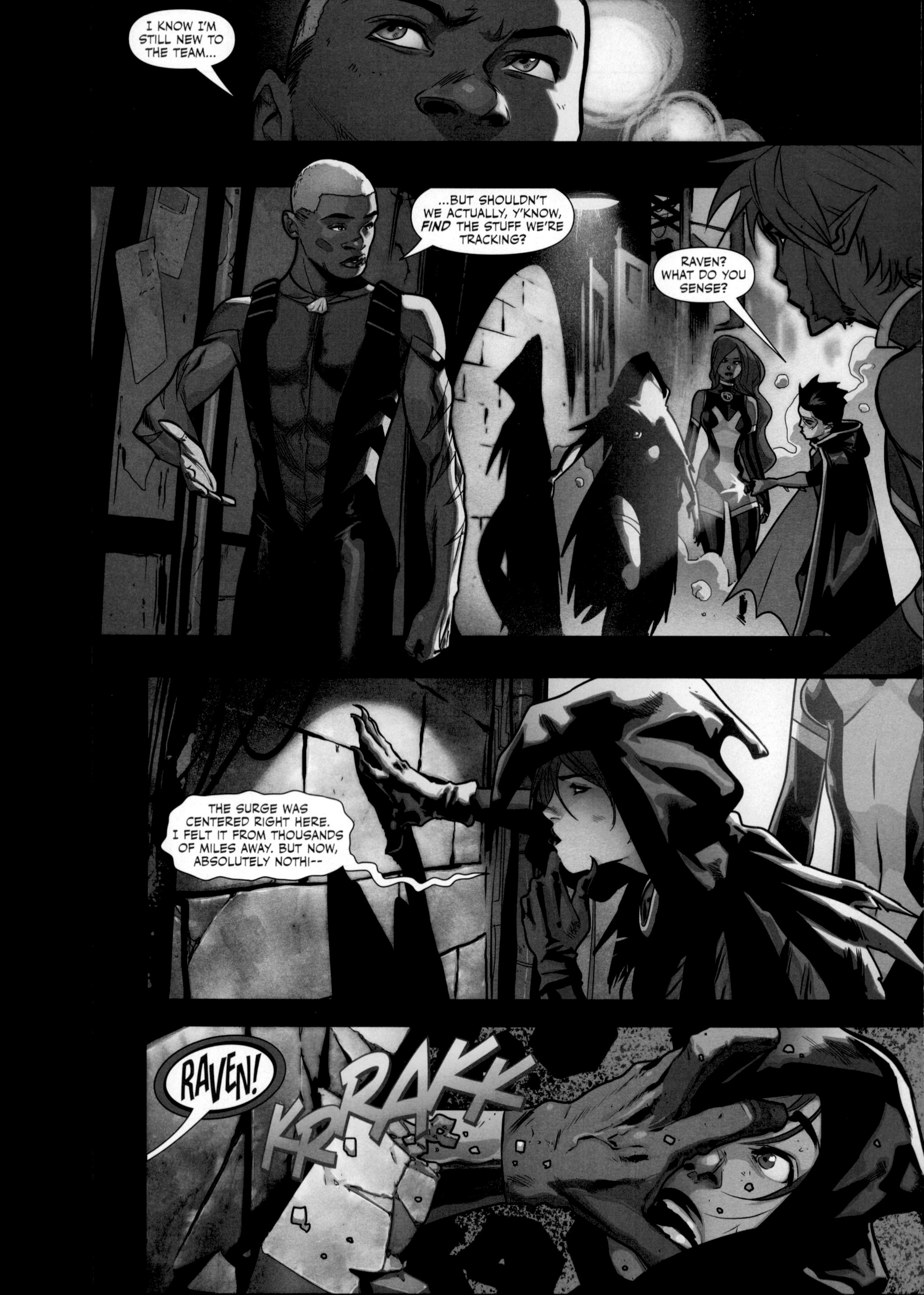

I KNOW I'M STILL NEW TO THE TEAM...
...BUT SHOULDN'T WE ACTUALLY, Y'KNOW, *FIND* THE STUFF WE'RE TRACKING?
RAVEN? WHAT DO YOU SENSE?
THE SURGE WAS CENTERED RIGHT HERE. I FELT IT FROM THOUSANDS OF MILES AWAY. BUT NOW, ABSOLUTELY NOTHI--
RAVEN!
KRRAKK

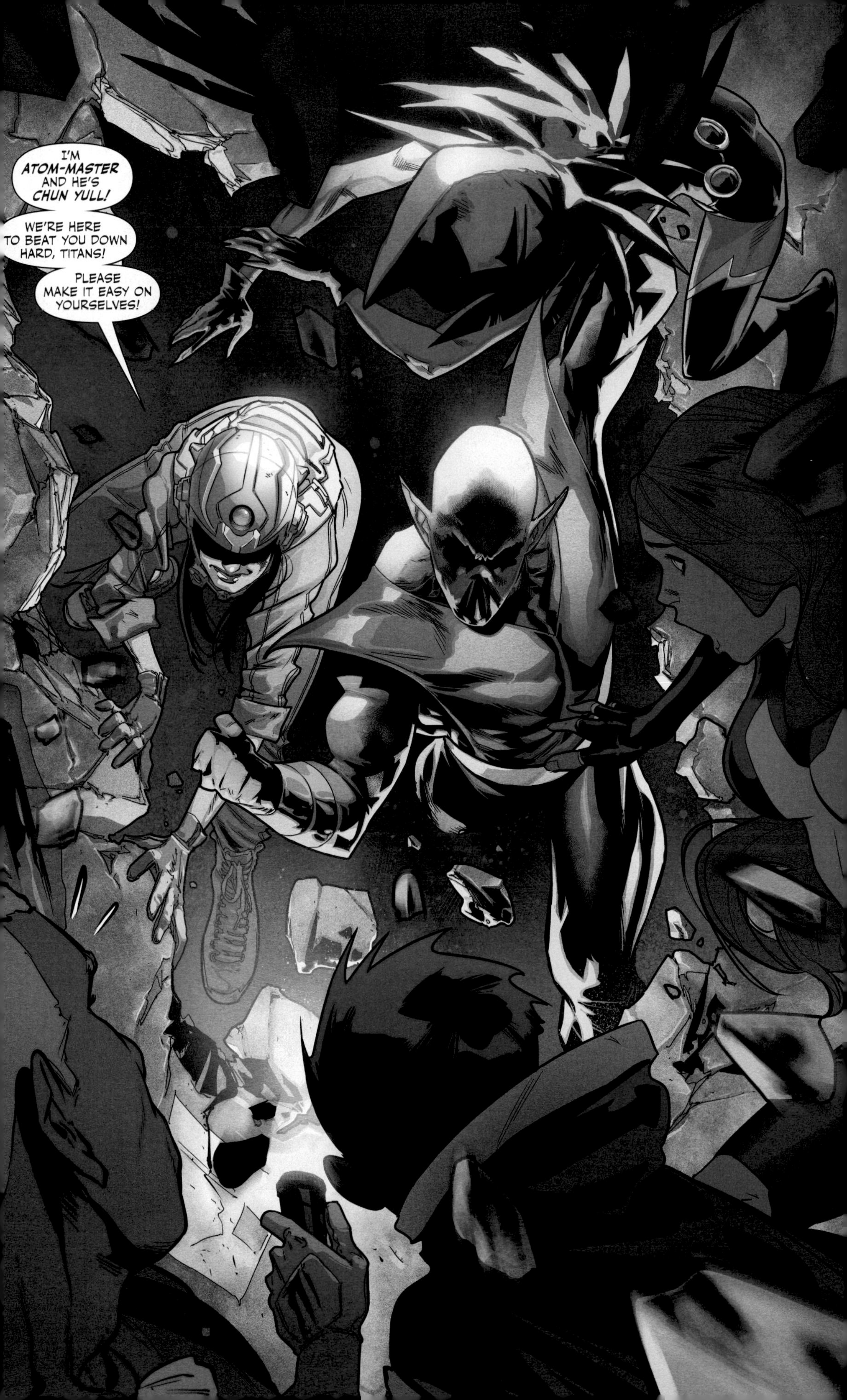
I'M ATOM-MASTER AND HE'S CHUN YULL!
WE'RE HERE TO BEAT YOU DOWN HARD, TITANS!
PLEASE MAKE IT EASY ON YOURSELVES!

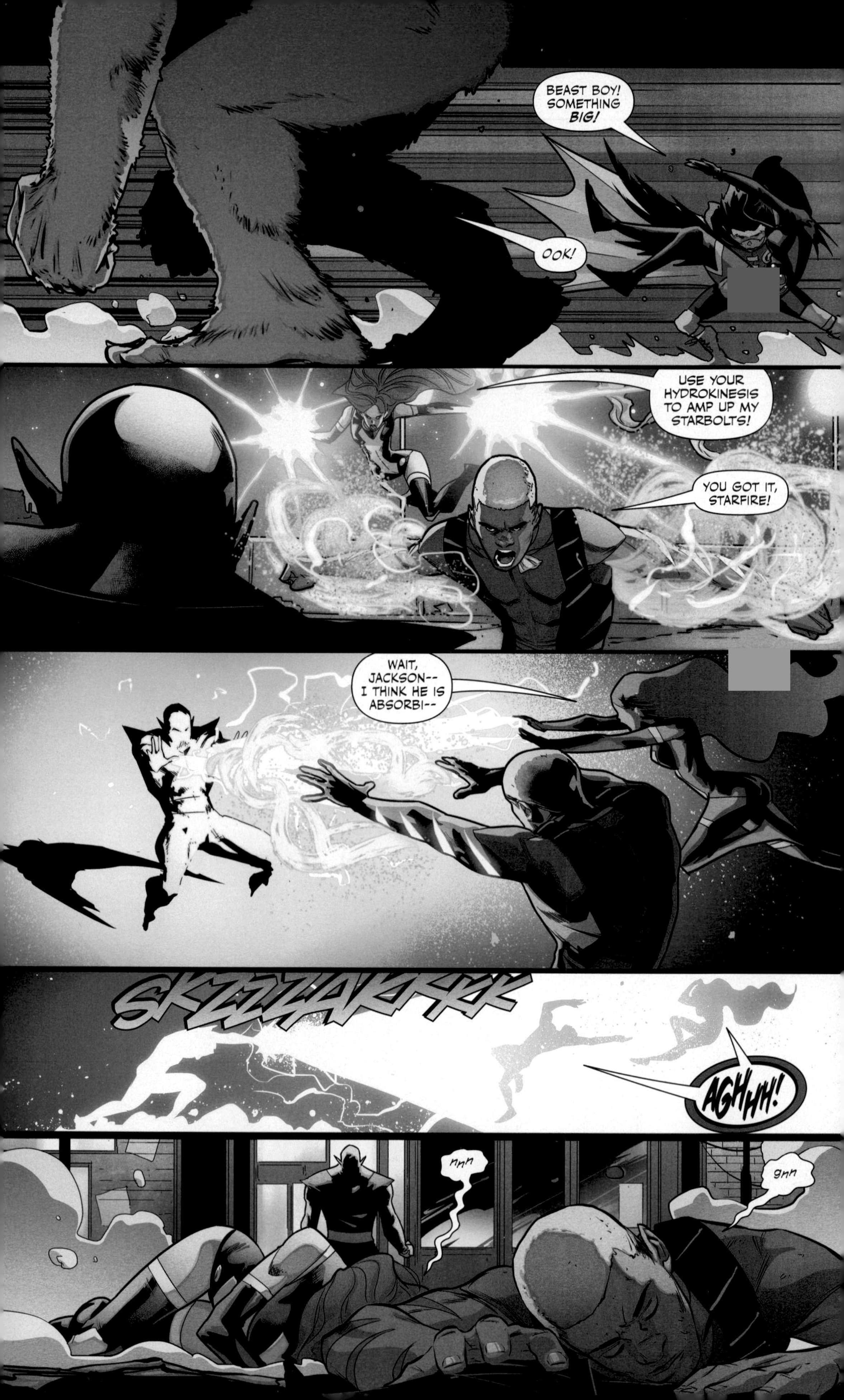

BEAST BOY! SOMETHING BIG!
OOK!
USE YOUR HYDROKINESIS TO AMP UP MY STARBOLTS!
YOU GOT IT, STARFIRE!
WAIT, JACKSON-- I THINK HE IS ABSORBI--
SKZZZAKRKK
AGHHH!
nnn
gnh

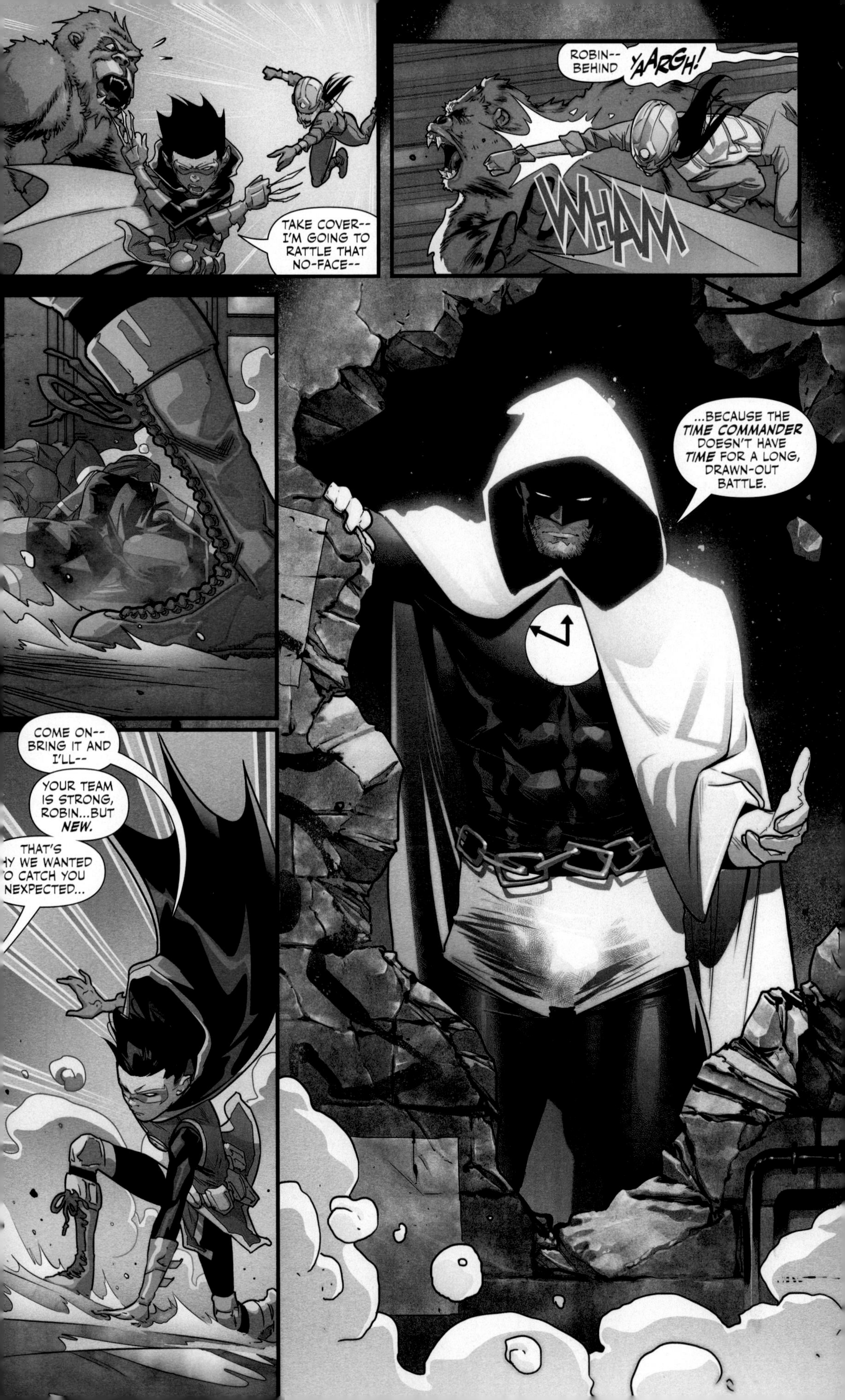

TAKE COVER-- I'M GOING TO RATTLE THAT NO-FACE--
ROBIN-- BEHIND
YAARGH!
WHAM
...BECAUSE THE TIME COMMANDER DOESN'T HAVE TIME FOR A LONG, DRAWN-OUT BATTLE.
COME ON-- BRING IT AND I'LL--
YOUR TEAM IS STRONG, ROBIN...BUT NEW.
THAT'S

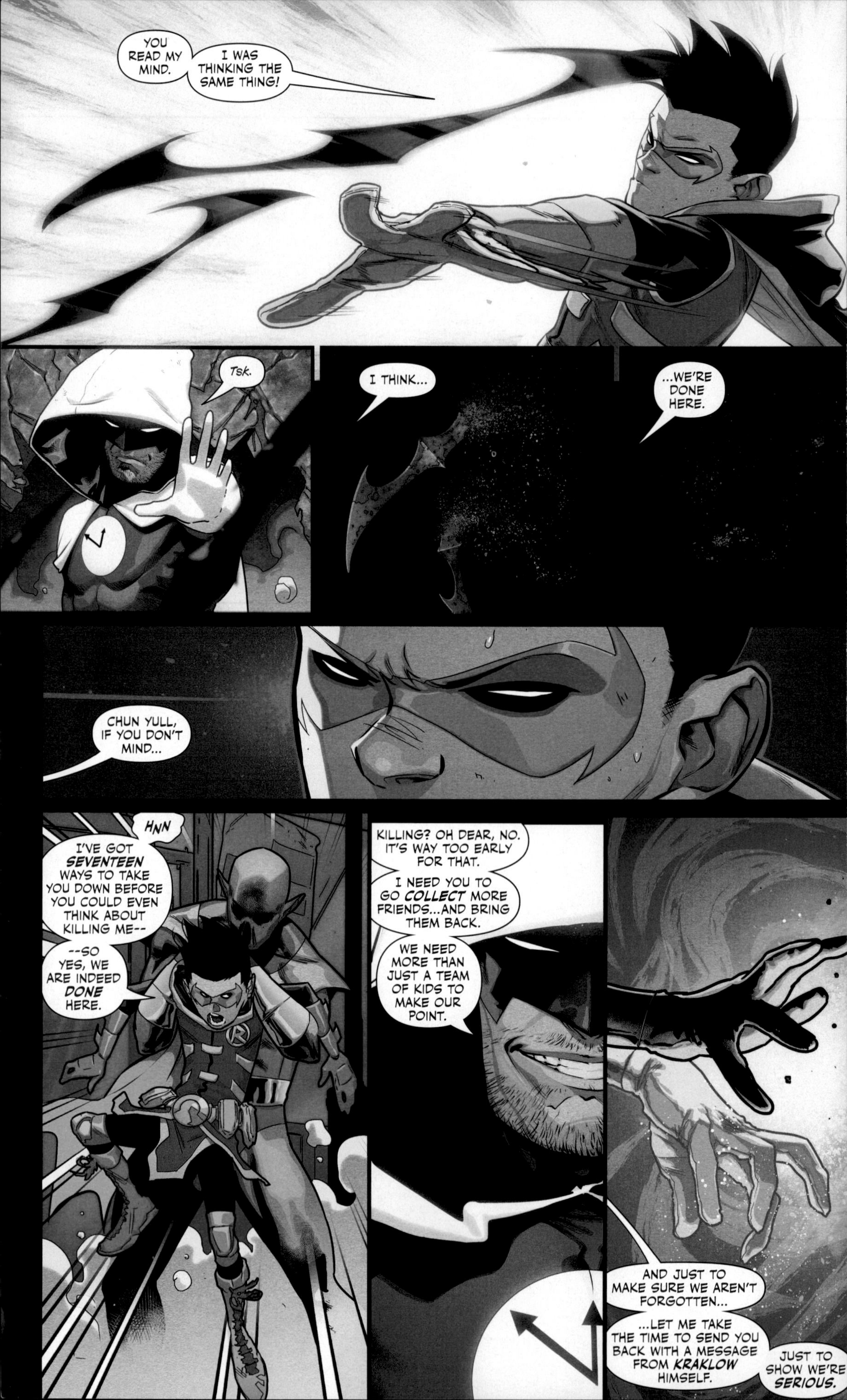
YOU READ MY MIND.
I WAS THINKING THE SAME THING!
Tsk.
I THINK...
...WE'RE DONE HERE.
CHUN YULL, IF YOU DON'T MIND...
HNN
I'VE GOT SEVENTEEN WAYS TO TAKE YOU DOWN BEFORE YOU COULD EVEN THINK ABOUT KILLING ME--
--SO YES, WE ARE INDEED DONE HERE.
KILLING? OH DEAR, NO. IT'S WAY TOO EARLY FOR THAT.
I NEED YOU TO GO COLLECT MORE FRIENDS...AND BRING THEM BACK.
WE NEED MORE THAN JUST A TEAM OF KIDS TO MAKE OUR POINT.
AND JUST TO MAKE SURE WE AREN'T FORGOTTEN...
...LET ME TAKE THE TIME TO SEND YOU BACK WITH A MESSAGE FROM KRAKLOW HIMSELF.
JUST TO SHOW WE'RE SERIOUS.

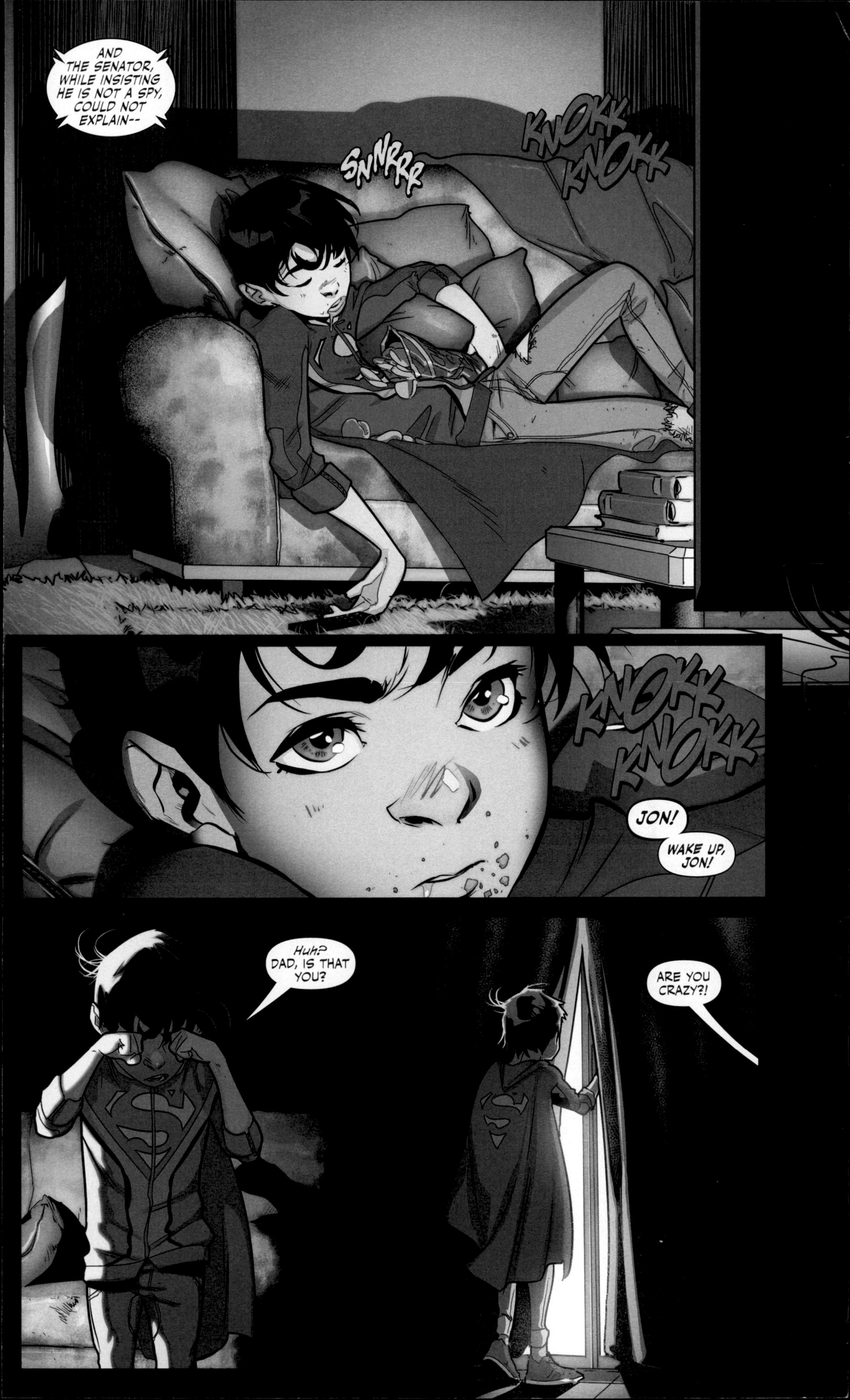
AND THE SENATOR, WHILE INSISTING HE IS NOT A SPY, COULD NOT EXPLAIN--
SNNRRR
KNOKK KNOKK
KNOKK KNOKK
JON!
WAKE UP, JON!
Huh? DAD, IS THAT YOU?
ARE YOU CRAZY?!

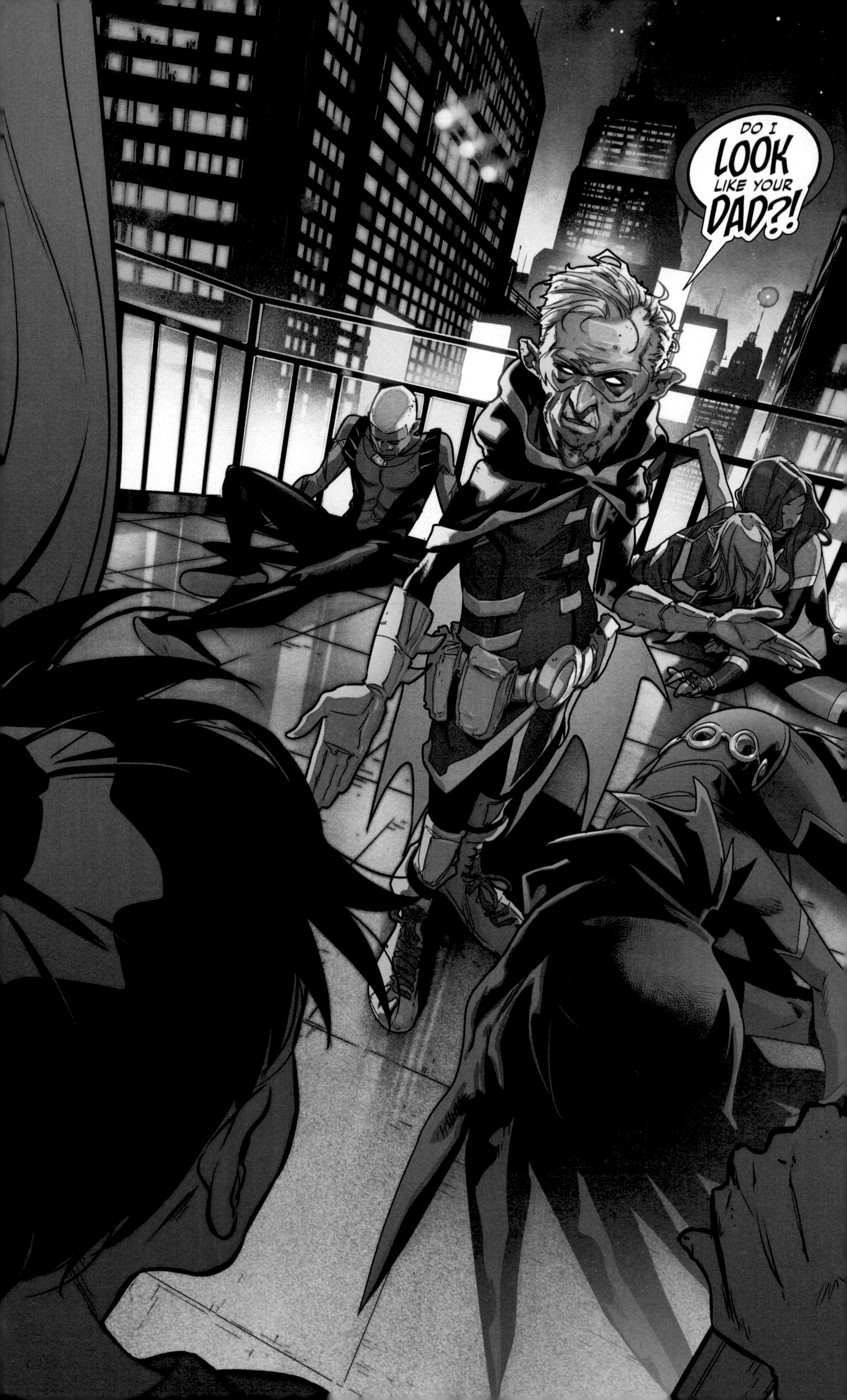
DO I LOOK LIKE YOUR DAD?!

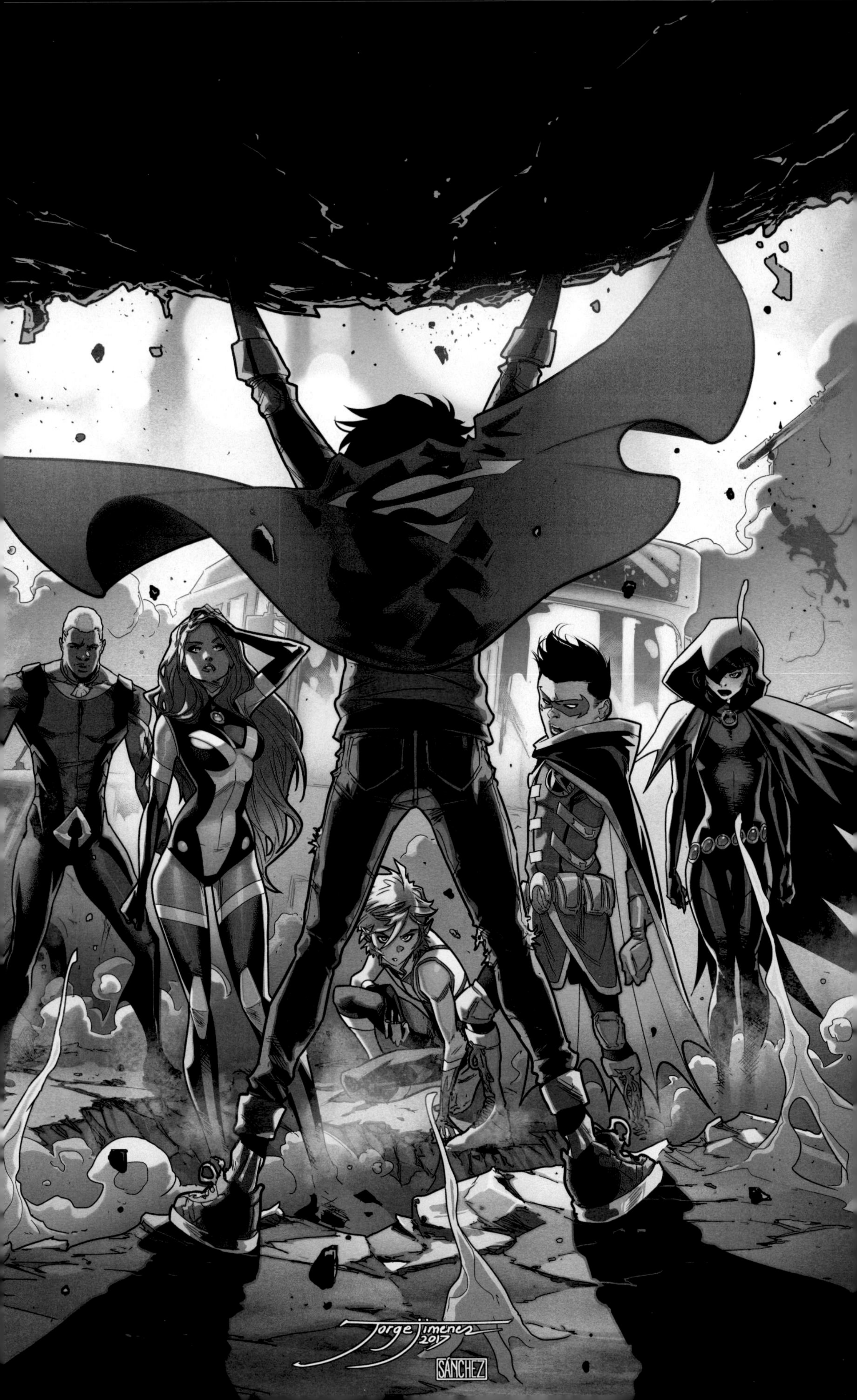
Jorge Jimenez 2017
SÁNCHEZ

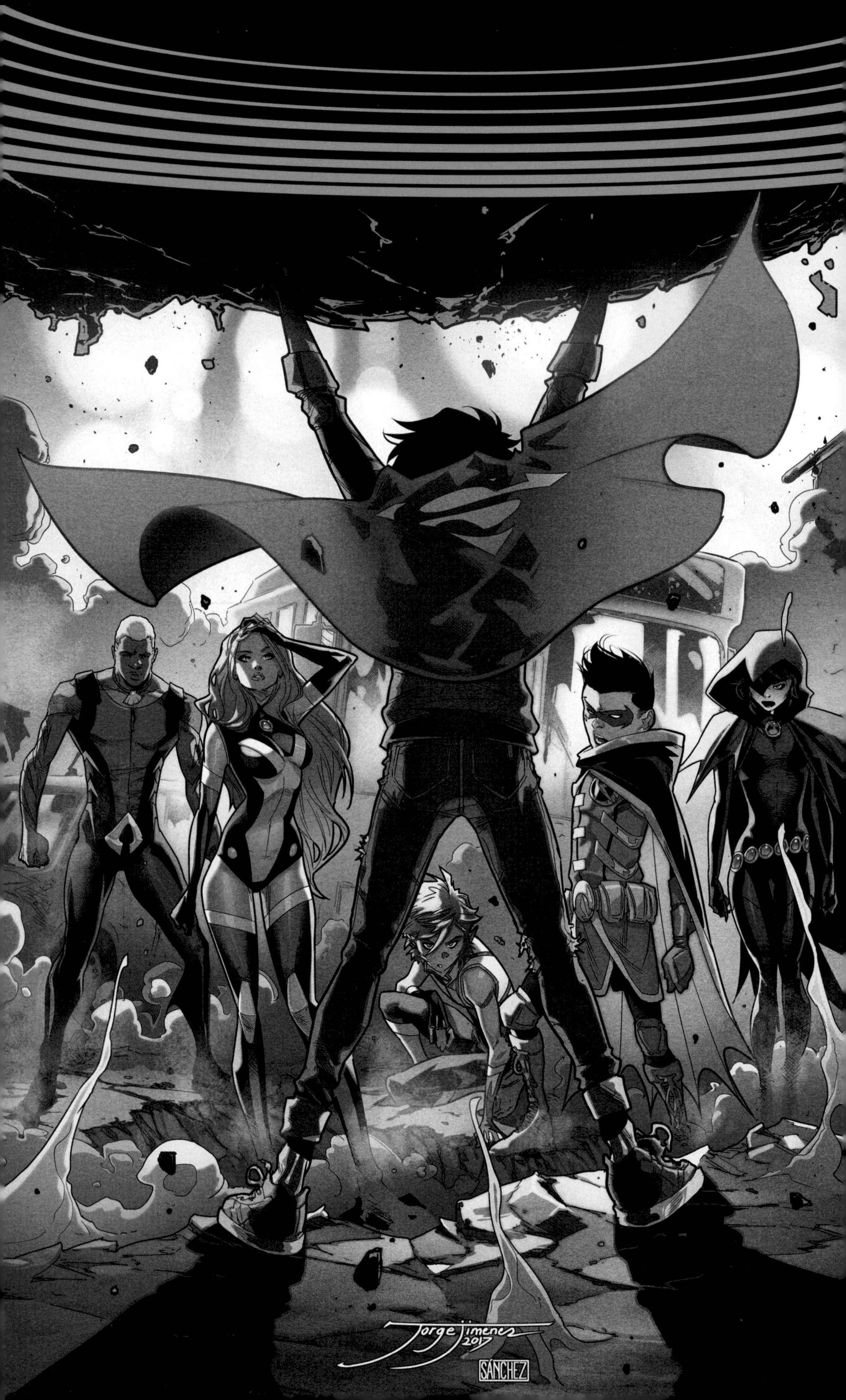
Jorge Jimenez 2017
SÁNCHEZ

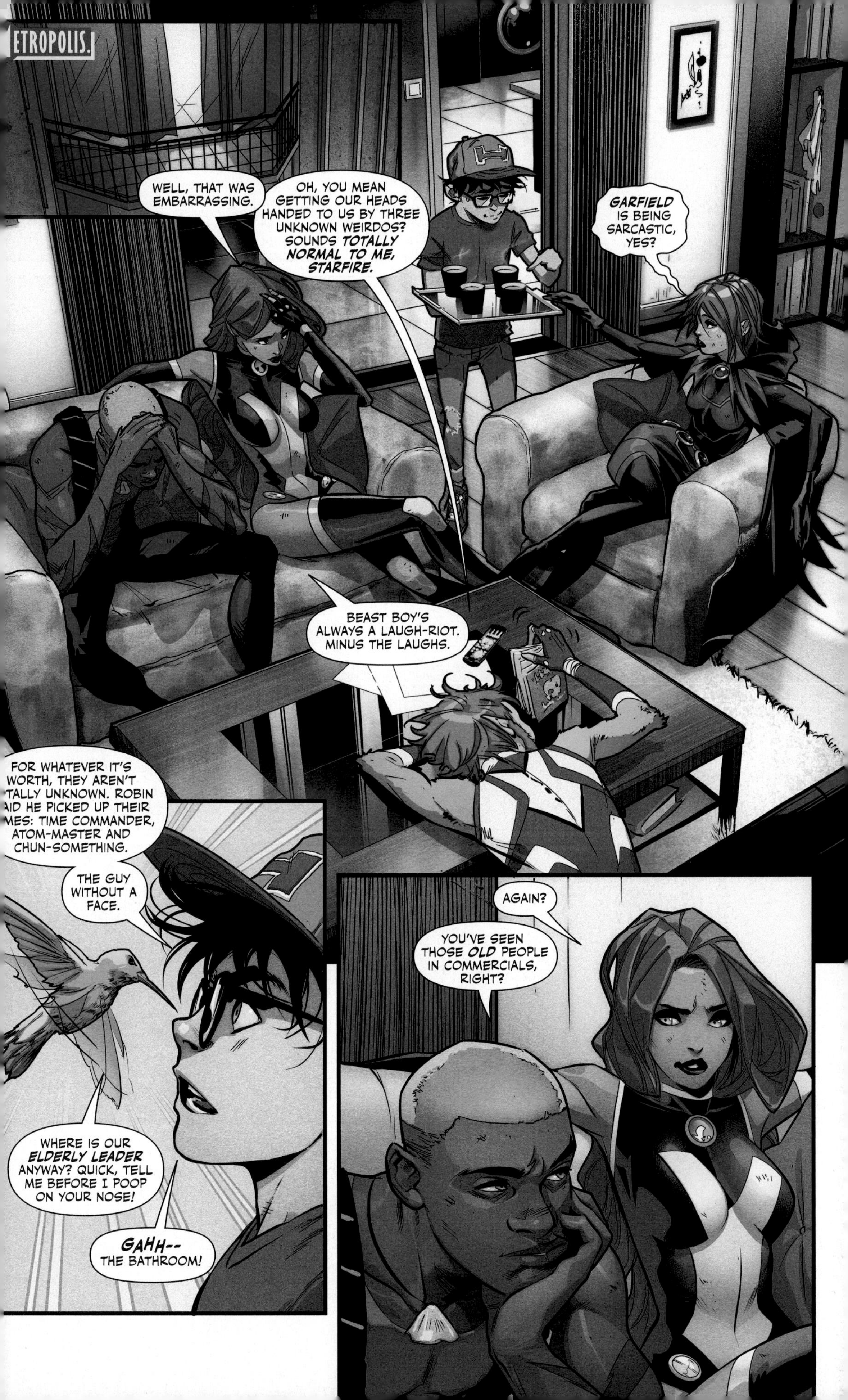
ETROPOLIS.
WELL, THAT WAS EMBARRASSING.
OH, YOU MEAN GETTING OUR HEADS HANDED TO US BY THREE UNKNOWN WEIRDOS? SOUNDS TOTALLY NORMAL TO ME, STARFIRE.
GARFIELD IS BEING SARCASTIC, YES?
BEAST BOY'S ALWAYS A LAUGH-RIOT. MINUS THE LAUGHS.
FOR WHATEVER IT'S WORTH, THEY AREN'T TALLY UNKNOWN. ROBIN AID HE PICKED UP THEIR MES: TIME COMMANDER, ATOM-MASTER AND CHUN-SOMETHING.
THE GUY WITHOUT A FACE.
WHERE IS OUR ELDERLY LEADER ANYWAY? QUICK, TELL ME BEFORE I POOP ON YOUR NOSE!
GAHH-- THE BATHROOM!
AGAIN?
YOU'VE SEEN THOSE OLD PEOPLE IN COMMERCIALS, RIGHT?

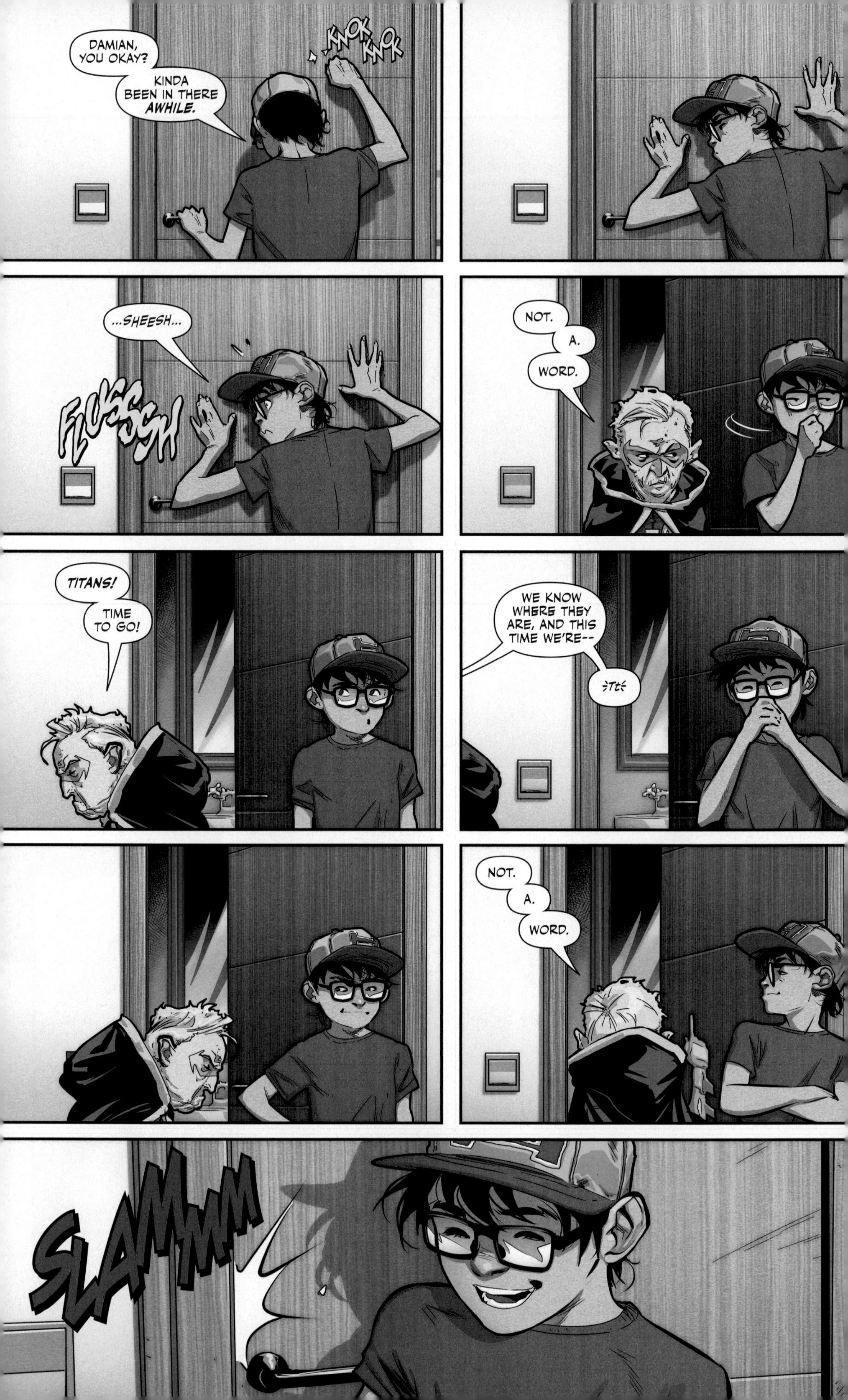
DAMIAN, YOU OKAY?
KINDA BEEN IN THERE AWHILE.
KNOK KNOK
...SHEESH...
FLUSSSH
NOT.
A.
WORD.
TITANS!
TIME TO GO!
WE KNOW WHERE THEY ARE, AND THIS TIME WE'RE--
TT
NOT.
A.
WORD.
SLAMMM

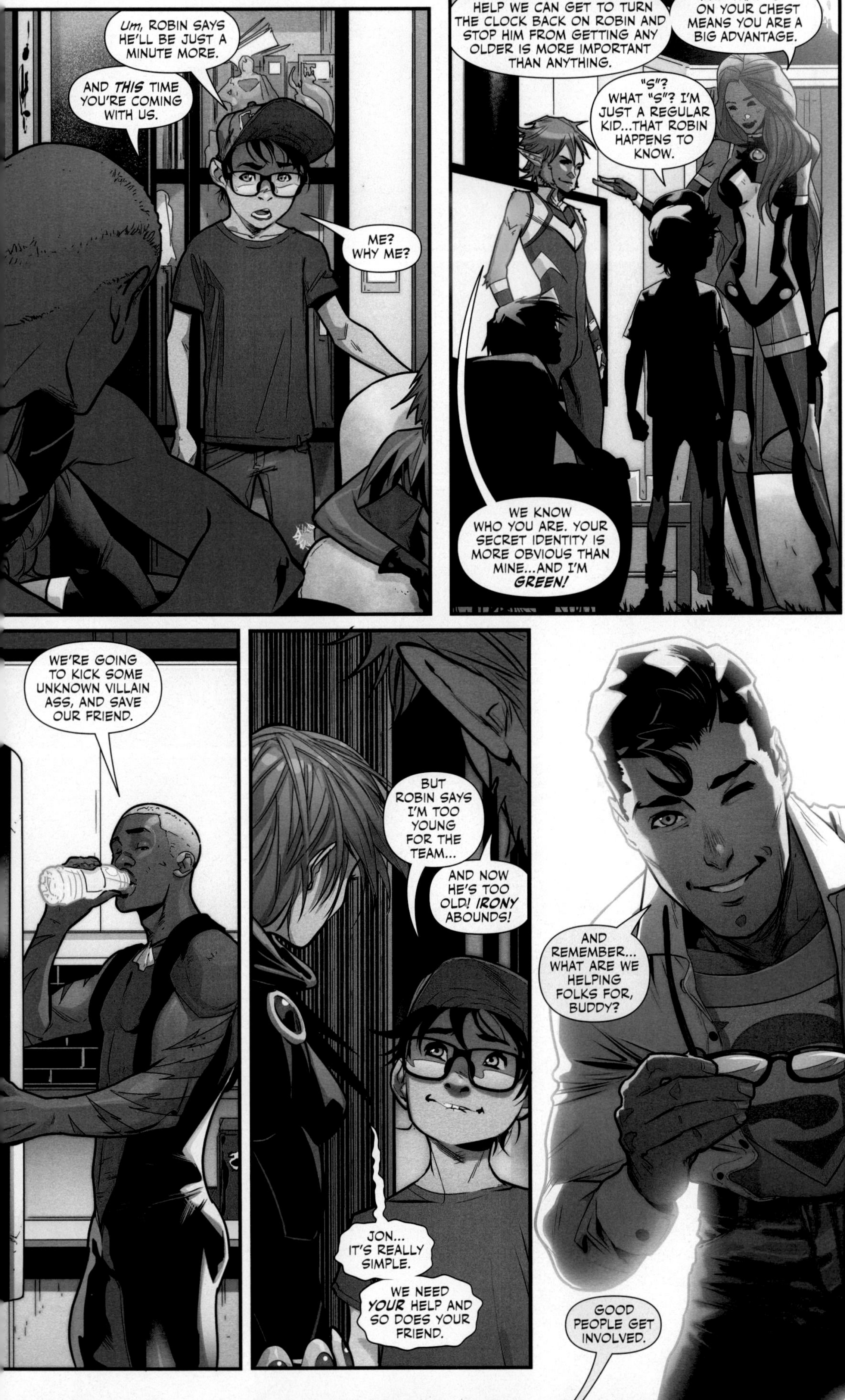
Um, ROBIN SAYS HE'LL BE JUST A MINUTE MORE.
AND ***THIS*** TIME YOU'RE COMING WITH US.
ME? WHY ME?
BECAUSE WHATEVER HELP WE CAN GET TO TURN THE CLOCK BACK ON ROBIN AND STOP HIM FROM GETTING ANY OLDER IS MORE IMPORTANT THAN ANYTHING.
AND THAT "S" ON YOUR CHEST MEANS YOU ARE A BIG ADVANTAGE.
"S"? WHAT "S"? I'M JUST A REGULAR KID...THAT ROBIN HAPPENS TO KNOW.
WE KNOW WHO YOU ARE. YOUR SECRET IDENTITY IS MORE OBVIOUS THAN MINE...AND I'M ***GREEN!***
WE'RE GOING TO KICK SOME UNKNOWN VILLAIN ASS, AND SAVE OUR FRIEND.
BUT ROBIN SAYS I'M TOO YOUNG FOR THE TEAM...
AND NOW HE'S TOO OLD! ***IRONY*** ABOUNDS!
JON... IT'S REALLY SIMPLE.
WE NEED ***YOUR*** HELP AND SO DOES YOUR FRIEND.
AND REMEMBER... WHAT ARE WE HELPING FOLKS FOR, BUDDY?
GOOD PEOPLE GET INVOLVED.

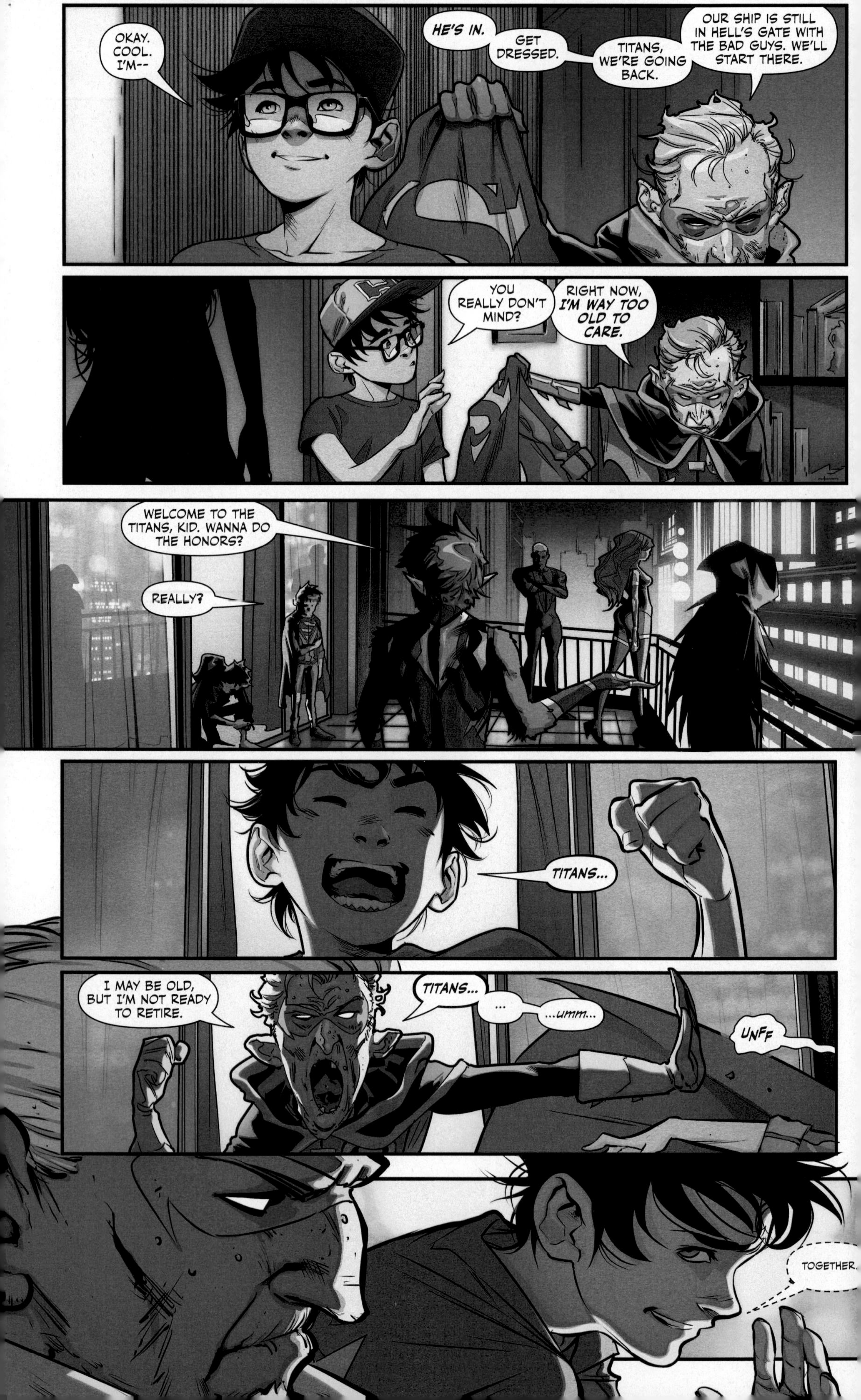
OKAY. COOL. I'M--
HE'S IN.
GET DRESSED.
TITANS, WE'RE GOING BACK.
OUR SHIP IS STILL IN HELL'S GATE WITH THE BAD GUYS. WE'LL START THERE.
YOU REALLY DON'T MIND?
RIGHT NOW, I'M WAY TOO OLD TO CARE.
WELCOME TO THE TITANS, KID. WANNA DO THE HONORS?
REALLY?
TITANS...
I MAY BE OLD, BUT I'M NOT READY TO RETIRE.
TITANS...
...
...umm...
UNFF
TOGETHER.

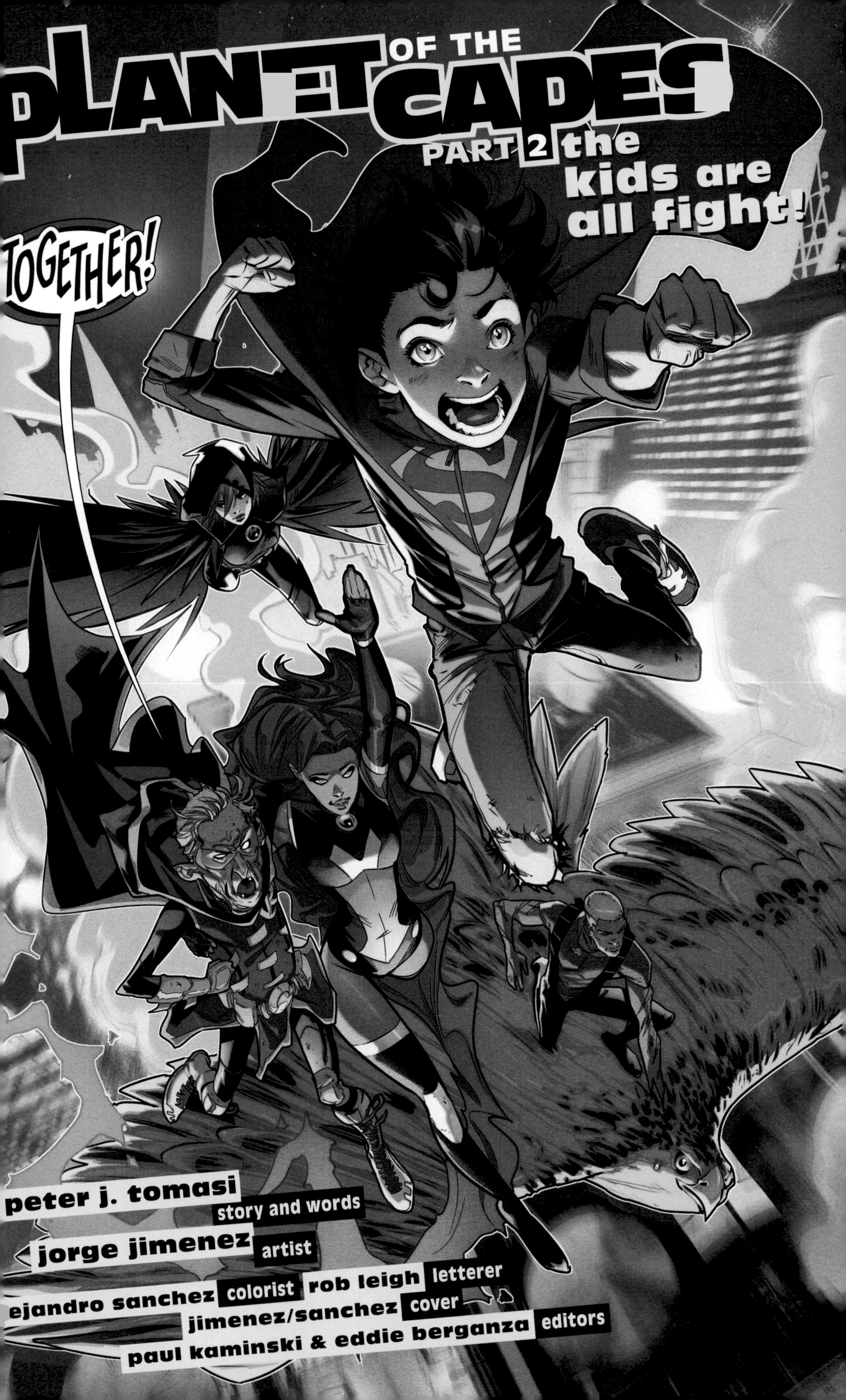
PLANET OF THE CAPES
PART 2 the kids are all fight!
TOGETHER!
peter j. tomasi story and words
jorge jimenez artist
ejandro sanchez colorist
rob leigh letterer
jimenez/sanchez cover
paul kaminski & eddie berganza editors

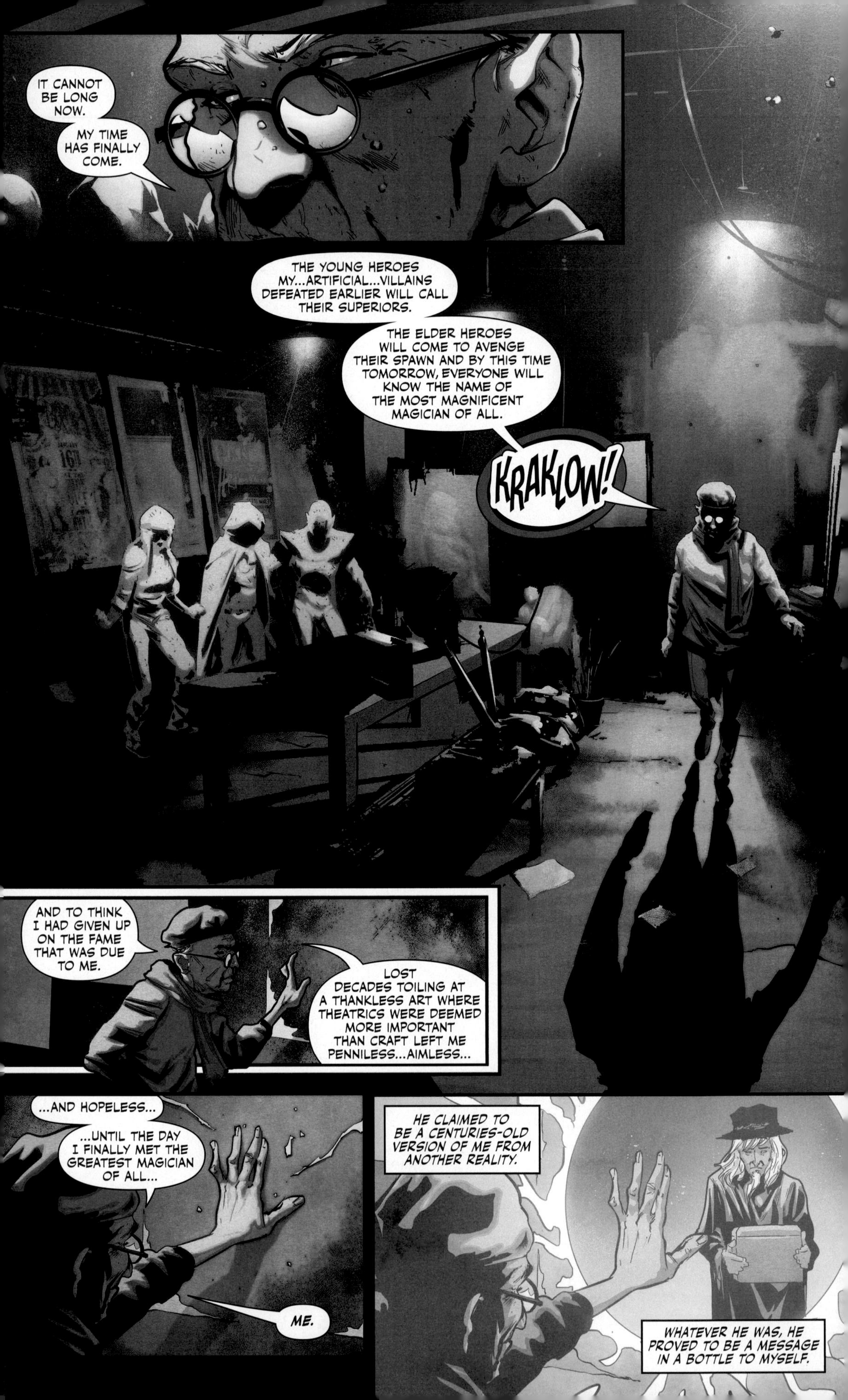
IT CANNOT BE LONG NOW.
MY TIME HAS FINALLY COME.
THE YOUNG HEROES MY...ARTIFICIAL...VILLAINS DEFEATED EARLIER WILL CALL THEIR SUPERIORS.
THE ELDER HEROES WILL COME TO AVENGE THEIR SPAWN AND BY THIS TIME TOMORROW, EVERYONE WILL KNOW THE NAME OF THE MOST MAGNIFICENT MAGICIAN OF ALL.
KRAKLOW!!
AND TO THINK I HAD GIVEN UP ON THE FAME THAT WAS DUE TO ME.
LOST DECADES TOILING AT A THANKLESS ART WHERE THEATRICS WERE DEEMED MORE IMPORTANT THAN CRAFT LEFT ME PENNILESS...AIMLESS...
...AND HOPELESS...
...UNTIL THE DAY I FINALLY MET THE GREATEST MAGICIAN OF ALL...
ME.
HE CLAIMED TO BE A CENTURIES-OLD VERSION OF ME FROM ANOTHER REALITY.
WHATEVER HE WAS, HE PROVED TO BE A MESSAGE IN A BOTTLE TO MYSELF.

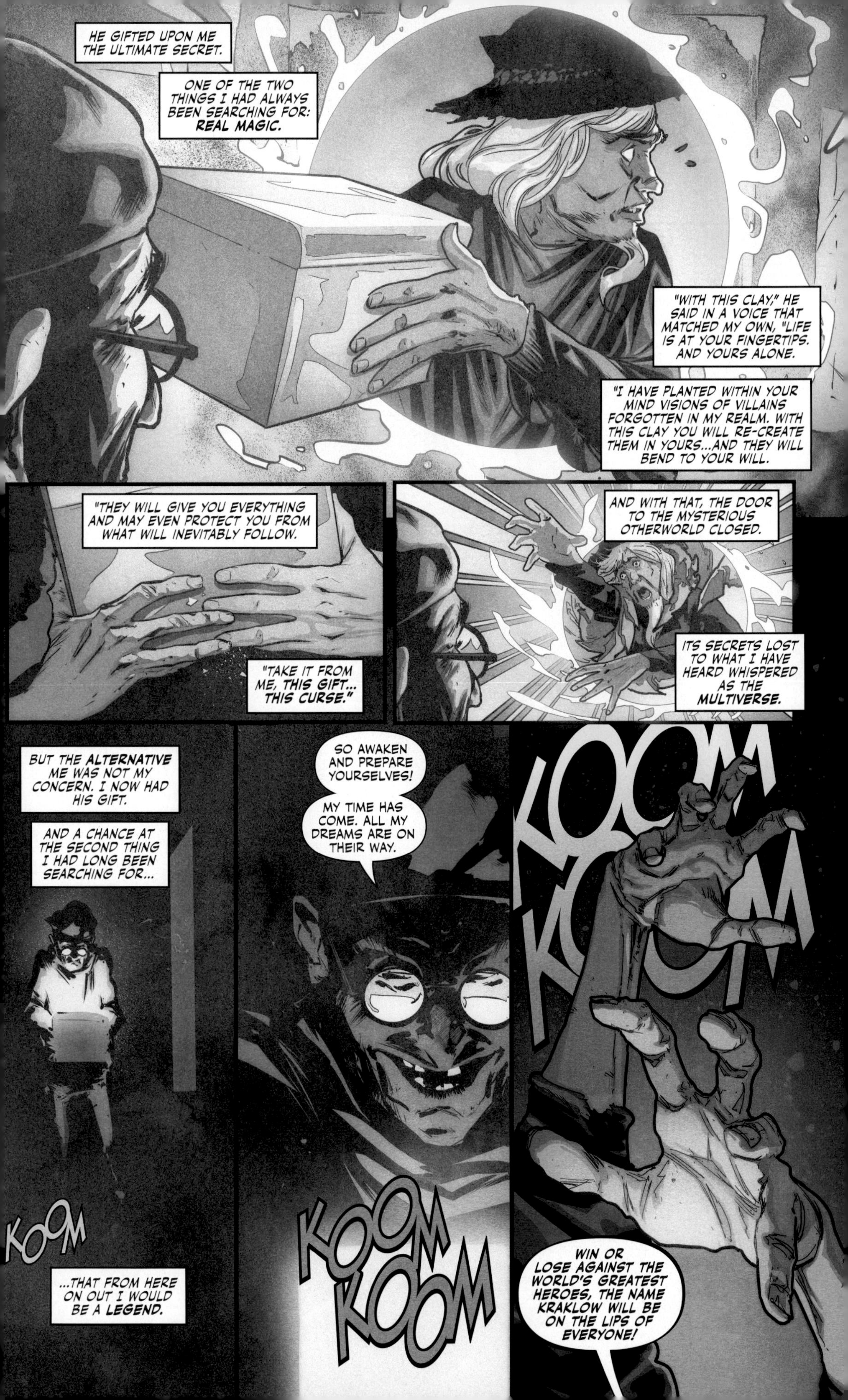
HE GIFTED UPON ME THE ULTIMATE SECRET.
ONE OF THE TWO THINGS I HAD ALWAYS BEEN SEARCHING FOR: REAL MAGIC.
"WITH THIS CLAY," HE SAID IN A VOICE THAT MATCHED MY OWN, "LIFE IS AT YOUR FINGERTIPS. AND YOURS ALONE.
"I HAVE PLANTED WITHIN YOUR MIND VISIONS OF VILLAINS FORGOTTEN IN MY REALM. WITH THIS CLAY YOU WILL RE-CREATE THEM IN YOURS...AND THEY WILL BEND TO YOUR WILL.
"THEY WILL GIVE YOU EVERYTHING AND MAY EVEN PROTECT YOU FROM WHAT WILL INEVITABLY FOLLOW.
"TAKE IT FROM ME, THIS GIFT... THIS CURSE."
AND WITH THAT, THE DOOR TO THE MYSTERIOUS OTHERWORLD CLOSED.
ITS SECRETS LOST TO WHAT I HAVE HEARD WHISPERED AS THE MULTIVERSE.
BUT THE ALTERNATIVE ME WAS NOT MY CONCERN. I NOW HAD HIS GIFT.
AND A CHANCE AT THE SECOND THING I HAD LONG BEEN SEARCHING FOR...
KOOM
...THAT FROM HERE ON OUT I WOULD BE A LEGEND.
SO AWAKEN AND PREPARE YOURSELVES!
MY TIME HAS COME. ALL MY DREAMS ARE ON THEIR WAY.
KOOM KOOM
KOOM KOOM
WIN OR LOSE AGAINST THE WORLD'S GREATEST HEROES, THE NAME KRAKLOW WILL BE ON THE LIPS OF EVERYONE!

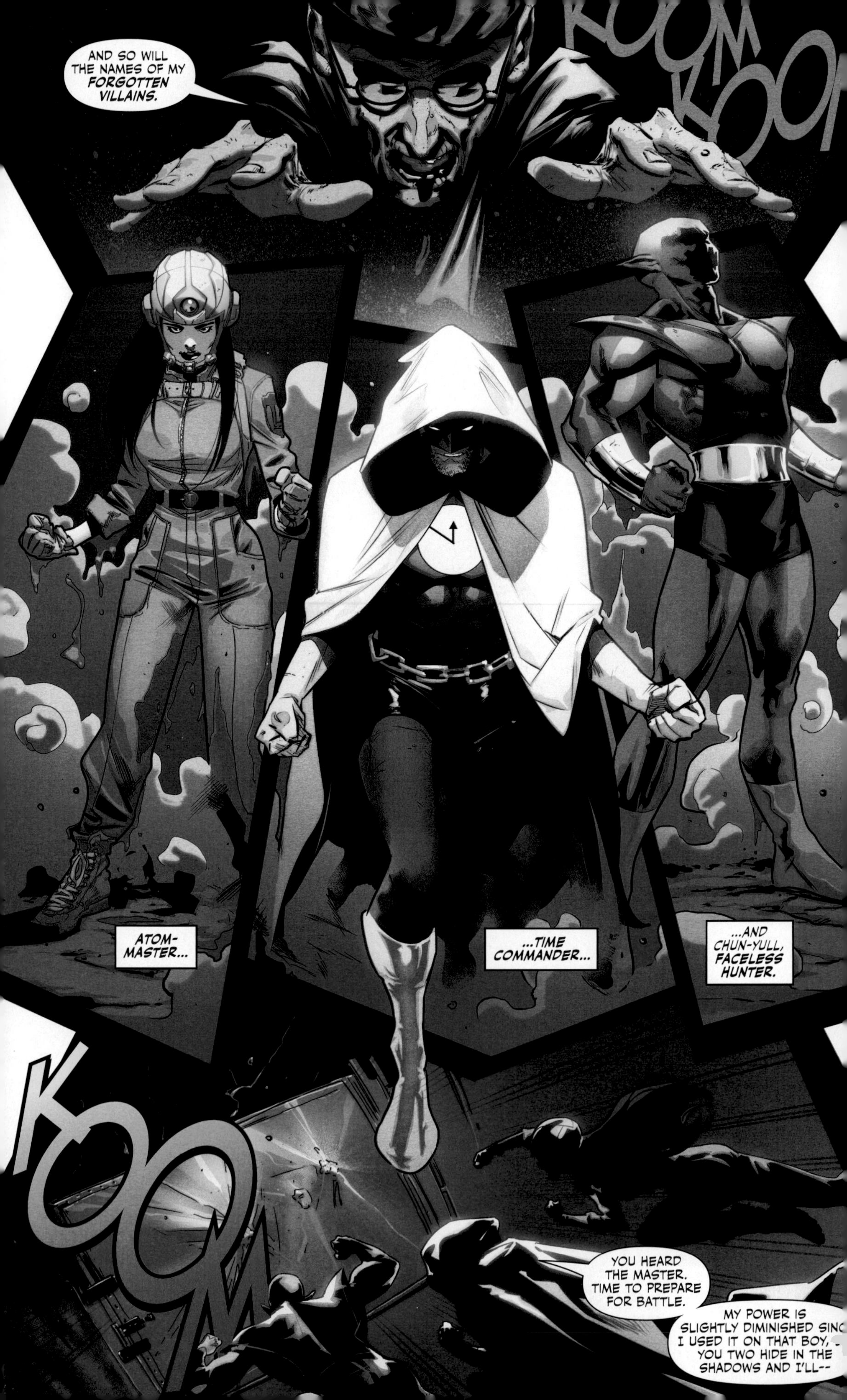
AND SO WILL THE NAMES OF MY FORGOTTEN VILLAINS.
KOOM
KOOM
ATOM-MASTER...
...TIME COMMANDER...
...AND CHUN-YULL, FACELESS HUNTER.
KOOM
YOU HEARD THE MASTER. TIME TO PREPARE FOR BATTLE.
MY POWER IS SLIGHTLY DIMINISHED SINC I USED IT ON THAT BOY, - YOU TWO HIDE IN THE SHADOWS AND I'LL--

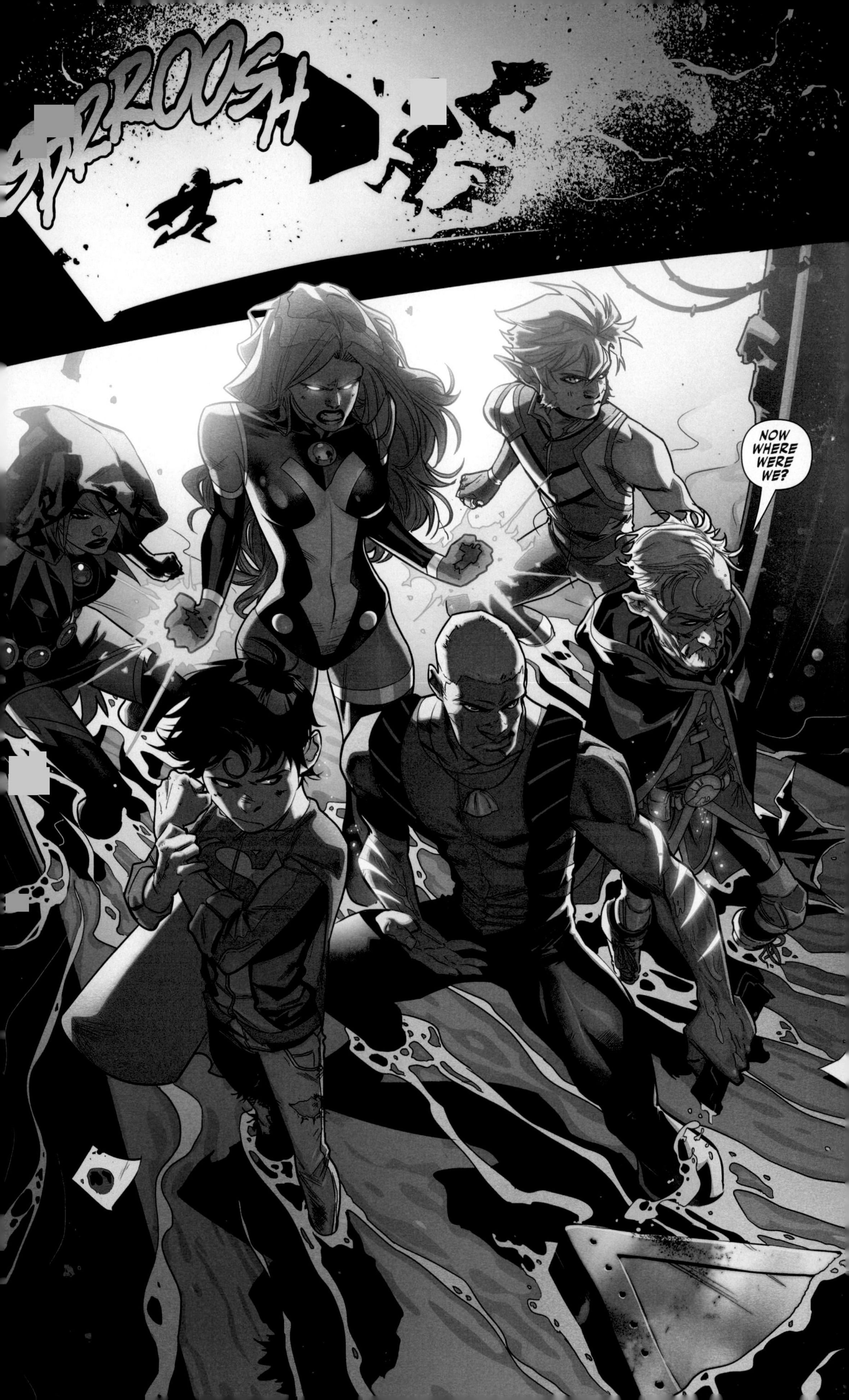
SPLROOSH
NOW WHERE WERE WE?

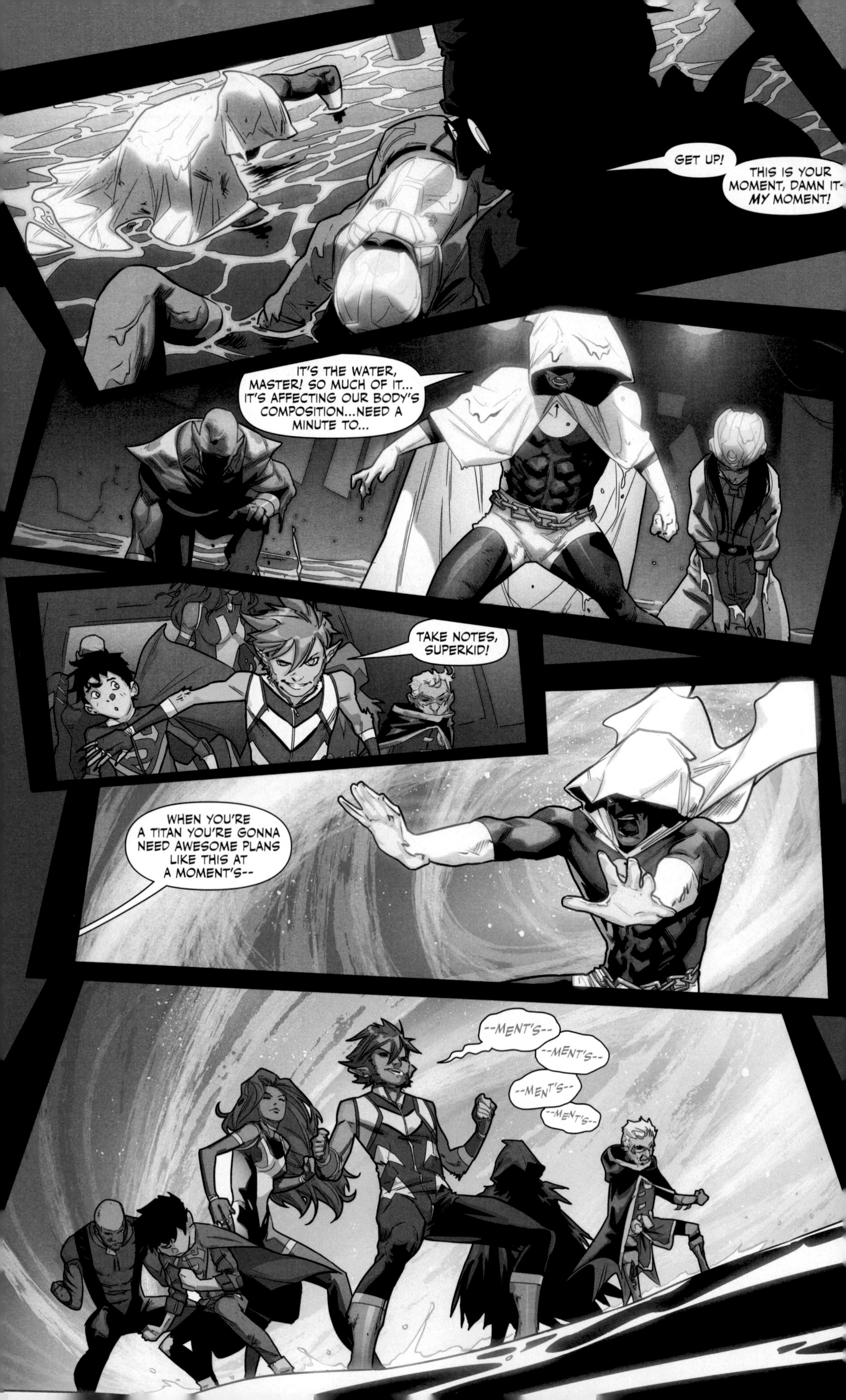
GET UP!
THIS IS YOUR MOMENT, DAMN IT-- MY MOMENT!
IT'S THE WATER, MASTER! SO MUCH OF IT... IT'S AFFECTING OUR BODY'S COMPOSITION...NEED A MINUTE TO...
TAKE NOTES, SUPERKID!
WHEN YOU'RE A TITAN YOU'RE GONNA NEED AWESOME PLANS LIKE THIS AT A MOMENT'S--
--MENT'S--
--MENT'S--
--MENT'S--
--MENT'S--

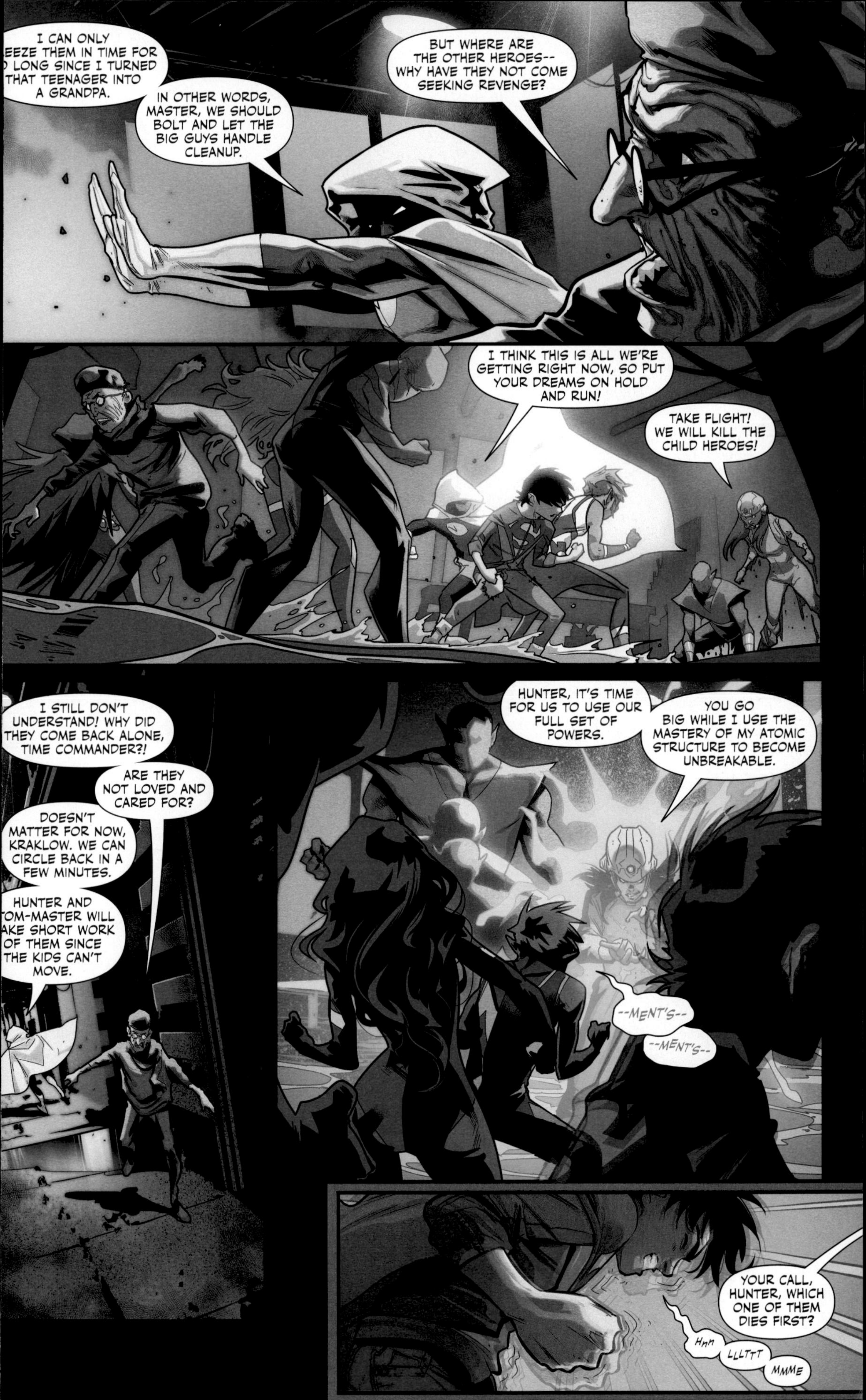
I CAN ONLY
EEZE THEM IN TIME FOR
D LONG SINCE I TURNED
THAT TEENAGER INTO
A GRANDPA.
IN OTHER WORDS, MASTER, WE SHOULD BOLT AND LET THE BIG GUYS HANDLE CLEANUP.
BUT WHERE ARE THE OTHER HEROES-- WHY HAVE THEY NOT COME SEEKING REVENGE?
I THINK THIS IS ALL WE'RE GETTING RIGHT NOW, SO PUT YOUR DREAMS ON HOLD AND RUN!
TAKE FLIGHT! WE WILL KILL THE CHILD HEROES!
I STILL DON'T UNDERSTAND! WHY DID THEY COME BACK ALONE, TIME COMMANDER?!
ARE THEY NOT LOVED AND CARED FOR?
DOESN'T MATTER FOR NOW, KRAKLOW. WE CAN CIRCLE BACK IN A FEW MINUTES.
HUNTER AND
TOM-MASTER WILL
AKE SHORT WORK
OF THEM SINCE
THE KIDS CAN'T
MOVE.
HUNTER, IT'S TIME FOR US TO USE OUR FULL SET OF POWERS.
YOU GO BIG WHILE I USE THE MASTERY OF MY ATOMIC STRUCTURE TO BECOME UNBREAKABLE.
--MENT'S--
--MENT'S--
YOUR CALL, HUNTER, WHICH ONE OF THEM DIES FIRST?
Hnn
LLLTTT
MMME

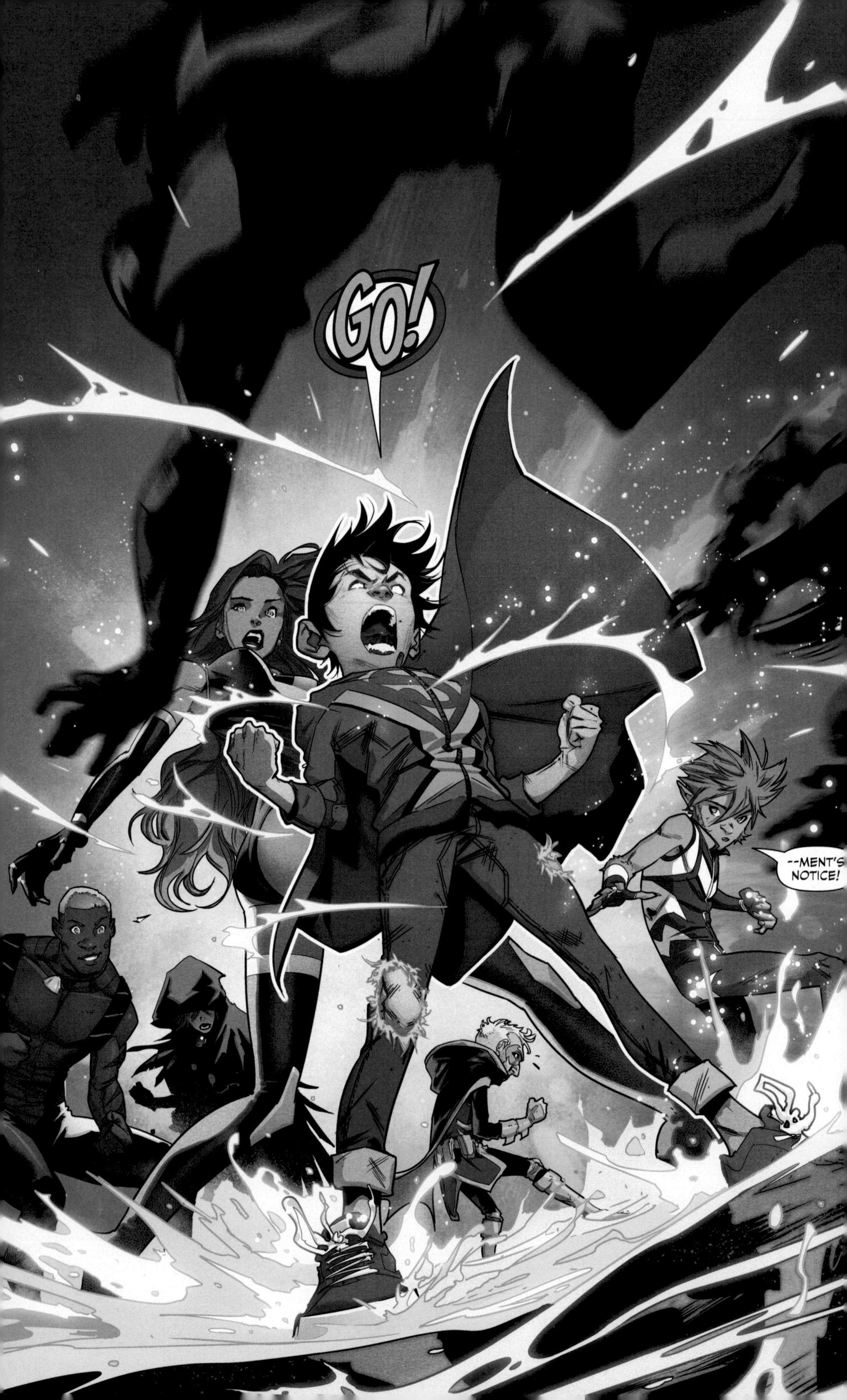
GO!
--MENT'S
NOTICE!

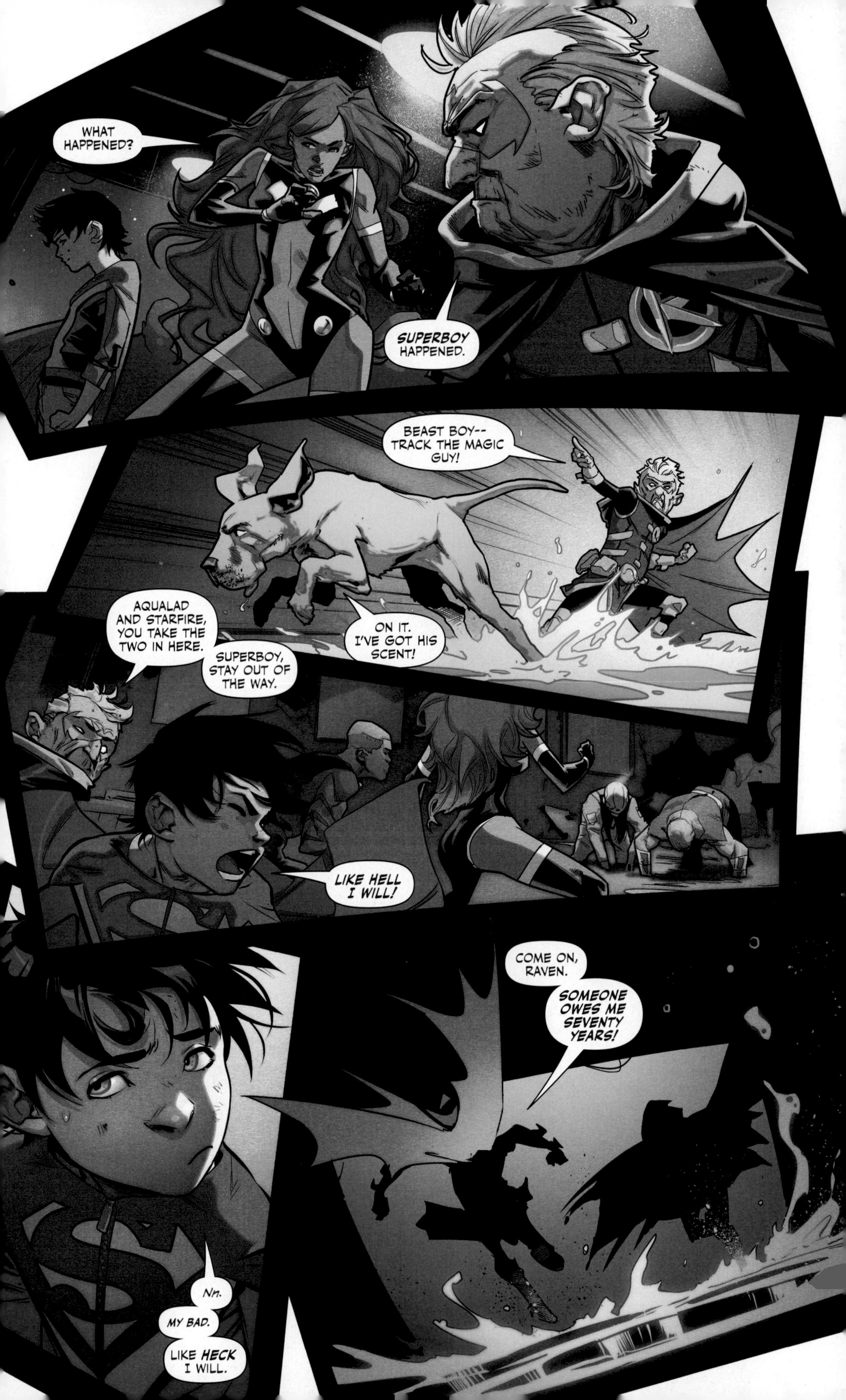
WHAT HAPPENED?
SUPERBOY HAPPENED.
BEAST BOY-- TRACK THE MAGIC GUY!
ON IT. I'VE GOT HIS SCENT!
AQUALAD AND STARFIRE, YOU TAKE THE TWO IN HERE.
SUPERBOY, STAY OUT OF THE WAY.
LIKE HELL I WILL!
Nn.
MY BAD.
LIKE HECK I WILL.
COME ON, RAVEN.
SOMEONE OWES ME SEVENTY YEARS!

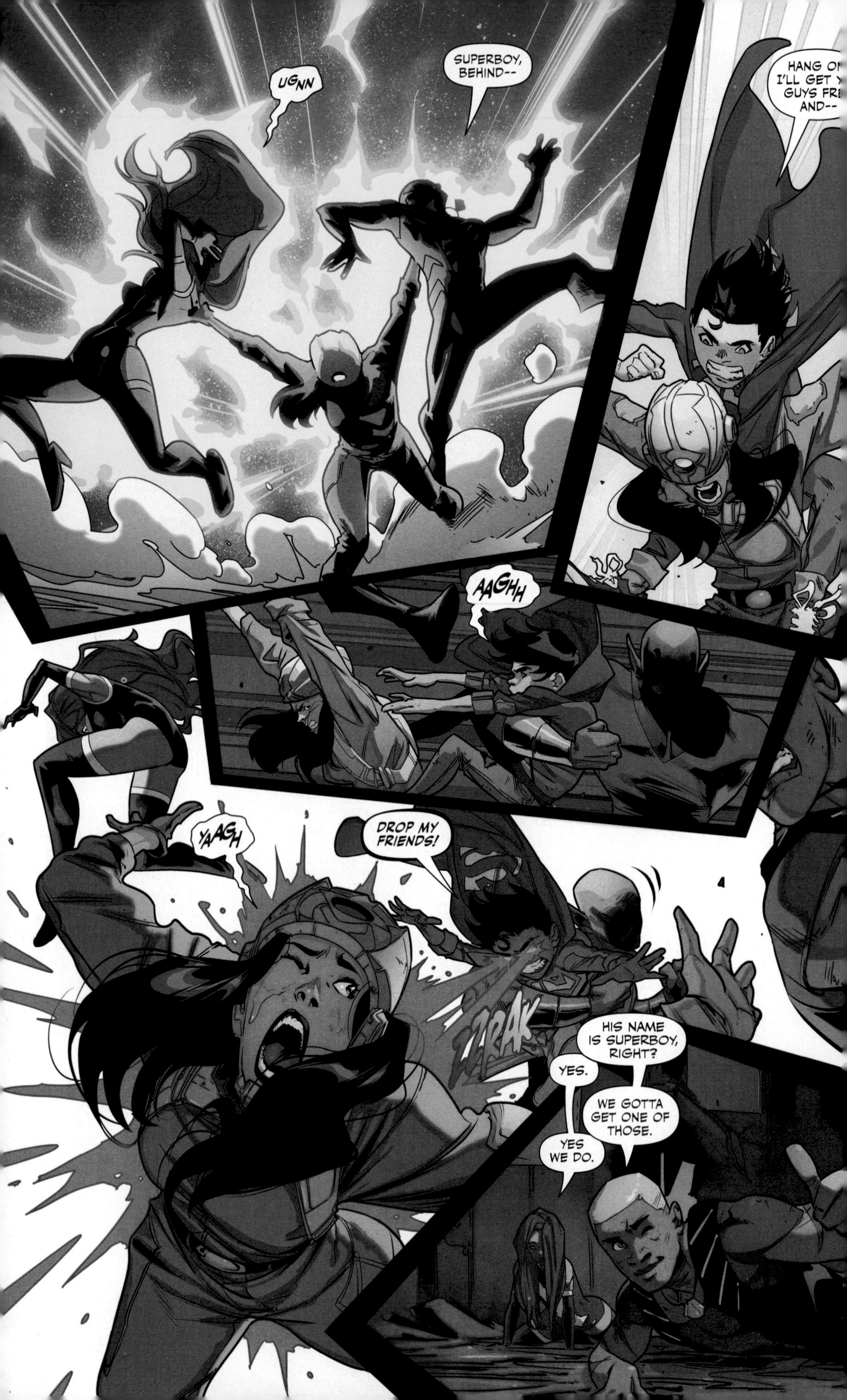
UGNN
SUPERBOY, BEHIND--
HANG O I'LL GET GUYS FR AND--
AAGHH
YAAGH
DROP MY FRIENDS!
HIS NAME IS SUPERBOY, RIGHT?
YES.
WE GOTTA GET ONE OF THOSE.
YES WE DO.

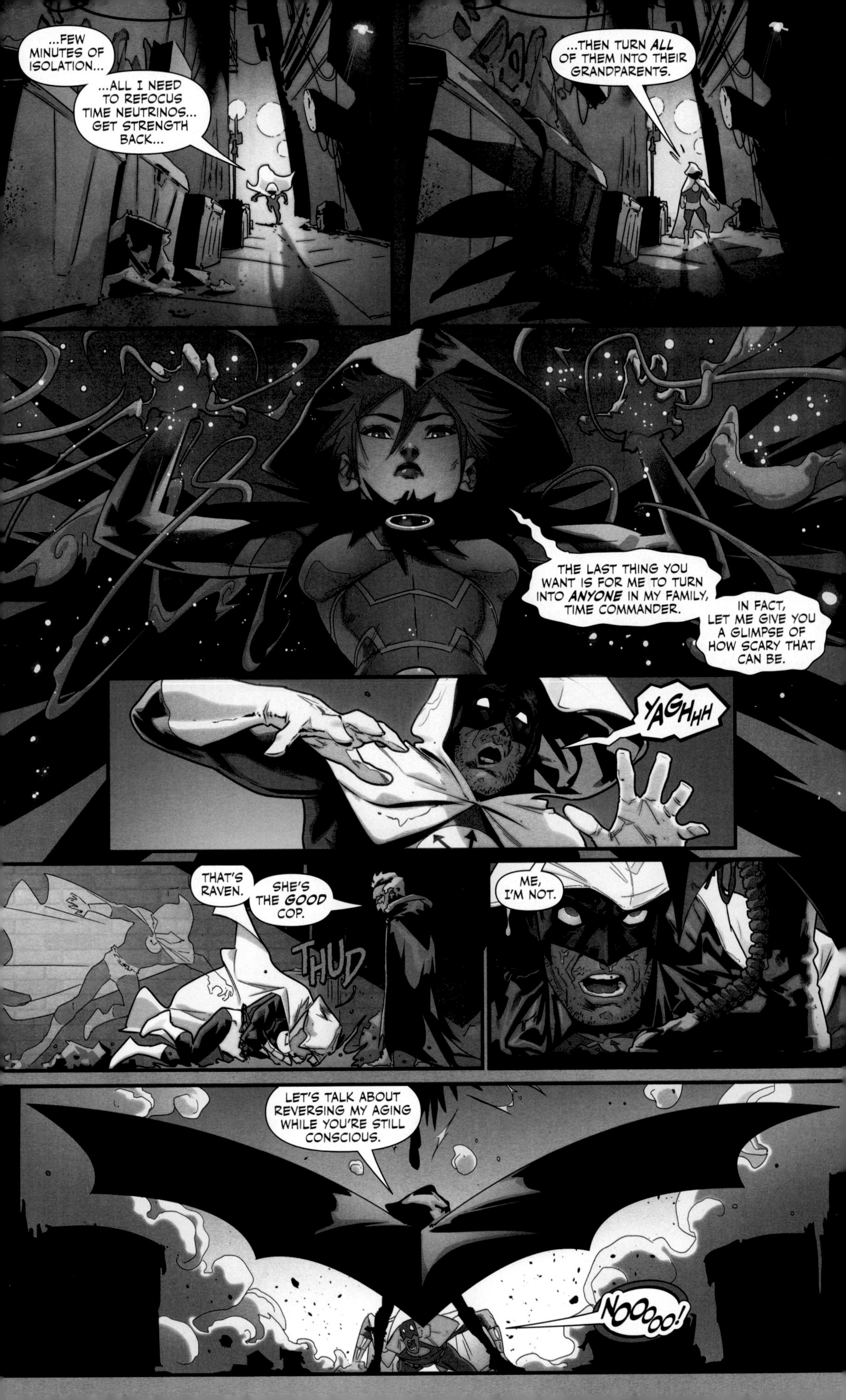

...FEW MINUTES OF ISOLATION...
...ALL I NEED TO REFOCUS TIME NEUTRINOS... GET STRENGTH BACK...
...THEN TURN *ALL* OF THEM INTO THEIR GRANDPARENTS.
THE LAST THING YOU WANT IS FOR ME TO TURN INTO *ANYONE* IN MY FAMILY, TIME COMMANDER.
IN FACT, LET ME GIVE YOU A GLIMPSE OF HOW SCARY THAT CAN BE.
YAGHHH
THAT'S RAVEN.
SHE'S THE *GOOD* COP.
THUD
ME, I'M NOT.
LET'S TALK ABOUT REVERSING MY AGING WHILE YOU'RE STILL CONSCIOUS.
NOOOOO!

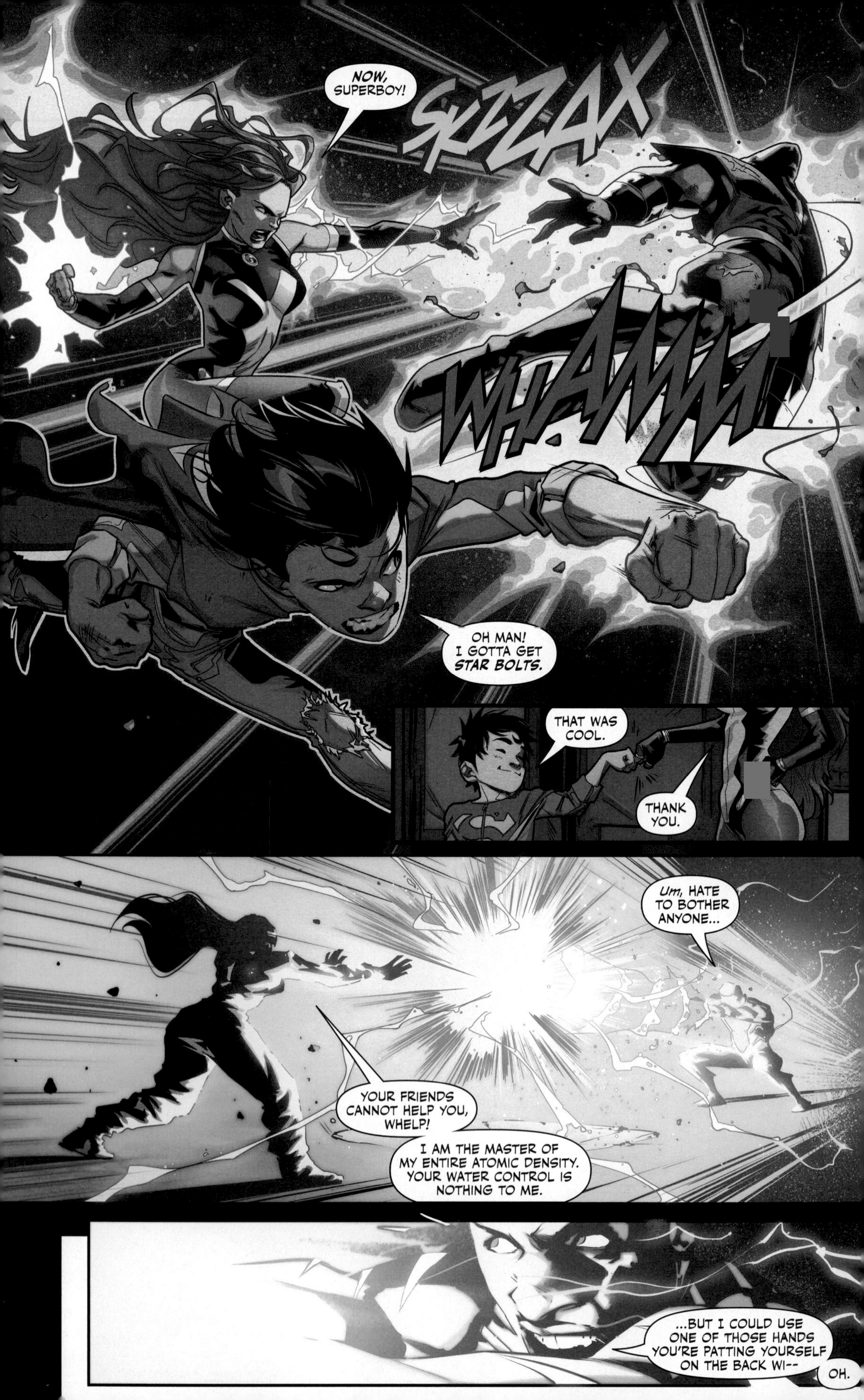
NOW, SUPERBOY!
SKZZAX
WHAMM
OH MAN! I GOTTA GET STAR BOLTS.
THAT WAS COOL.
THANK YOU.
Um, HATE TO BOTHER ANYONE...
YOUR FRIENDS CANNOT HELP YOU, WHELP!
I AM THE MASTER OF MY ENTIRE ATOMIC DENSITY. YOUR WATER CONTROL IS NOTHING TO ME.
...BUT I COULD USE ONE OF THOSE HANDS YOU'RE PATTING YOURSELF ON THE BACK WI--
OH.

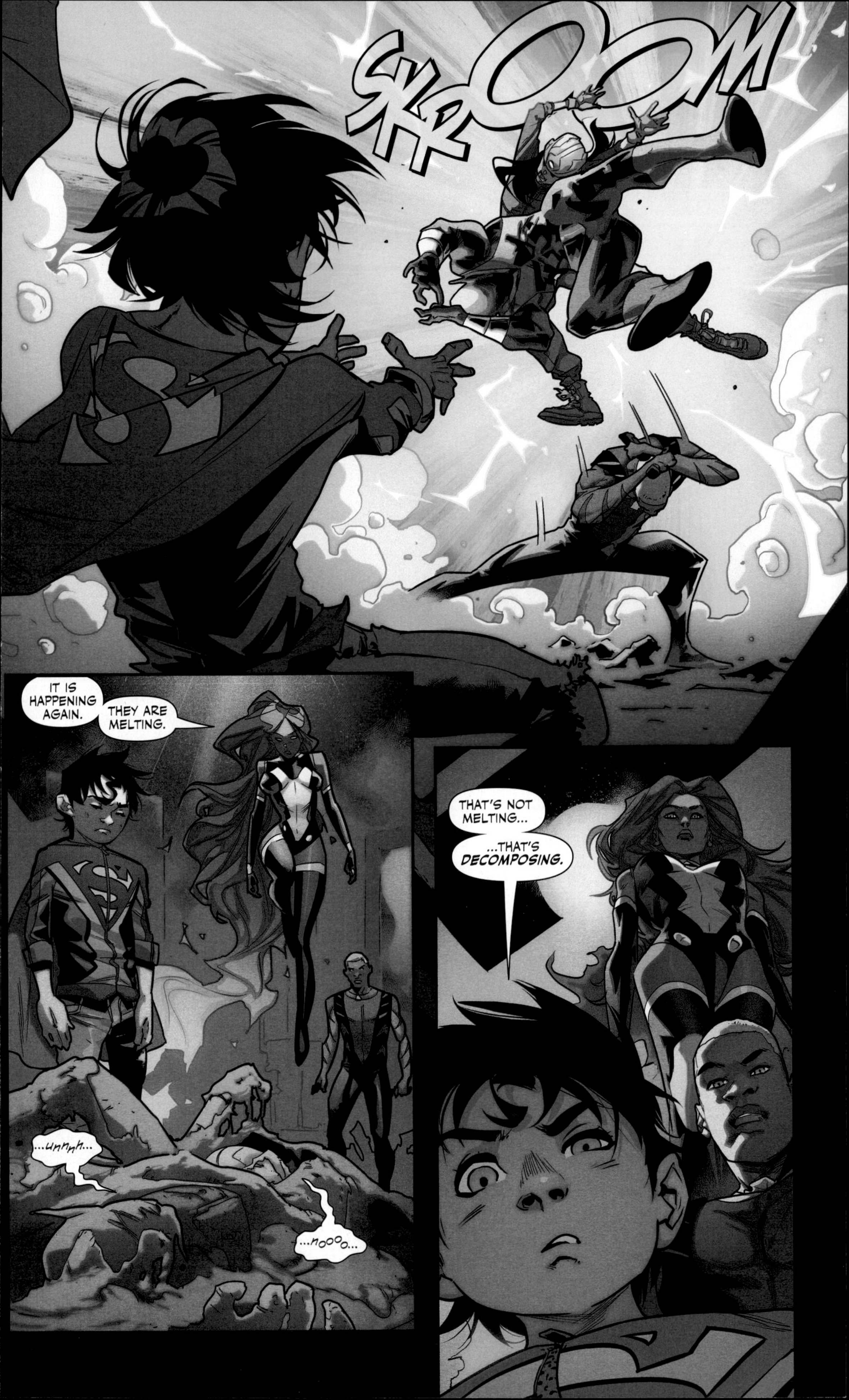
SKROOOM
IT IS HAPPENING AGAIN.
THEY ARE MELTING.
...unnnh...
...nooooo...
THAT'S NOT MELTING...
...THAT'S DECOMPOSING.

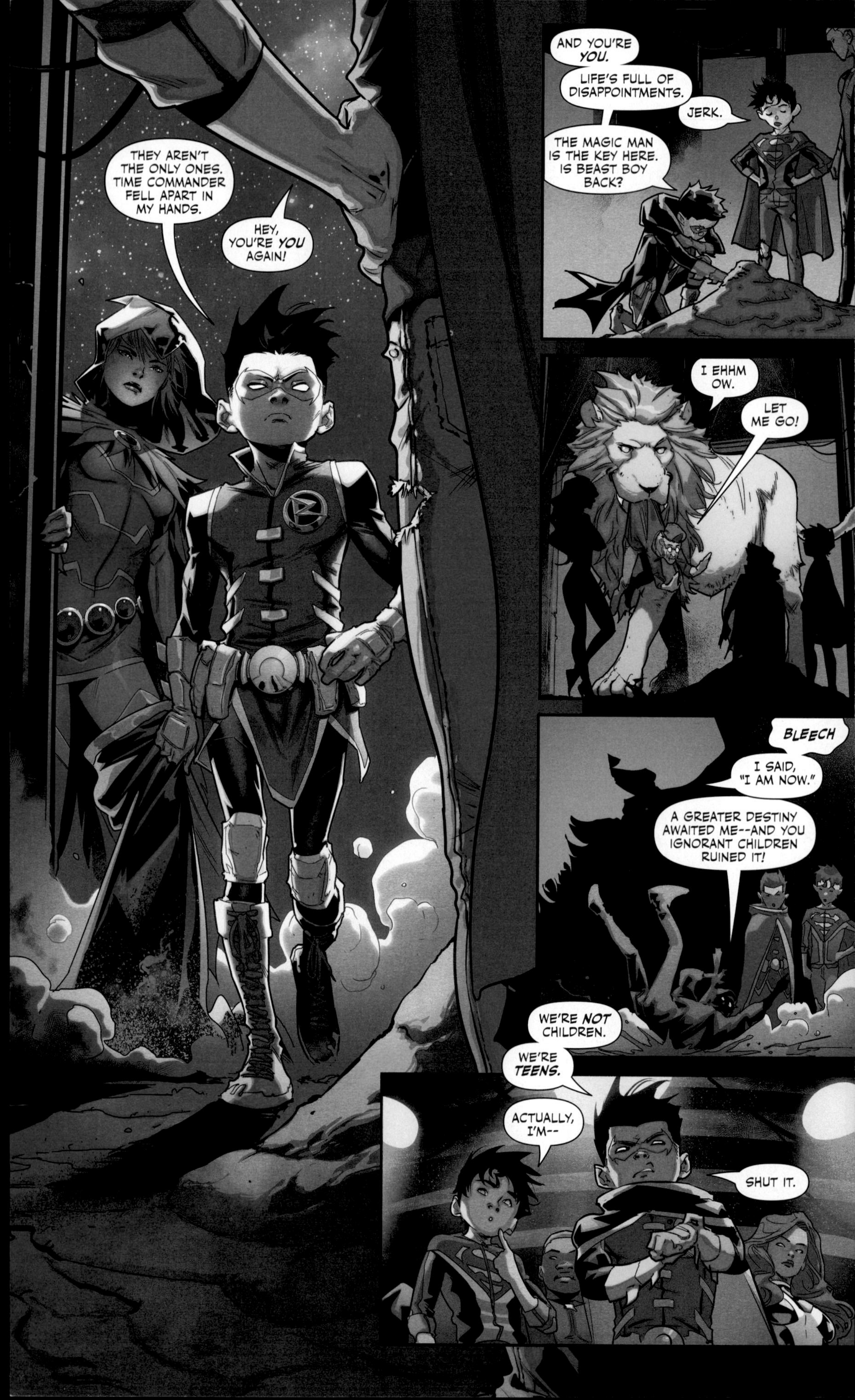
THEY AREN'T THE ONLY ONES. TIME COMMANDER FELL APART IN MY HANDS.
HEY, YOU'RE YOU AGAIN!
AND YOU'RE YOU.
LIFE'S FULL OF DISAPPOINTMENTS.
JERK.
THE MAGIC MAN IS THE KEY HERE. IS BEAST BOY BACK?
I EHHM OW.
LET ME GO!
BLEECH
I SAID, "I AM NOW."
A GREATER DESTINY AWAITED ME--AND YOU IGNORANT CHILDREN RUINED IT!
WE'RE NOT CHILDREN.
WE'RE TEENS.
ACTUALLY, I'M--
SHUT IT.

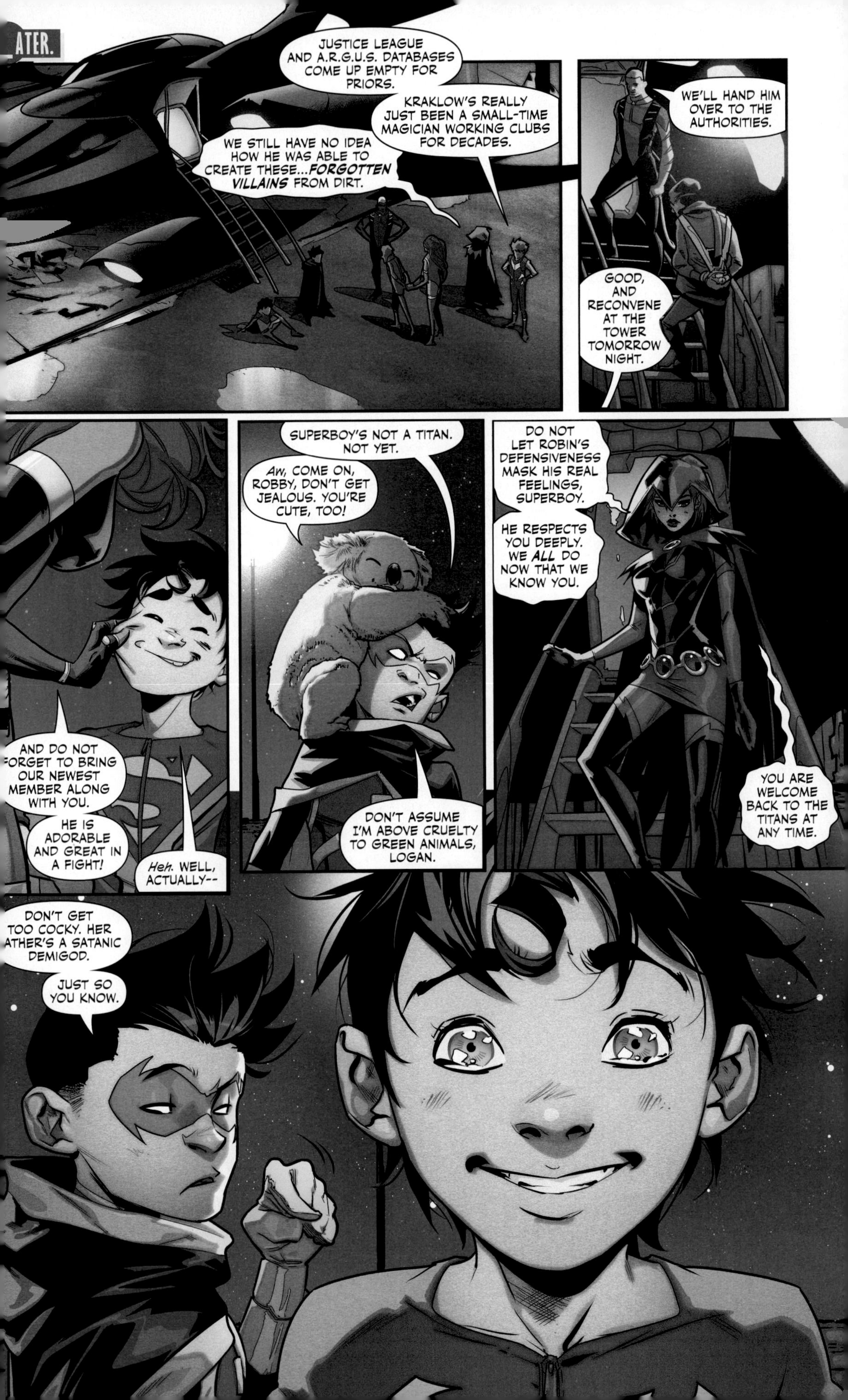
ATER.
JUSTICE LEAGUE AND A.R.G.U.S. DATABASES COME UP EMPTY FOR PRIORS.
KRAKLOW'S REALLY JUST BEEN A SMALL-TIME MAGICIAN WORKING CLUBS FOR DECADES.
WE STILL HAVE NO IDEA HOW HE WAS ABLE TO CREATE THESE...FORGOTTEN VILLAINS FROM DIRT.
WE'LL HAND HIM OVER TO THE AUTHORITIES.
GOOD, AND RECONVENE AT THE TOWER TOMORROW NIGHT.
AND DO NOT FORGET TO BRING OUR NEWEST MEMBER ALONG WITH YOU.
HE IS ADORABLE AND GREAT IN A FIGHT!
Heh. WELL, ACTUALLY--
SUPERBOY'S NOT A TITAN. NOT YET.
Aw, COME ON, ROBBY, DON'T GET JEALOUS. YOU'RE CUTE, TOO!
DON'T ASSUME I'M ABOVE CRUELTY TO GREEN ANIMALS, LOGAN.
DO NOT LET ROBIN'S DEFENSIVENESS MASK HIS REAL FEELINGS, SUPERBOY.
HE RESPECTS YOU DEEPLY. WE ALL DO NOW THAT WE KNOW YOU.
YOU ARE WELCOME BACK TO THE TITANS AT ANY TIME.
DON'T GET TOO COCKY. HER ATHER'S A SATANIC DEMIGOD.
JUST SO YOU KNOW.

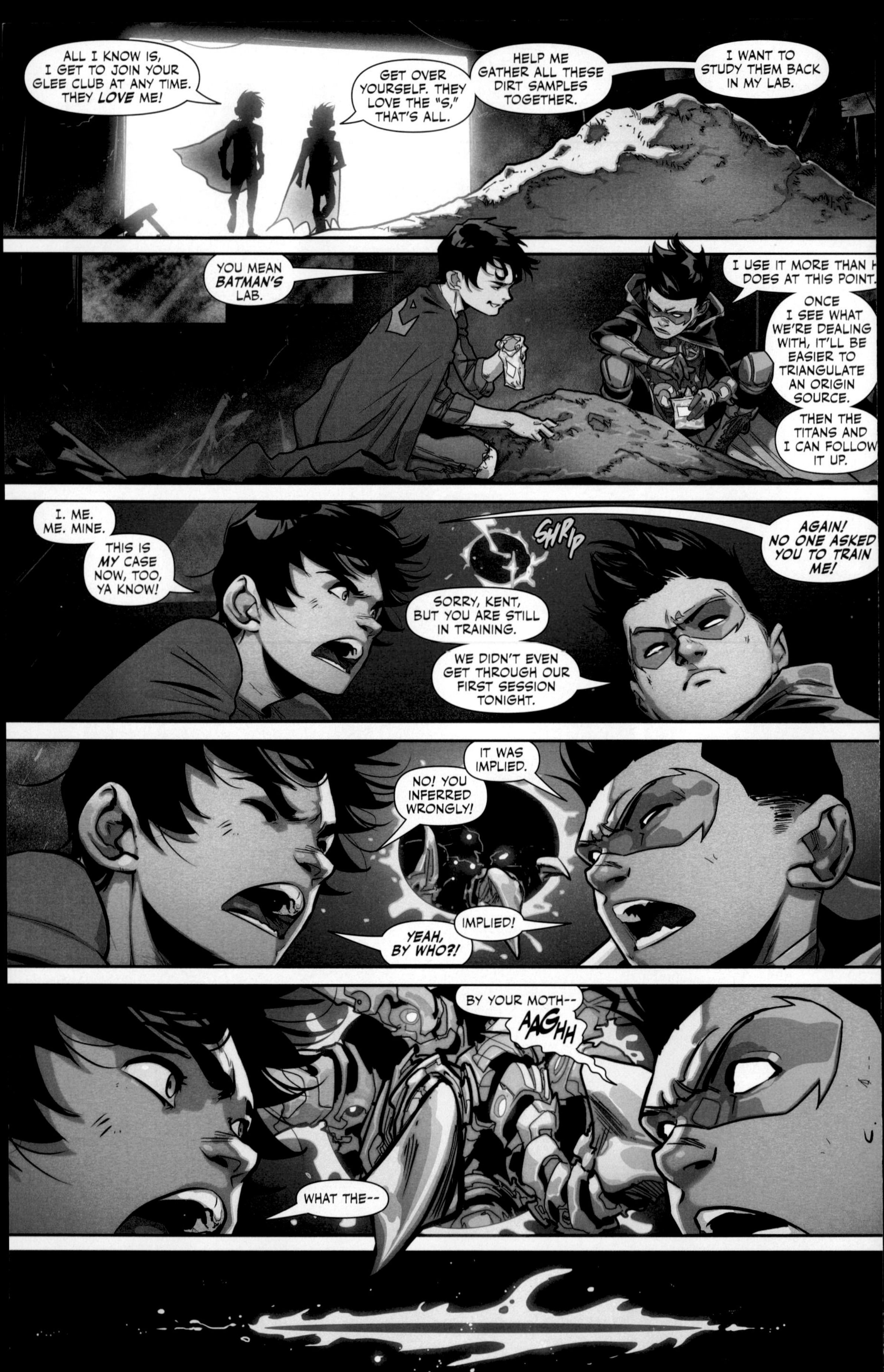
ALL I KNOW IS, I GET TO JOIN YOUR GLEE CLUB AT ANY TIME. THEY LOVE ME!
GET OVER YOURSELF. THEY LOVE THE "S," THAT'S ALL.
HELP ME GATHER ALL THESE DIRT SAMPLES TOGETHER.
I WANT TO STUDY THEM BACK IN MY LAB.
YOU MEAN BATMAN'S LAB.
I USE IT MORE THAN HE DOES AT THIS POINT.
ONCE I SEE WHAT WE'RE DEALING WITH, IT'LL BE EASIER TO TRIANGULATE AN ORIGIN SOURCE.
THEN THE TITANS AND I CAN FOLLOW IT UP.
I. ME. ME. MINE.
THIS IS MY CASE NOW, TOO, YA KNOW!
SHRIP
SORRY, KENT, BUT YOU ARE STILL IN TRAINING.
WE DIDN'T EVEN GET THROUGH OUR FIRST SESSION TONIGHT.
AGAIN! NO ONE ASKED YOU TO TRAIN ME!
IT WAS IMPLIED.
NO! YOU INFERRED WRONGLY!
IMPLIED!
YEAH, BY WHO?!
BY YOUR MOTH--
AAGHH
WHAT THE--

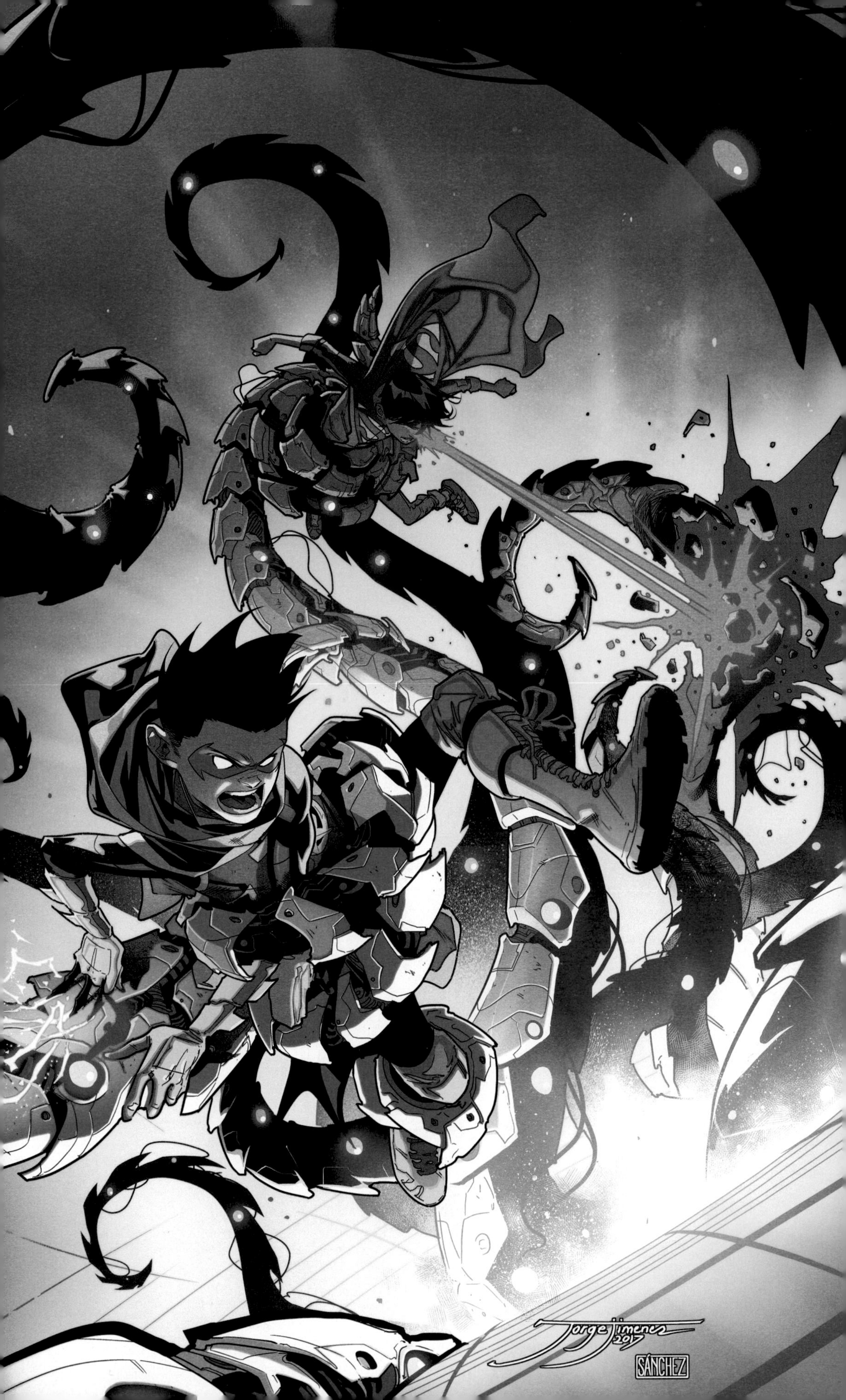
Jorge Jimenez 2017
SÁNCHEZ

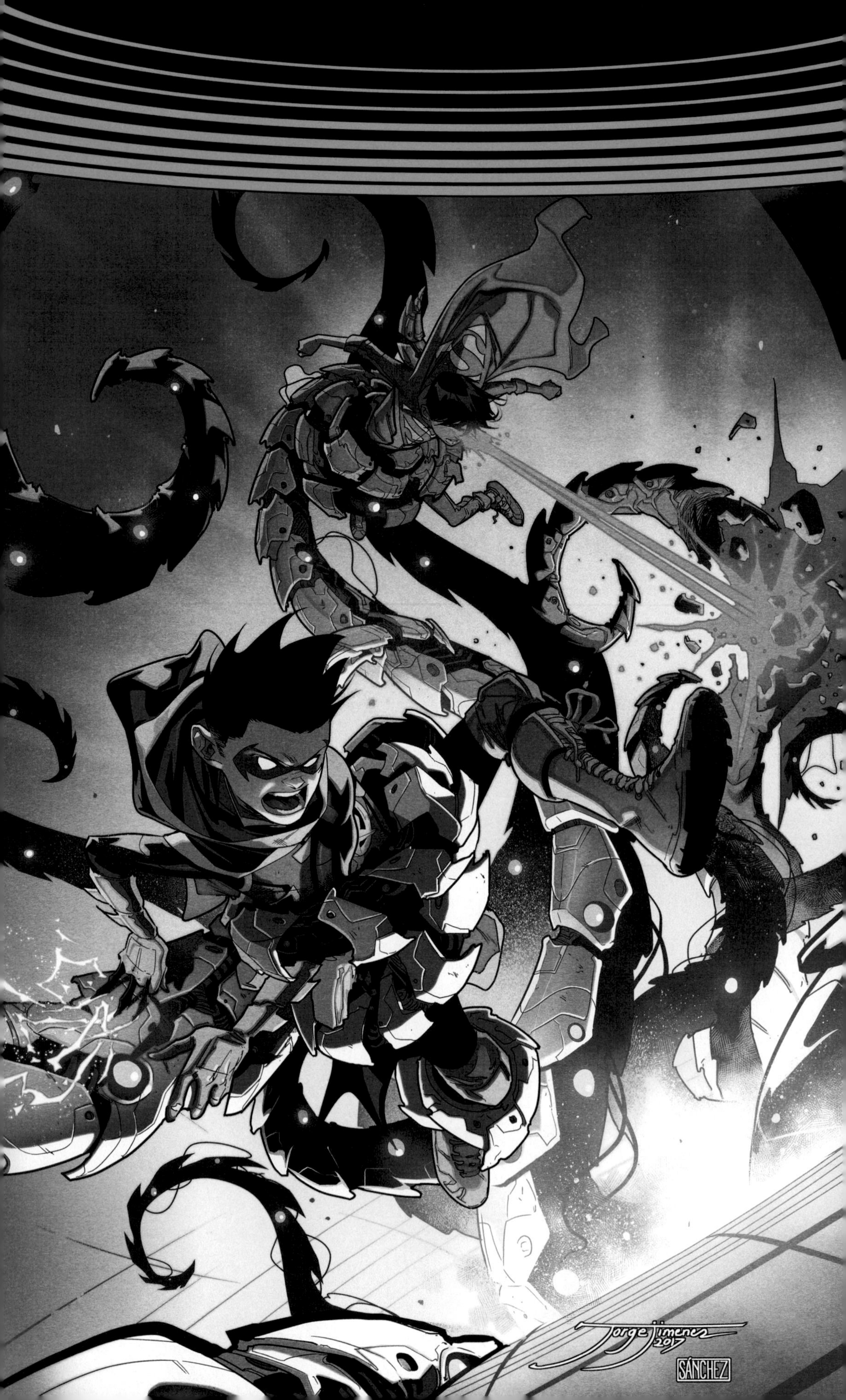
Jorge Jimenez 2017
SÁNCHEZ

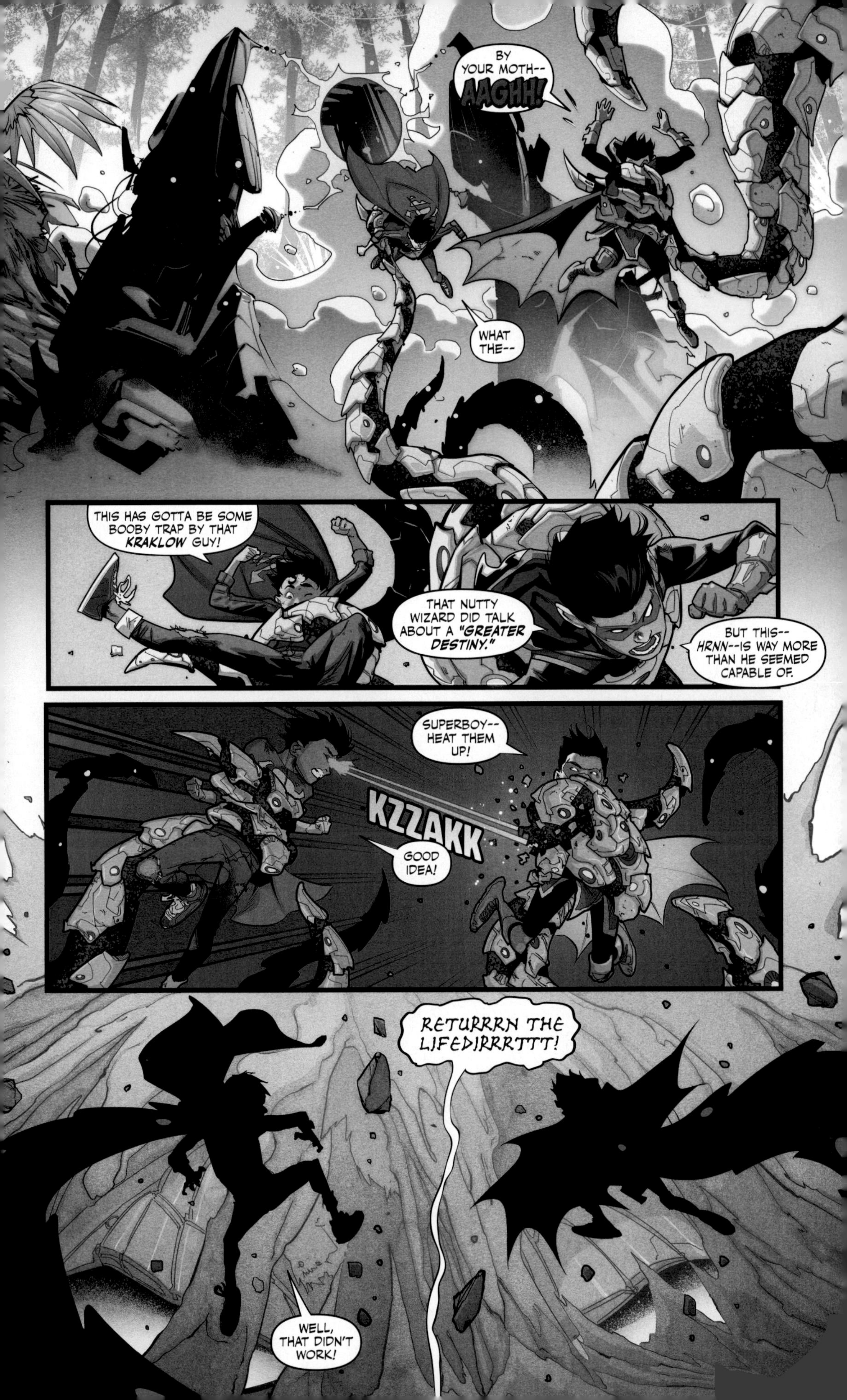
BY YOUR MOTH-- AAGHH!
WHAT THE--
THIS HAS GOTTA BE SOME BOOBY TRAP BY THAT KRAKLOW GUY!
THAT NUTTY WIZARD DID TALK ABOUT A "GREATER DESTINY."
BUT THIS-- HRNN--IS WAY MORE THAN HE SEEMED CAPABLE OF.
SUPERBOY-- HEAT THEM UP!
KZZAKK
GOOD IDEA!
RETURRRN THE LIFEDIRRRTTTT!
WELL, THAT DIDN'T WORK!

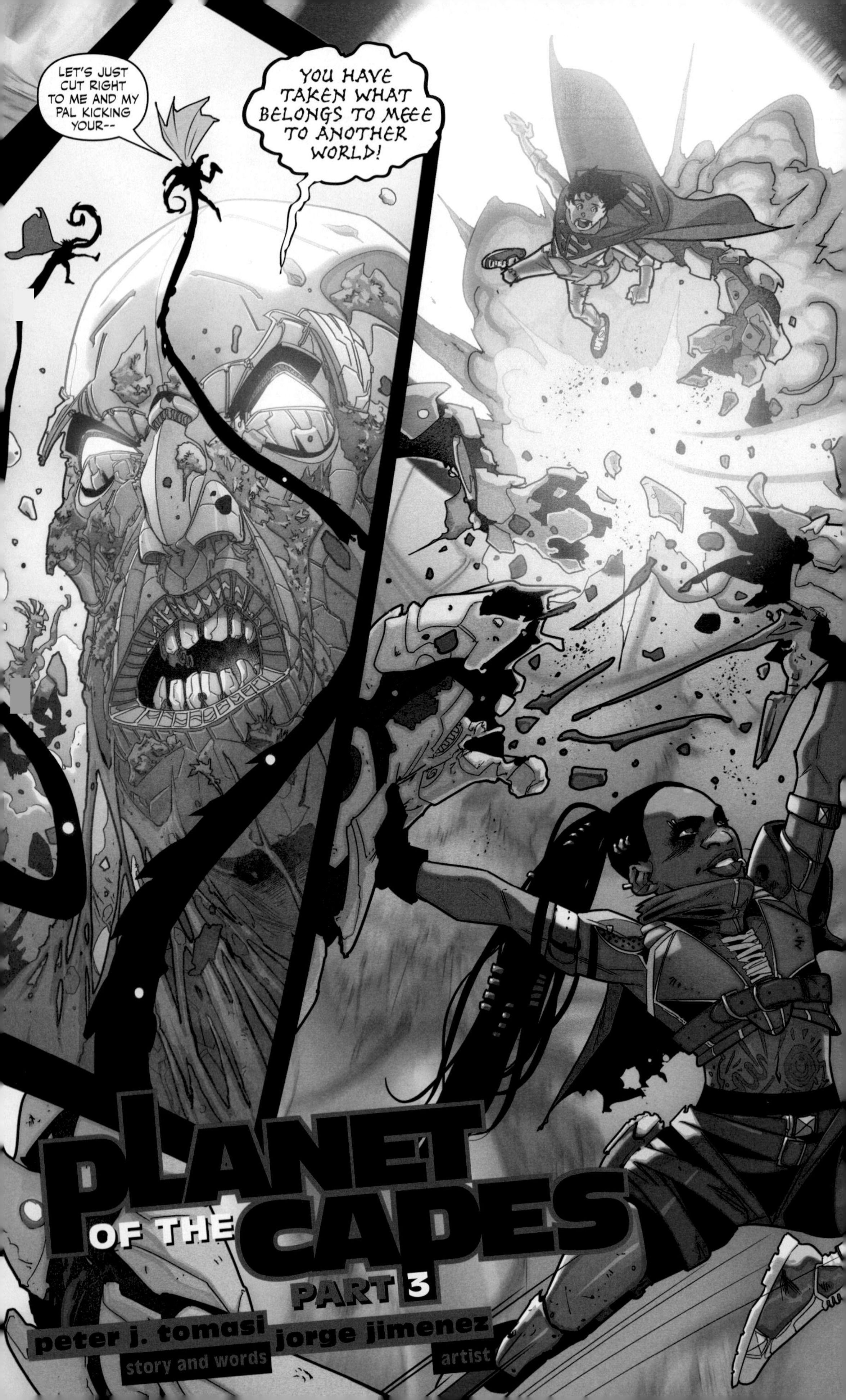
LET'S JUST CUT RIGHT TO ME AND MY PAL KICKING YOUR--
YOU HAVE TAKEN WHAT BELONGS TO MEEE TO ANOTHER WORLD!
PLANET OF THE CAPES
PART 3
peter j. tomasi
story and words
jorge jimenez
artist

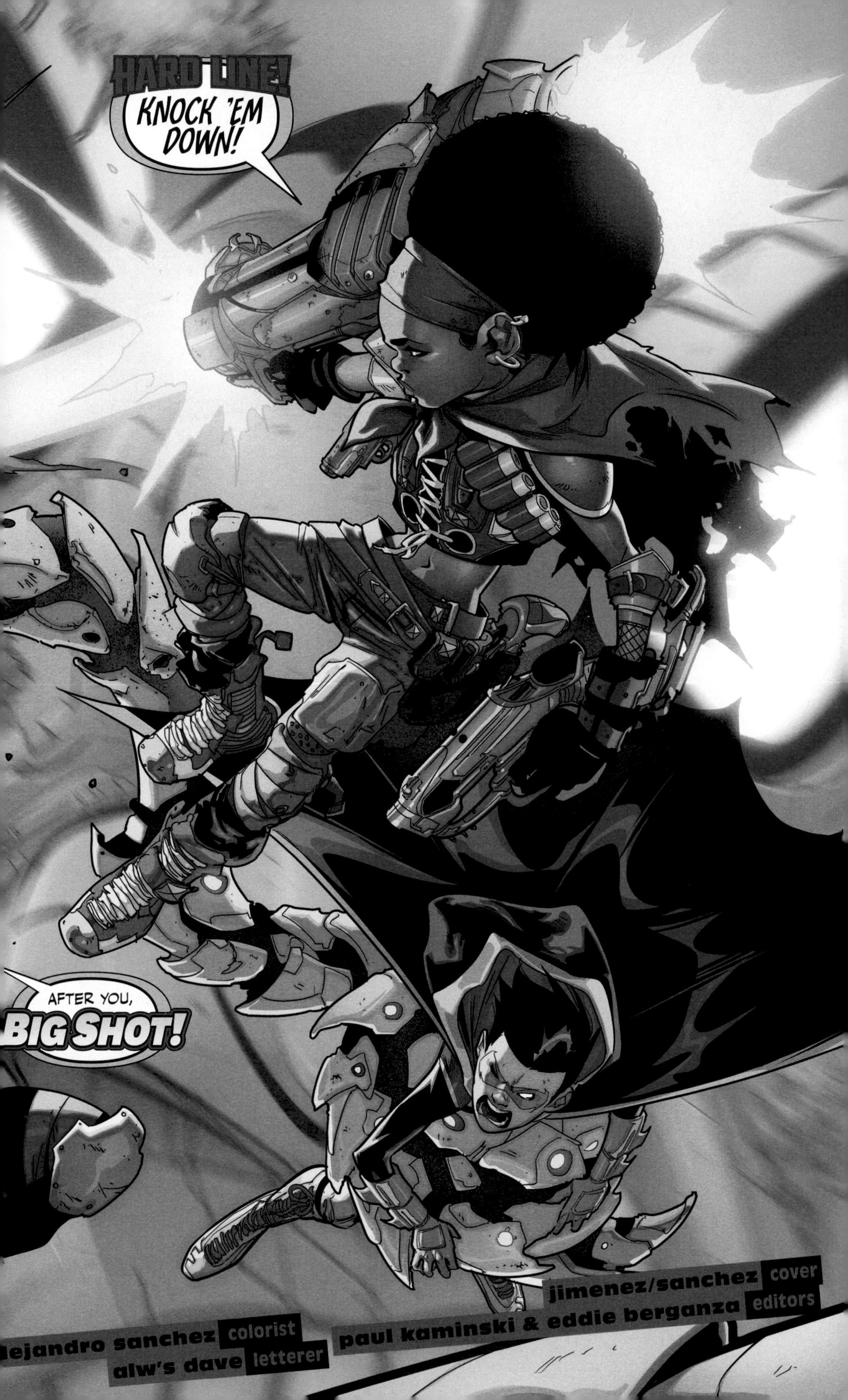

HARD LINE!
KNOCK 'EM DOWN!
AFTER YOU, BIG SHOT!
jimenez/sanchez cover
paul kaminski & eddie berganza editors
lejandro sanchez colorist
alw's dave letterer

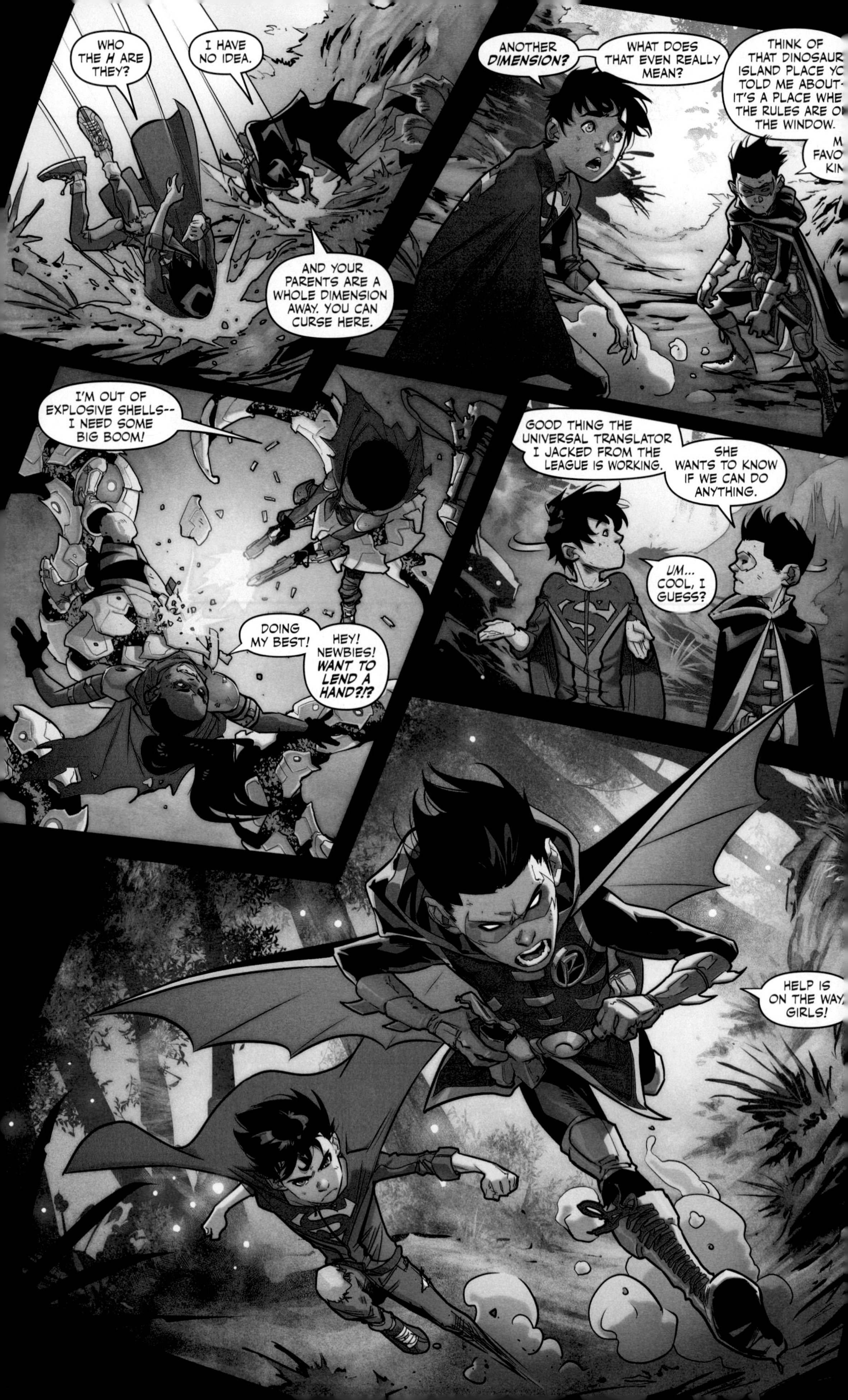
WHO THE *H* ARE THEY?
I HAVE NO IDEA.
AND YOUR PARENTS ARE A WHOLE DIMENSION AWAY. YOU CAN CURSE HERE.
ANOTHER *DIMENSION?*
WHAT DOES THAT EVEN REALLY MEAN?
THINK OF THAT DINOSAUR ISLAND PLACE YO TOLD ME ABOUT- IT'S A PLACE WHE THE RULES ARE O THE WINDOW.
I'M OUT OF EXPLOSIVE SHELLS-- I NEED SOME BIG BOOM!
DOING MY BEST!
HEY! NEWBIES! *WANT TO LEND A HAND?!?*
GOOD THING THE UNIVERSAL TRANSLATOR I JACKED FROM THE LEAGUE IS WORKING.
SHE WANTS TO KNOW IF WE CAN DO ANYTHING.
UM... COOL, I GUESS?
HELP IS ON THE WAY, GIRLS!

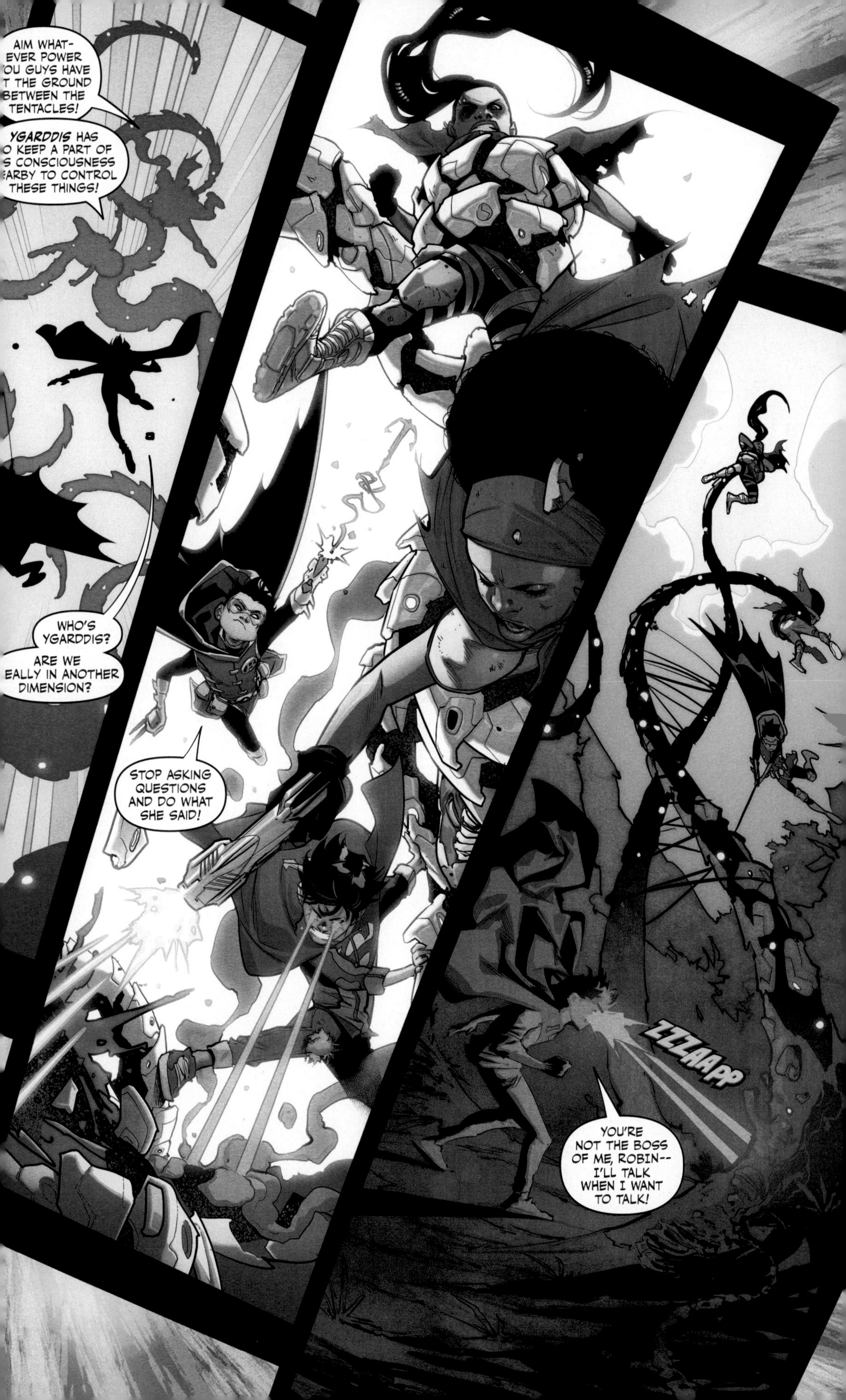
AIM WHAT-EVER POWER OU GUYS HAVE T THE GROUND BETWEEN THE TENTACLES!
YGARDDIS HAS O KEEP A PART OF S CONSCIOUSNESS EARBY TO CONTROL THESE THINGS!
WHO'S YGARDDIS?
ARE WE EALLY IN ANOTHER DIMENSION?
STOP ASKING QUESTIONS AND DO WHAT SHE SAID!
ZZZAAPP
YOU'RE NOT THE BOSS OF ME, ROBIN-- I'LL TALK WHEN I WANT TO TALK!

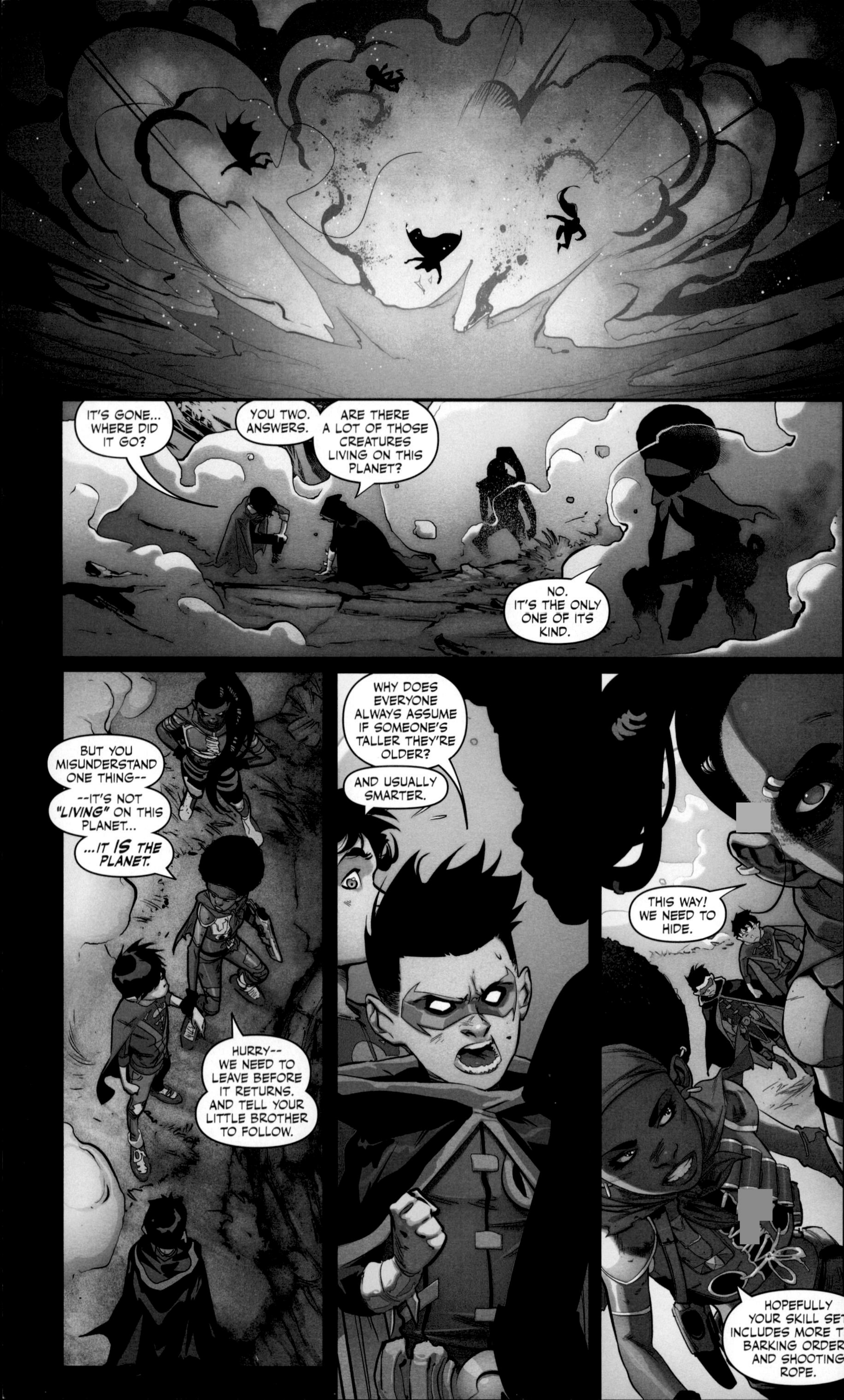
IT'S GONE... WHERE DID IT GO?
YOU TWO. ANSWERS.
ARE THERE A LOT OF THOSE CREATURES LIVING ON THIS PLANET?
NO. IT'S THE ONLY ONE OF ITS KIND.
BUT YOU MISUNDERSTAND ONE THING--
--IT'S NOT "LIVING" ON THIS PLANET...
...IT IS THE PLANET.
HURRY-- WE NEED TO LEAVE BEFORE IT RETURNS. AND TELL YOUR LITTLE BROTHER TO FOLLOW.
WHY DOES EVERYONE ALWAYS ASSUME IF SOMEONE'S TALLER THEY'RE OLDER?
AND USUALLY SMARTER.
THIS WAY! WE NEED TO HIDE.
HOPEFULLY YOUR SKILL SET INCLUDES MORE T
BARKING ORDER
AND SHOOTING ROPE.

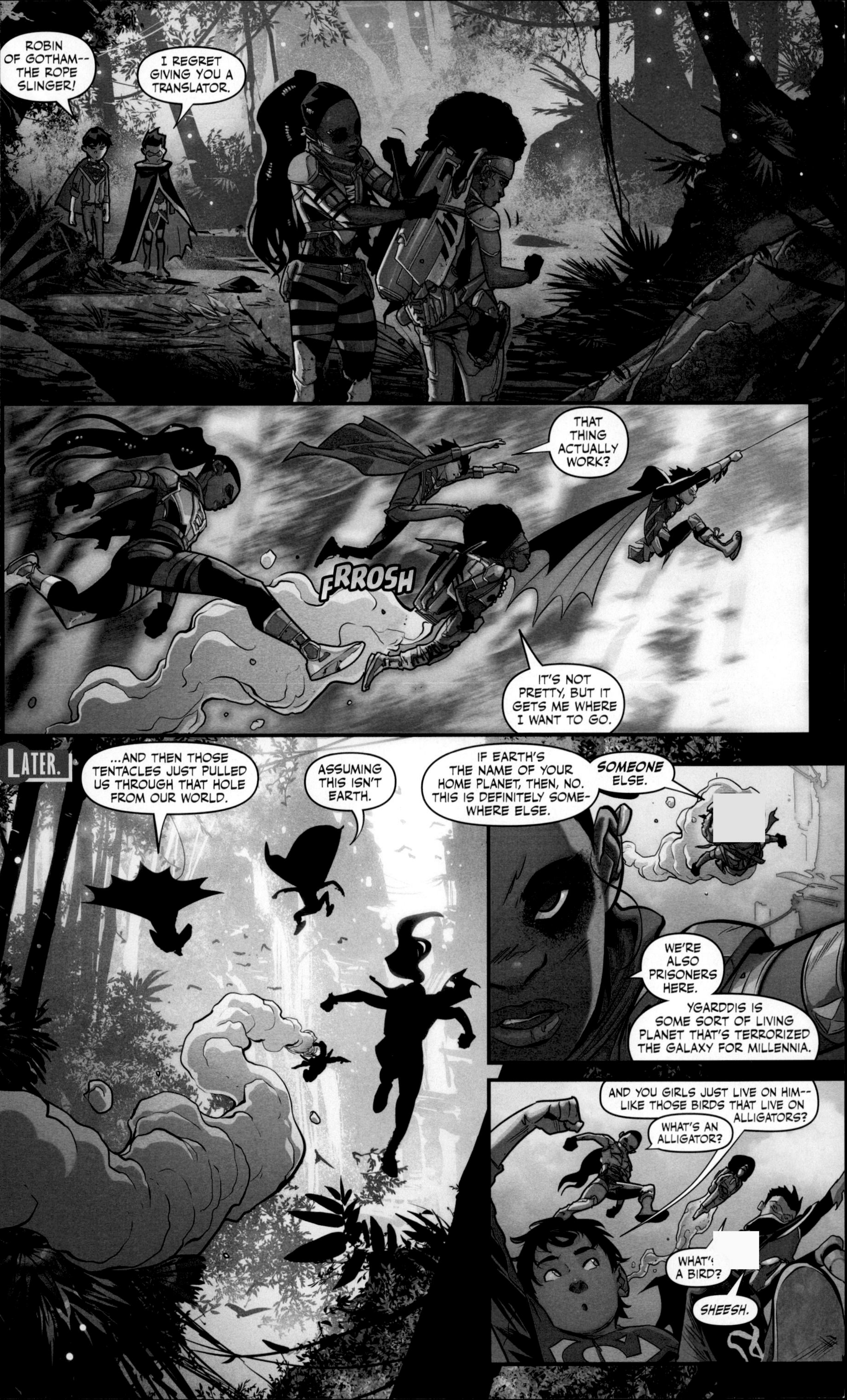
ROBIN OF GOTHAM-- THE ROPE SLINGER!
I REGRET GIVING YOU A TRANSLATOR.
THAT THING ACTUALLY WORK?
FRROSH
IT'S NOT PRETTY, BUT IT GETS ME WHERE I WANT TO GO.
LATER.
...AND THEN THOSE TENTACLES JUST PULLED US THROUGH THAT HOLE FROM OUR WORLD.
ASSUMING THIS ISN'T EARTH.
IF EARTH'S THE NAME OF YOUR HOME PLANET, THEN, NO. THIS IS DEFINITELY SOME-WHERE ELSE.
SOMEONE ELSE.
WE'RE ALSO PRISONERS HERE.
YGARDDIS IS SOME SORT OF LIVING PLANET THAT'S TERRORIZED THE GALAXY FOR MILLENNIA.
AND YOU GIRLS JUST LIVE ON HIM-- LIKE THOSE BIRDS THAT LIVE ON ALLIGATORS?
WHAT'S AN ALLIGATOR?
WHAT'S A BIRD?
SHEESH.

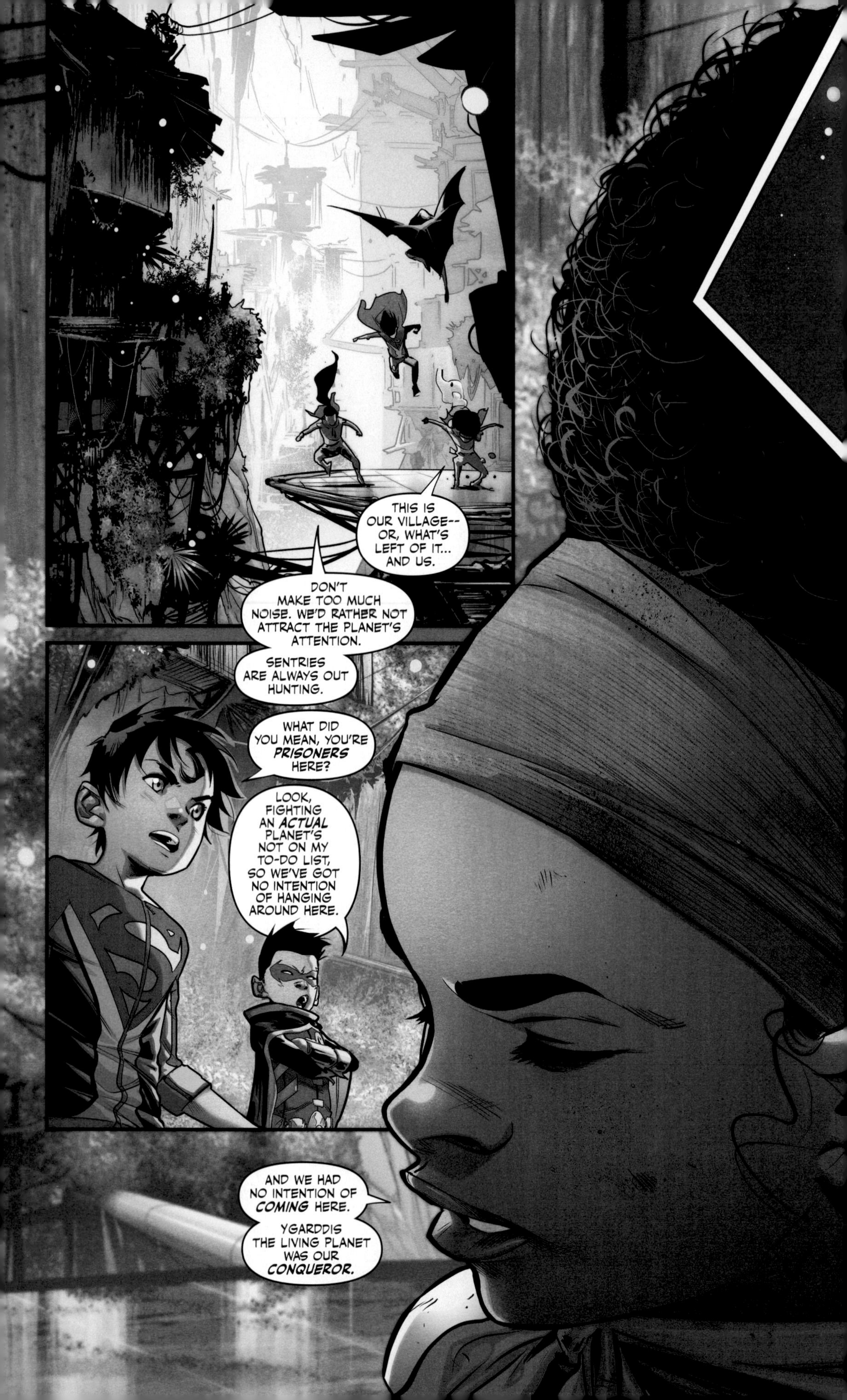
THIS IS OUR VILLAGE-- OR, WHAT'S LEFT OF IT... AND US.
DON'T MAKE TOO MUCH NOISE. WE'D RATHER NOT ATTRACT THE PLANET'S ATTENTION.
SENTRIES ARE ALWAYS OUT HUNTING.
WHAT DID YOU MEAN, YOU'RE PRISONERS HERE?
LOOK, FIGHTING AN ACTUAL PLANET'S NOT ON MY TO-DO LIST, SO WE'VE GOT NO INTENTION OF HANGING AROUND HERE.
AND WE HAD NO INTENTION OF COMING HERE.
YGARDDIS THE LIVING PLANET WAS OUR CONQUEROR.

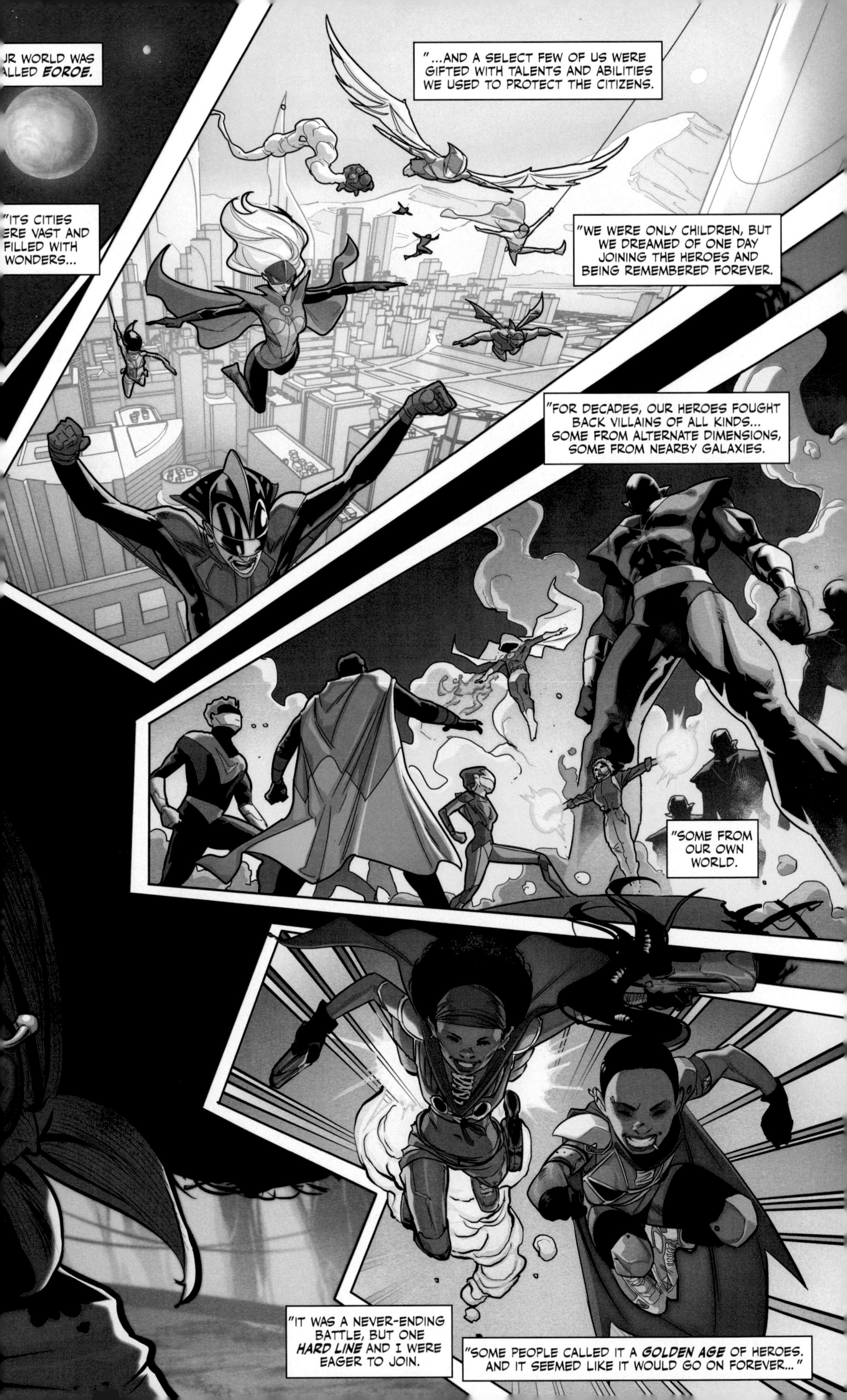

UR WORLD WAS
ALLED *EOROE.*
"...AND A SELECT FEW OF US WERE GIFTED WITH TALENTS AND ABILITIES WE USED TO PROTECT THE CITIZENS.
"ITS CITIES ERE VAST AND FILLED WITH WONDERS...
"WE WERE ONLY CHILDREN, BUT WE DREAMED OF ONE DAY JOINING THE HEROES AND BEING REMEMBERED FOREVER.
"FOR DECADES, OUR HEROES FOUGHT BACK VILLAINS OF ALL KINDS... SOME FROM ALTERNATE DIMENSIONS, SOME FROM NEARBY GALAXIES.
"SOME FROM OUR OWN WORLD.
"IT WAS A NEVER-ENDING BATTLE, BUT ONE *HARD LINE* AND I WERE EAGER TO JOIN.
"SOME PEOPLE CALLED IT A *GOLDEN AGE* OF HEROES. AND IT SEEMED LIKE IT WOULD GO ON FOREVER..."

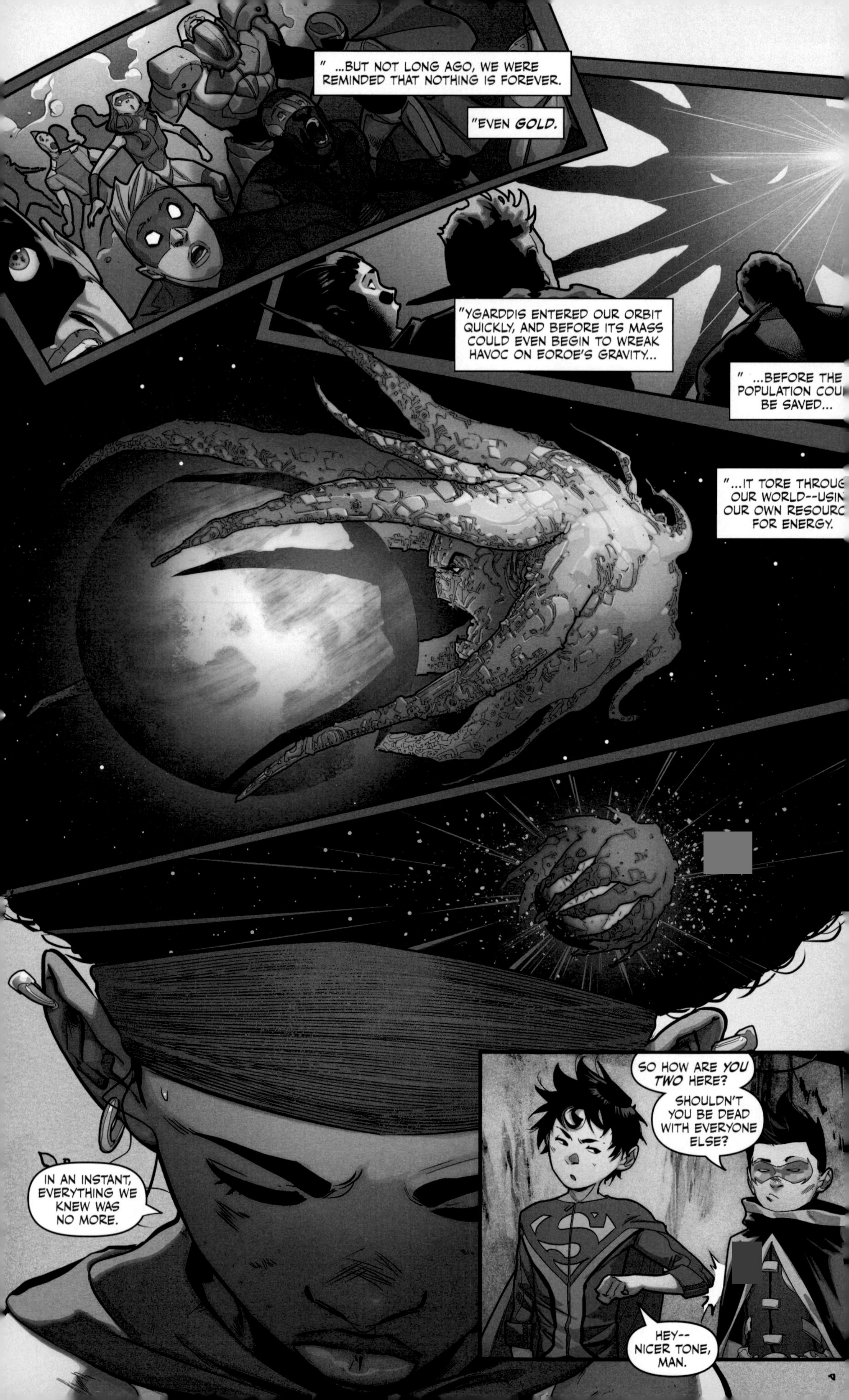

" ...BUT NOT LONG AGO, WE WERE REMINDED THAT NOTHING IS FOREVER.
"EVEN *GOLD.*
"YGARDDIS ENTERED OUR ORBIT QUICKLY, AND BEFORE ITS MASS COULD EVEN BEGIN TO WREAK HAVOC ON EOROE'S GRAVITY...
" ...BEFORE THE POPULATION COU BE SAVED...
"...IT TORE THROUG OUR WORLD--USIN OUR OWN RESOURC FOR ENERGY.
IN AN INSTANT, EVERYTHING WE KNEW WAS NO MORE.
SO HOW ARE *YOU TWO* HERE?
SHOULDN'T YOU BE DEAD WITH EVERYONE ELSE?
HEY-- NICER TONE, MAN.

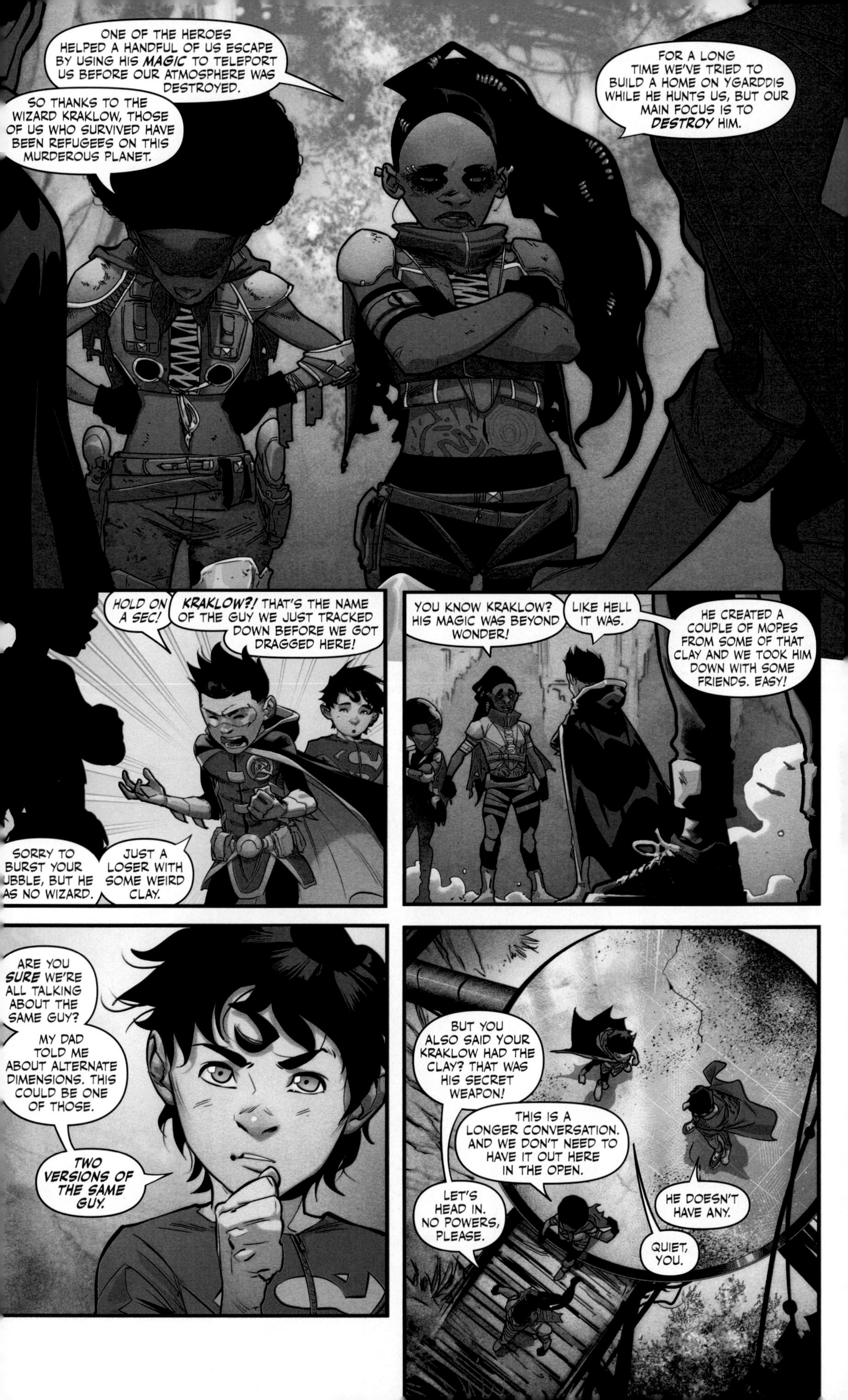
ONE OF THE HEROES HELPED A HANDFUL OF US ESCAPE BY USING HIS MAGIC TO TELEPORT US BEFORE OUR ATMOSPHERE WAS DESTROYED.
SO THANKS TO THE WIZARD KRAKLOW, THOSE OF US WHO SURVIVED HAVE BEEN REFUGEES ON THIS MURDEROUS PLANET.
FOR A LONG TIME WE'VE TRIED TO BUILD A HOME ON YGARDDIS WHILE HE HUNTS US, BUT OUR MAIN FOCUS IS TO DESTROY HIM.
HOLD ON A SEC!
KRAKLOW?! THAT'S THE NAME OF THE GUY WE JUST TRACKED DOWN BEFORE WE GOT DRAGGED HERE!
SORRY TO BURST YOUR UBBLE, BUT HE AS NO WIZARD.
JUST A LOSER WITH SOME WEIRD CLAY.
YOU KNOW KRAKLOW? HIS MAGIC WAS BEYOND WONDER!
LIKE HELL IT WAS.
HE CREATED A COUPLE OF MOPES FROM SOME OF THAT CLAY AND WE TOOK HIM DOWN WITH SOME FRIENDS. EASY!
ARE YOU SURE WE'RE ALL TALKING ABOUT THE SAME GUY?
MY DAD TOLD ME ABOUT ALTERNATE DIMENSIONS. THIS COULD BE ONE OF THOSE.
TWO VERSIONS OF THE SAME GUY.
BUT YOU ALSO SAID YOUR KRAKLOW HAD THE CLAY? THAT WAS HIS SECRET WEAPON!
THIS IS A LONGER CONVERSATION. AND WE DON'T NEED TO HAVE IT OUT HERE IN THE OPEN.
LET'S HEAD IN. NO POWERS, PLEASE.
HE DOESN'T HAVE ANY.
QUIET, YOU.

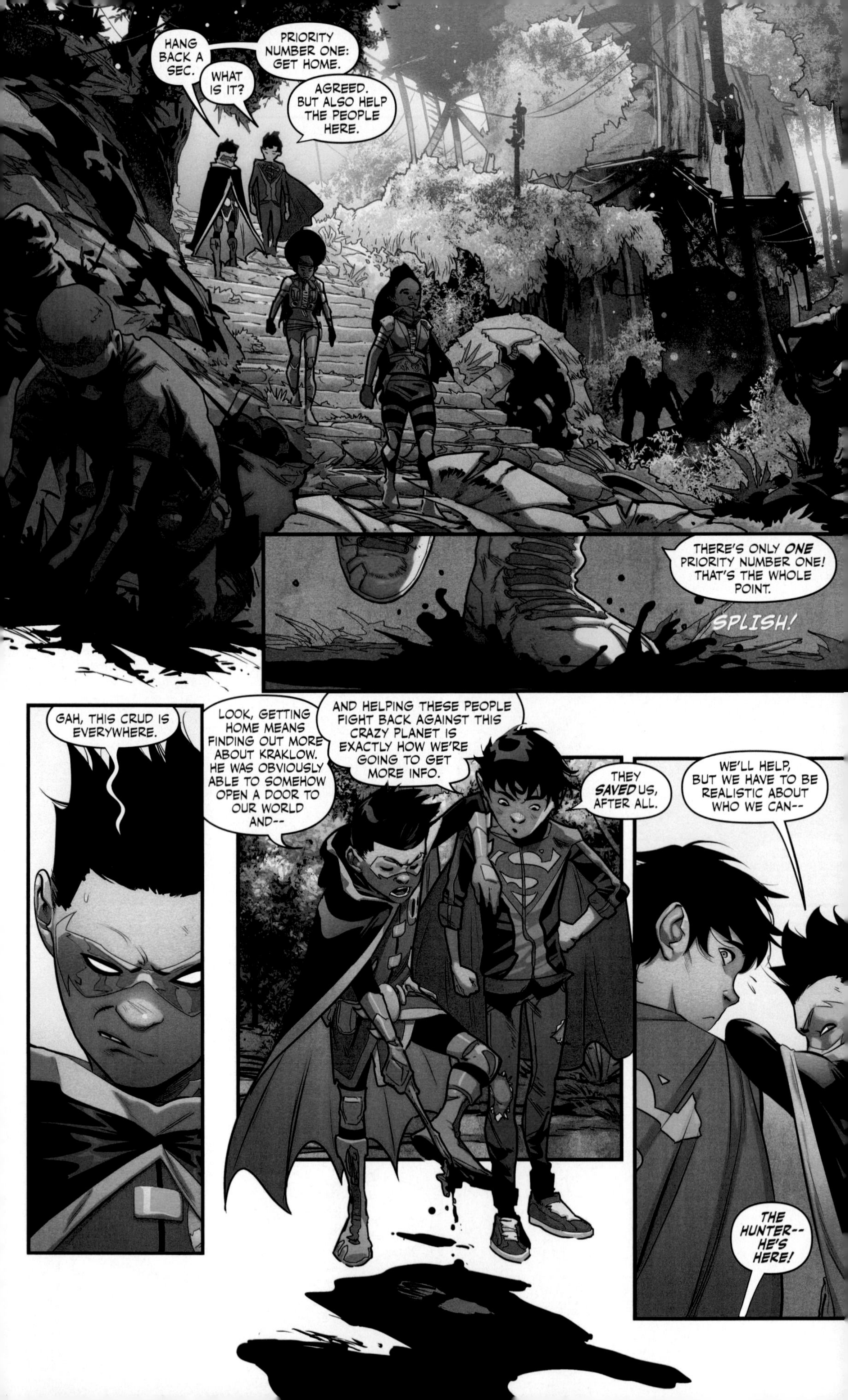
HANG BACK A SEC.
WHAT IS IT?
PRIORITY NUMBER ONE: GET HOME.
AGREED. BUT ALSO HELP THE PEOPLE HERE.
THERE'S ONLY ONE PRIORITY NUMBER ONE! THAT'S THE WHOLE POINT.
SPLISH!
GAH, THIS CRUD IS EVERYWHERE.
LOOK, GETTING HOME MEANS FINDING OUT MORE ABOUT KRAKLOW. HE WAS OBVIOUSLY ABLE TO SOMEHOW OPEN A DOOR TO OUR WORLD AND--
AND HELPING THESE PEOPLE FIGHT BACK AGAINST THIS CRAZY PLANET IS EXACTLY HOW WE'RE GOING TO GET MORE INFO.
THEY SAVED US, AFTER ALL.
WE'LL HELP, BUT WE HAVE TO BE REALISTIC ABOUT WHO WE CAN--
THE HUNTER-- HE'S HERE!

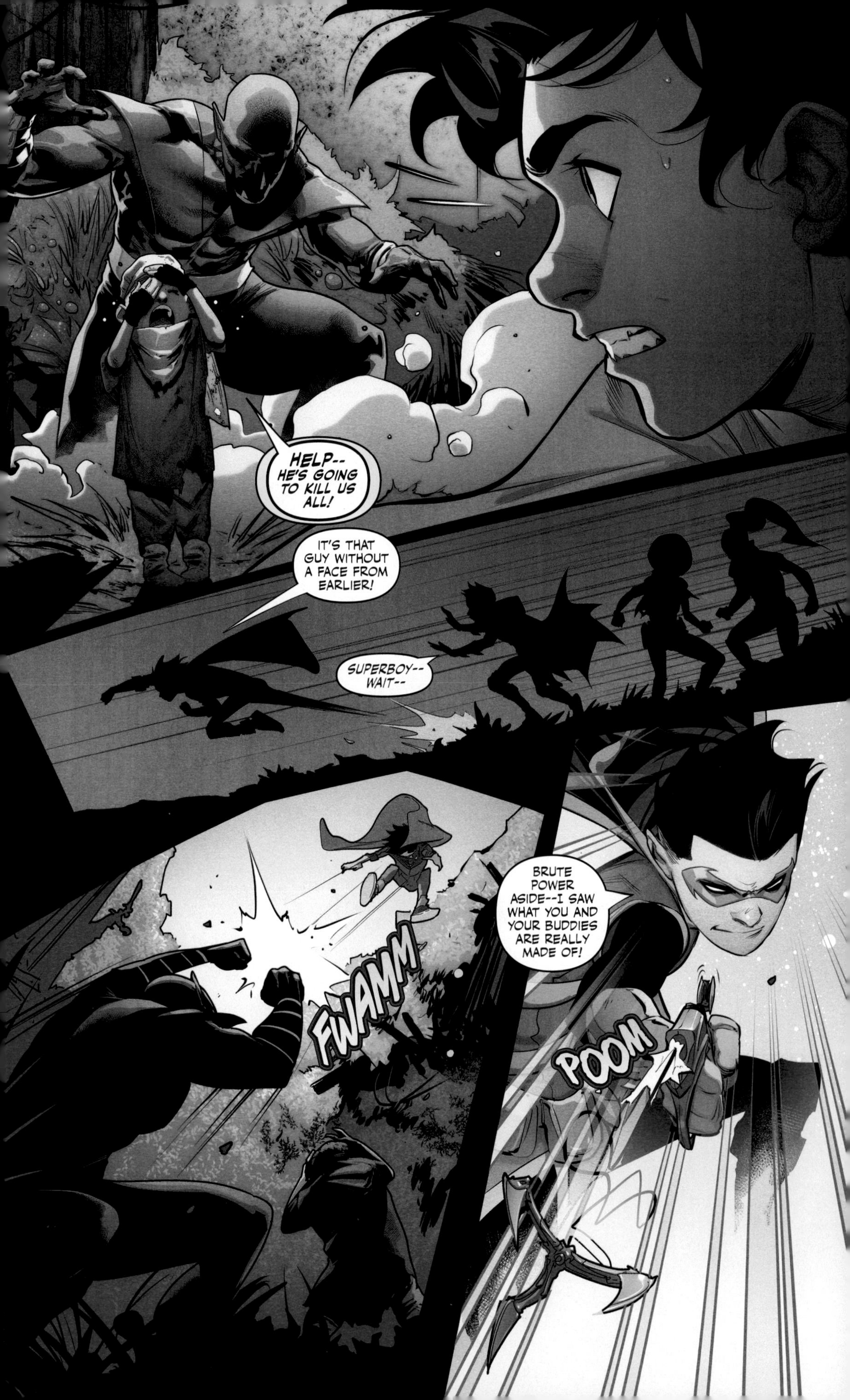
HELP-- HE'S GOING TO KILL US ALL!
IT'S THAT GUY WITHOUT A FACE FROM EARLIER!
SUPERBOY-- WAIT--
FWAMM
BRUTE POWER ASIDE--I SAW WHAT YOU AND YOUR BUDDIES ARE REALLY MADE OF!
POOM

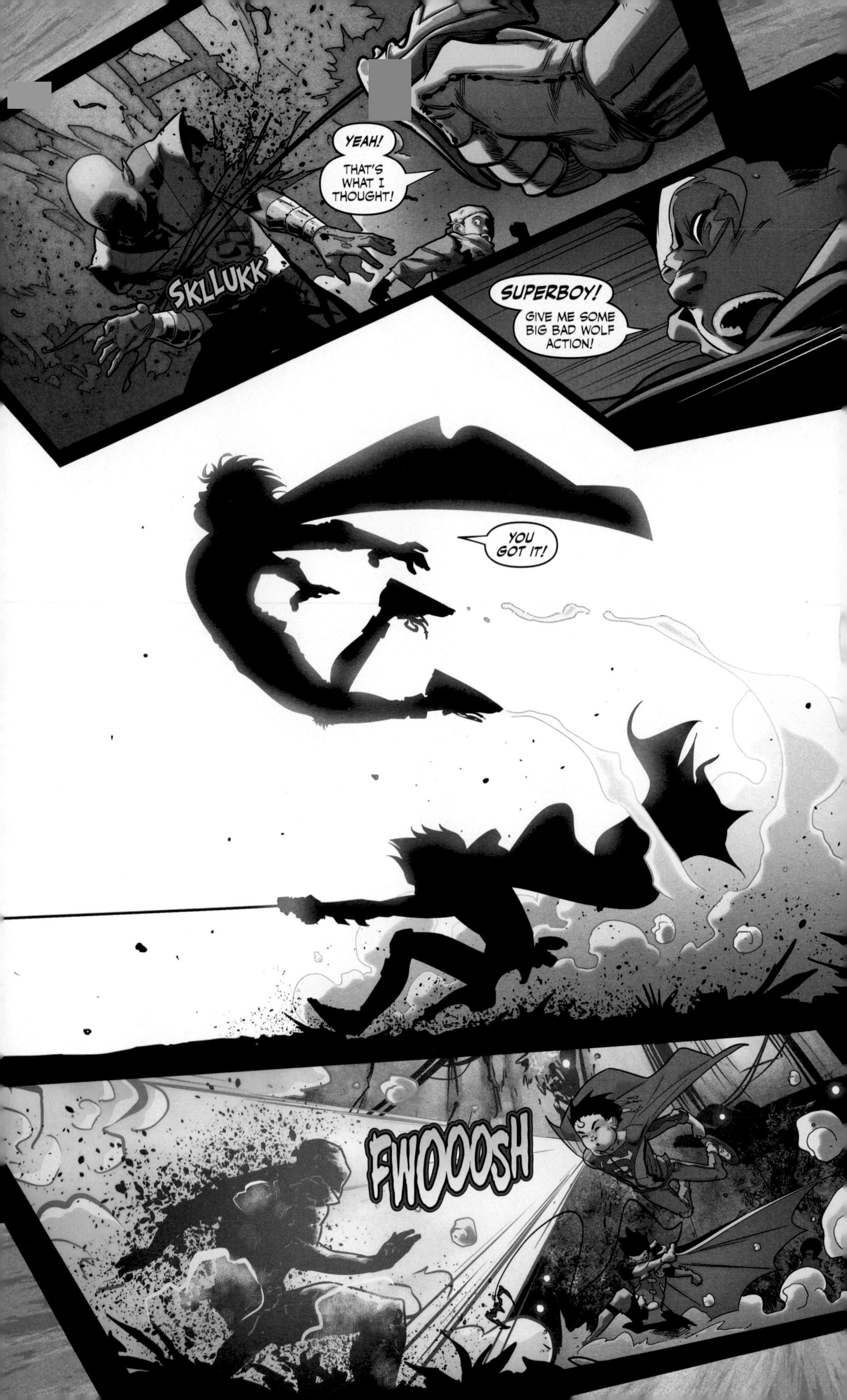
SKLLUKK
YEAH!
THAT'S WHAT I THOUGHT!
SUPERBOY!
GIVE ME SOME BIG BAD WOLF ACTION!
YOU GOT IT!
FWOOOSH

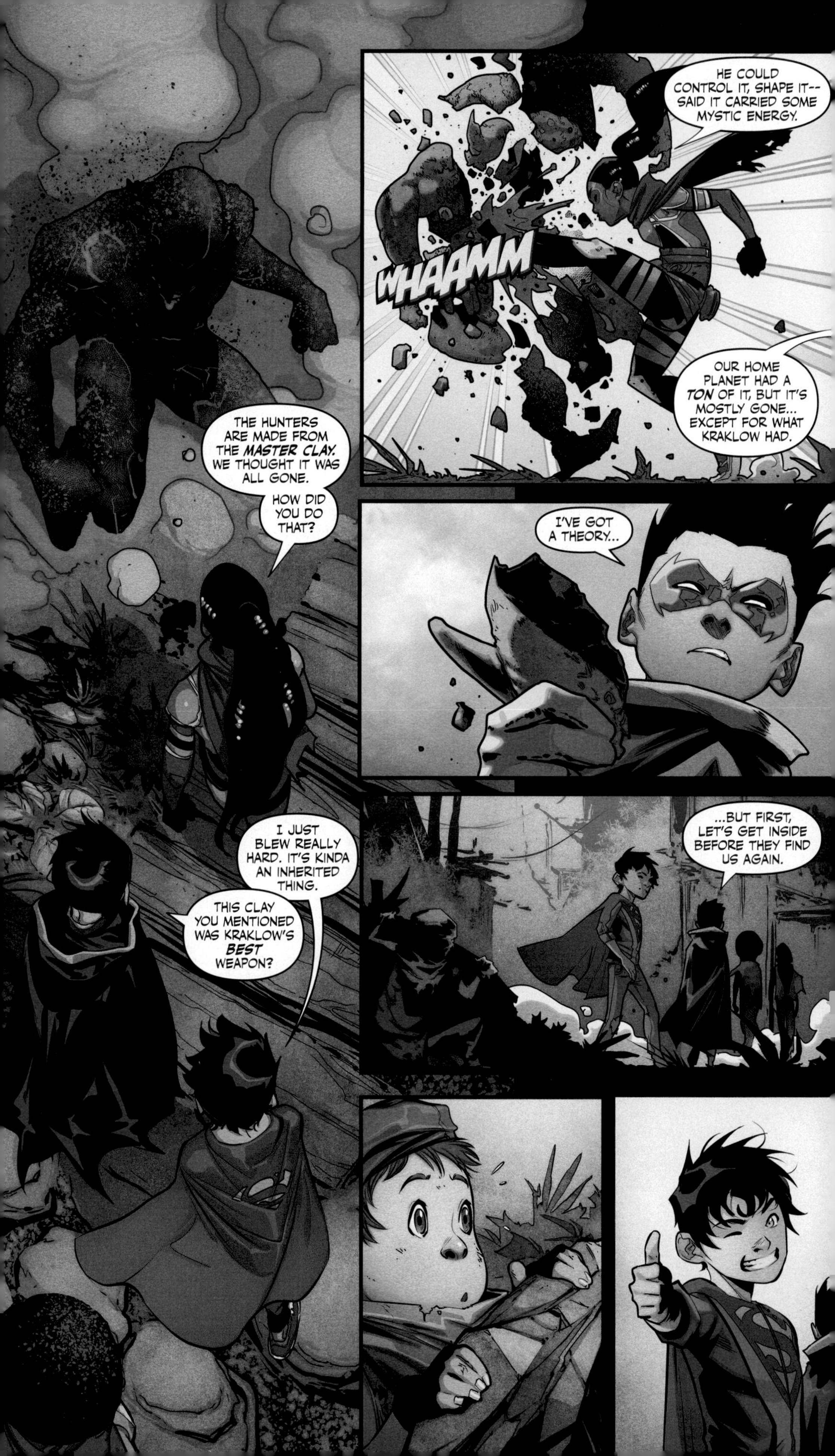
HE COULD CONTROL IT, SHAPE IT-- SAID IT CARRIED SOME MYSTIC ENERGY.
WHAAMM
OUR HOME PLANET HAD A TON OF IT, BUT IT'S MOSTLY GONE... EXCEPT FOR WHAT KRAKLOW HAD.
THE HUNTERS ARE MADE FROM THE MASTER CLAY. WE THOUGHT IT WAS ALL GONE.
HOW DID YOU DO THAT?
I JUST BLEW REALLY HARD. IT'S KINDA AN INHERITED THING.
THIS CLAY YOU MENTIONED WAS KRAKLOW'S BEST WEAPON?
I'VE GOT A THEORY...
...BUT FIRST, LET'S GET INSIDE BEFORE THEY FIND US AGAIN.

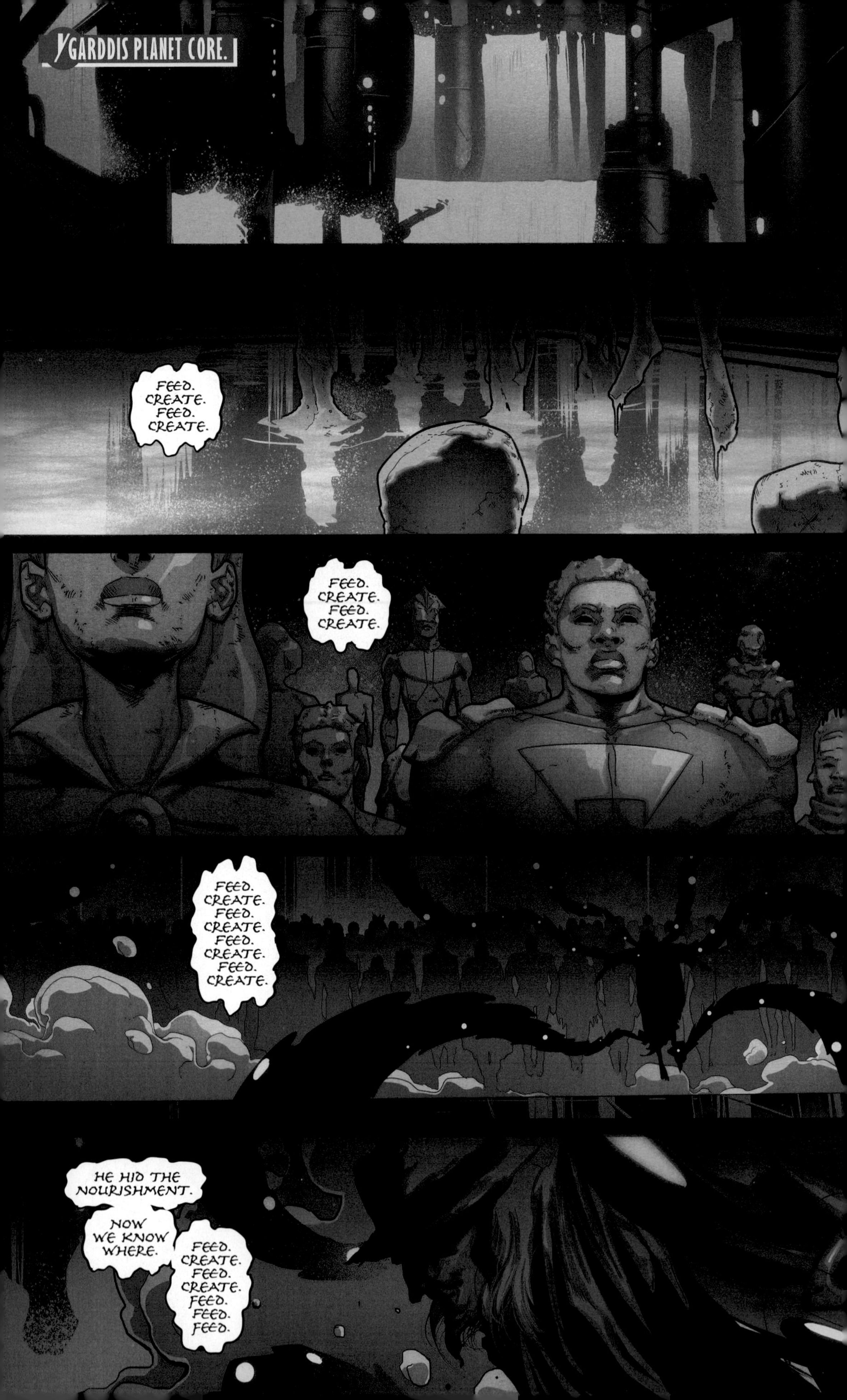
YGARDDIS PLANET CORE.
FEED. CREATE. FEED. CREATE.
FEED. CREATE. FEED. CREATE.
FEED. CREATE. FEED. CREATE. FEED. CREATE. FEED. CREATE.
HE HID THE NOURISHMENT.
NOW WE KNOW WHERE.
FEED. CREATE. FEED. CREATE. FEED. FEED. FEED.

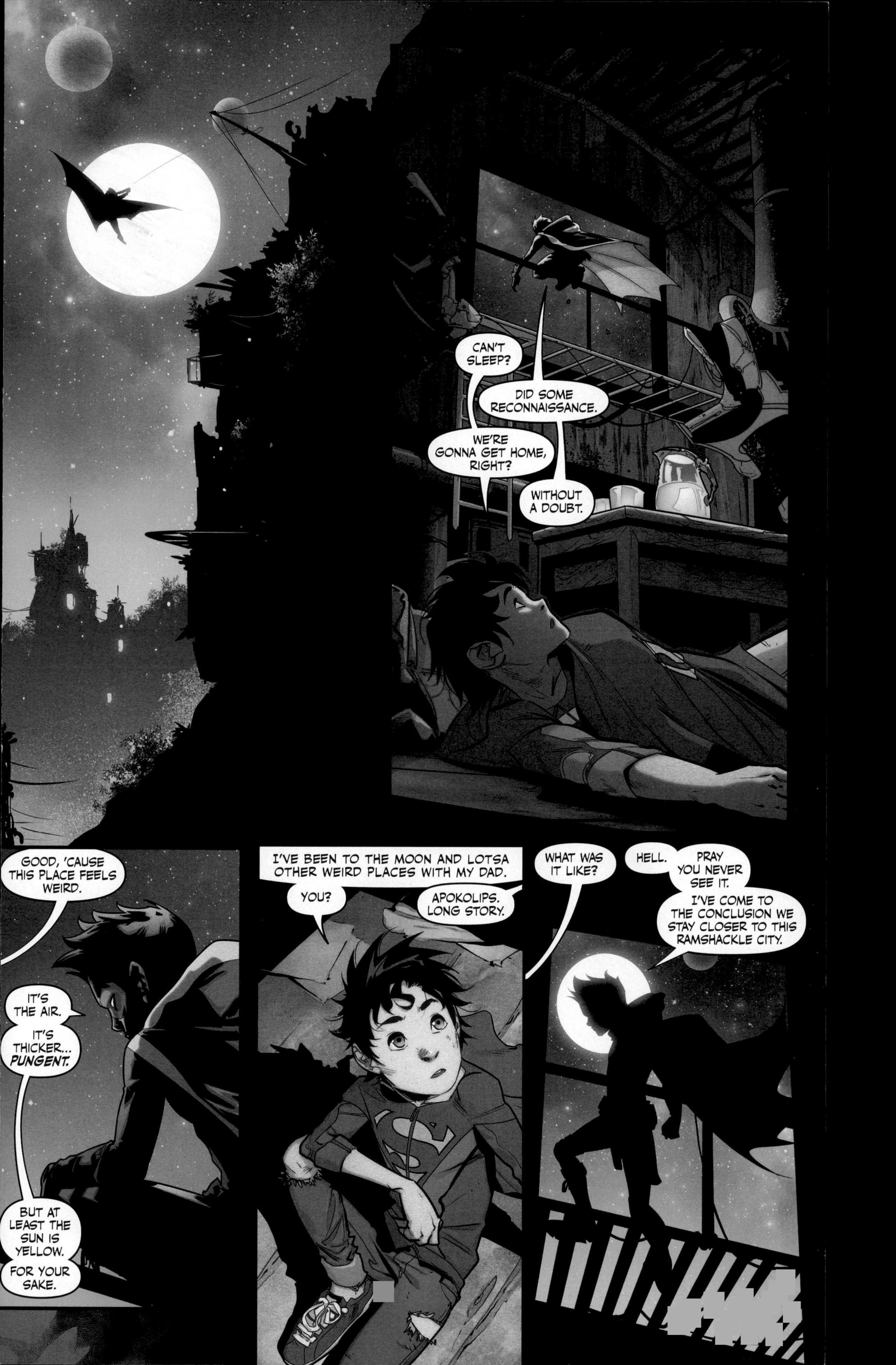
CAN'T SLEEP?
DID SOME RECONNAISSANCE.
WE'RE GONNA GET HOME, RIGHT?
WITHOUT A DOUBT.
GOOD, 'CAUSE THIS PLACE FEELS WEIRD.
IT'S THE AIR.
IT'S THICKER... *PUNGENT.*
BUT AT LEAST THE SUN IS YELLOW.
FOR YOUR SAKE.
I'VE BEEN TO THE MOON AND LOTSA OTHER WEIRD PLACES WITH MY DAD.
YOU?
APOKOLIPS. LONG STORY.
WHAT WAS IT LIKE?
HELL.
PRAY YOU NEVER SEE IT.
I'VE COME TO THE CONCLUSION WE STAY CLOSER TO THIS RAMSHACKLE CITY.

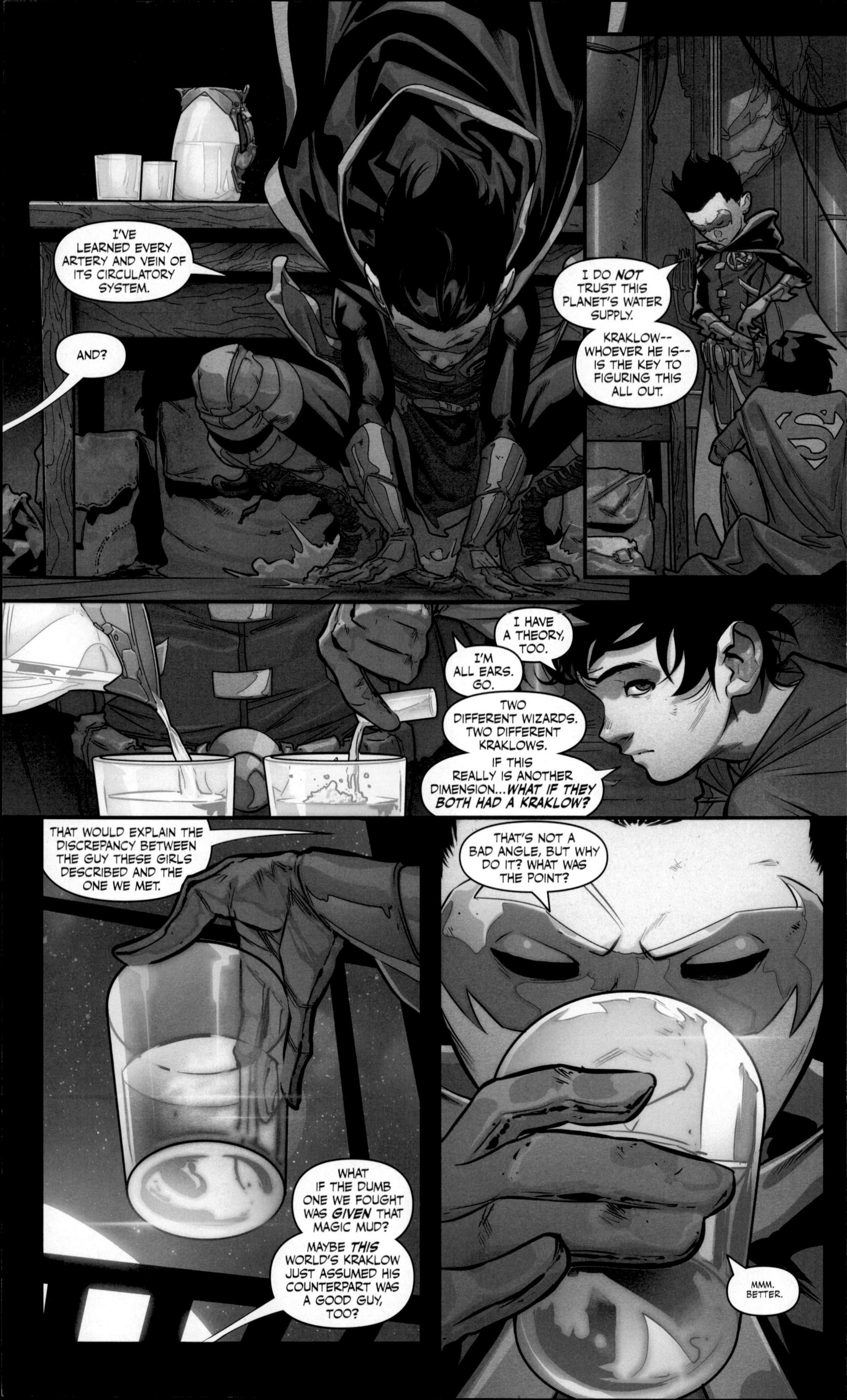
I'VE LEARNED EVERY ARTERY AND VEIN OF ITS CIRCULATORY SYSTEM.
AND?
I DO NOT TRUST THIS PLANET'S WATER SUPPLY.
KRAKLOW-- WHOEVER HE IS-- IS THE KEY TO FIGURING THIS ALL OUT.
I HAVE A THEORY, TOO.
I'M ALL EARS. GO.
TWO DIFFERENT WIZARDS. TWO DIFFERENT KRAKLOWS.
IF THIS REALLY IS ANOTHER DIMENSION...WHAT IF THEY BOTH HAD A KRAKLOW?
THAT WOULD EXPLAIN THE DISCREPANCY BETWEEN THE GUY THESE GIRLS DESCRIBED AND THE ONE WE MET.
THAT'S NOT A BAD ANGLE, BUT WHY DO IT? WHAT WAS THE POINT?
WHAT IF THE DUMB ONE WE FOUGHT WAS GIVEN THAT MAGIC MUD?
MAYBE THIS WORLD'S KRAKLOW JUST ASSUMED HIS COUNTERPART WAS A GOOD GUY, TOO?
MMM. BETTER.

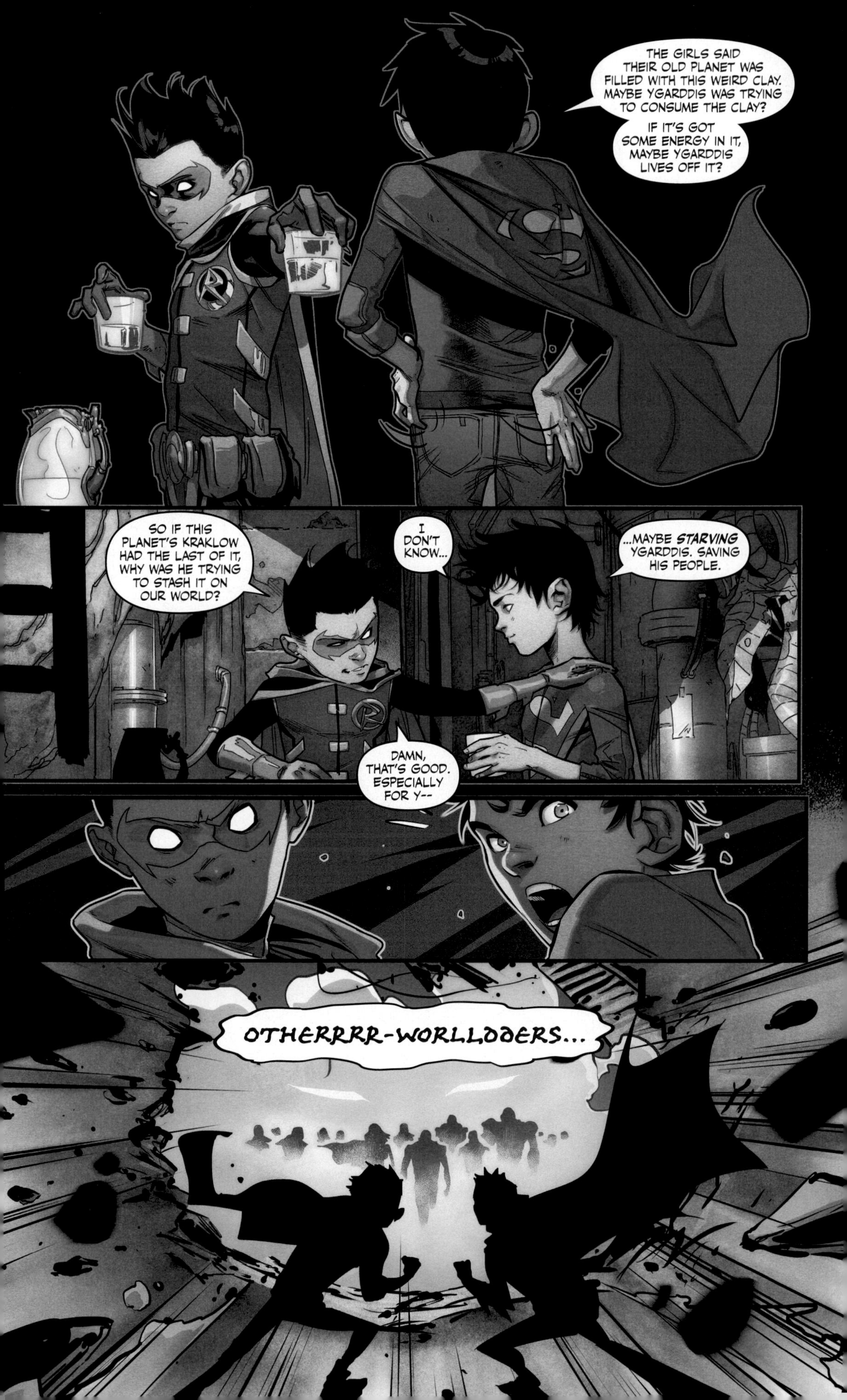
THE GIRLS SAID THEIR OLD PLANET WAS FILLED WITH THIS WEIRD CLAY. MAYBE YGARDDIS WAS TRYING TO CONSUME THE CLAY?
IF IT'S GOT SOME ENERGY IN IT, MAYBE YGARDDIS LIVES OFF IT?
SO IF THIS PLANET'S KRAKLOW HAD THE LAST OF IT, WHY WAS HE TRYING TO STASH IT ON OUR WORLD?
I DON'T KNOW...
...MAYBE STARVING YGARDDIS. SAVING HIS PEOPLE.
DAMN, THAT'S GOOD. ESPECIALLY FOR Y--
OTHERRRR-WORLLDDERS...

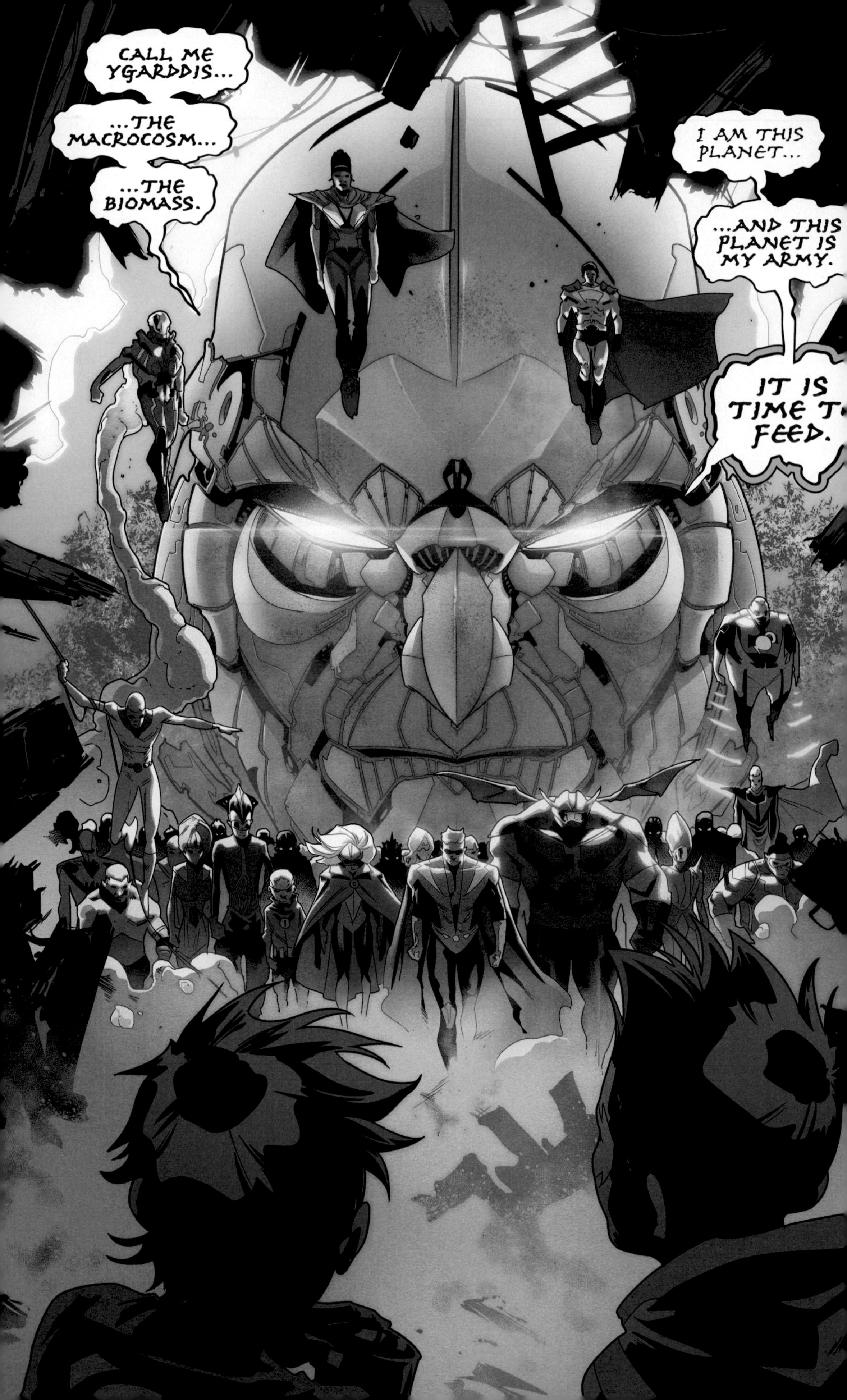
CALL ME YGARDDIS...
...THE MACROCOSM...
...THE BIOMASS.
I AM THIS PLANET...
...AND THIS PLANET IS MY ARMY.
IT IS TIME T FEED.

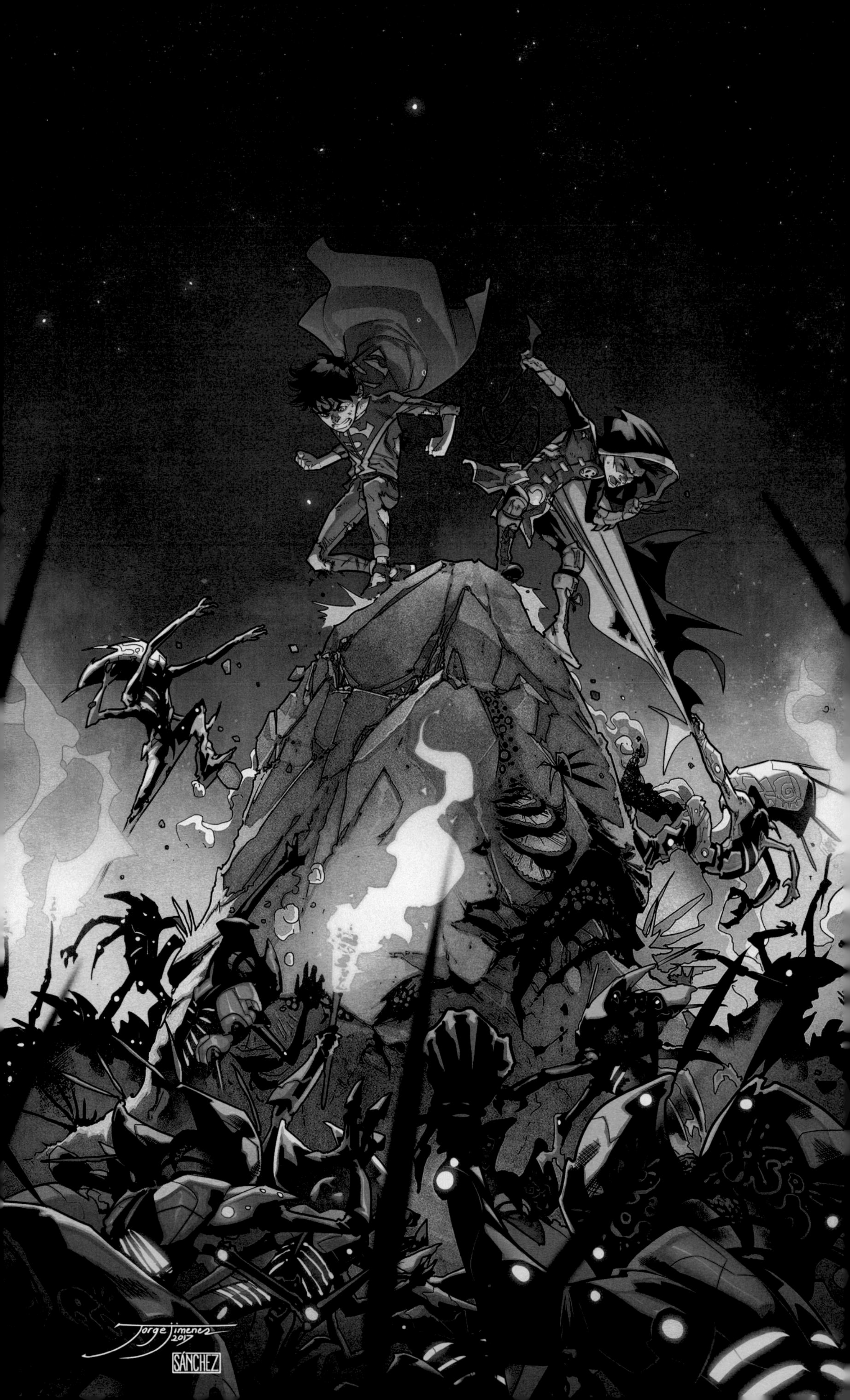
Jorge Jimenez 2017
SÁNCHEZ

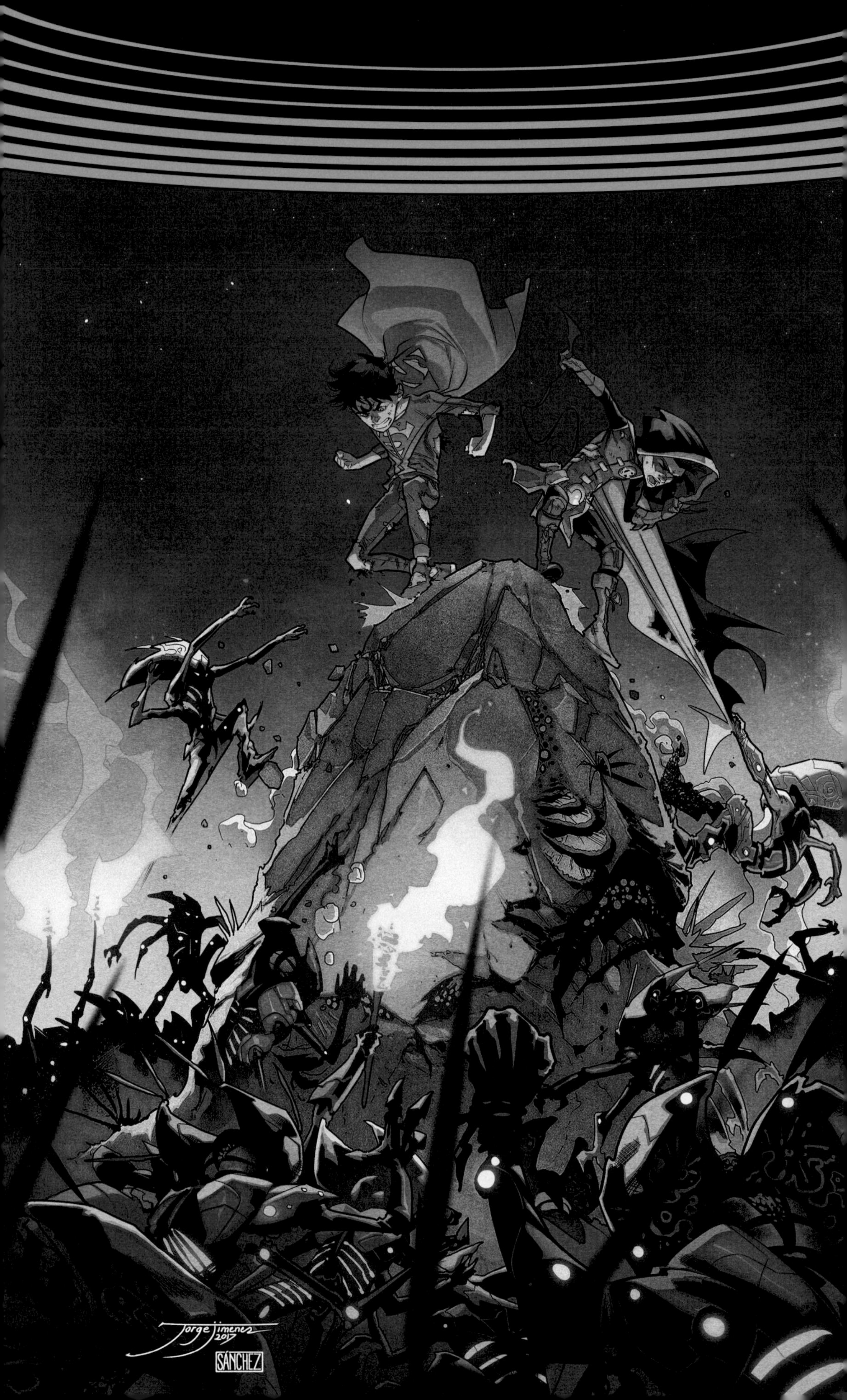
Jorge Jimenez 2017
SÁNCHEZ

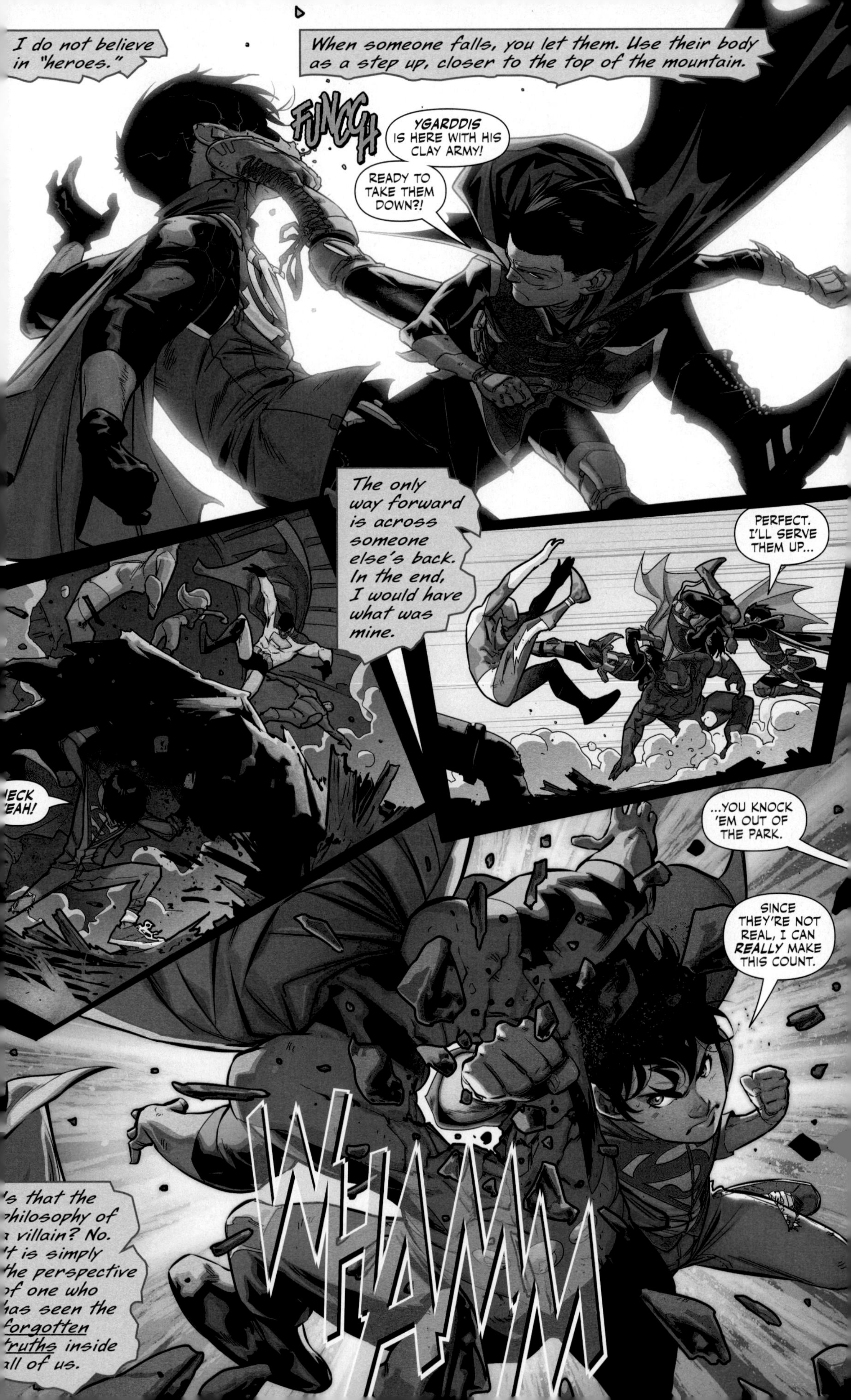
I do not believe in "heroes."
When someone falls, you let them. Use their body as a step up, closer to the top of the mountain.
FUNCCH
YGARDDIS IS HERE WITH HIS CLAY ARMY!
READY TO TAKE THEM DOWN?!
The only way forward is across someone else's back. In the end, I would have what was mine.
PERFECT. I'LL SERVE THEM UP...
...YOU KNOCK 'EM OUT OF THE PARK.
SINCE THEY'RE NOT REAL, I CAN REALLY MAKE THIS COUNT.
WHAMM

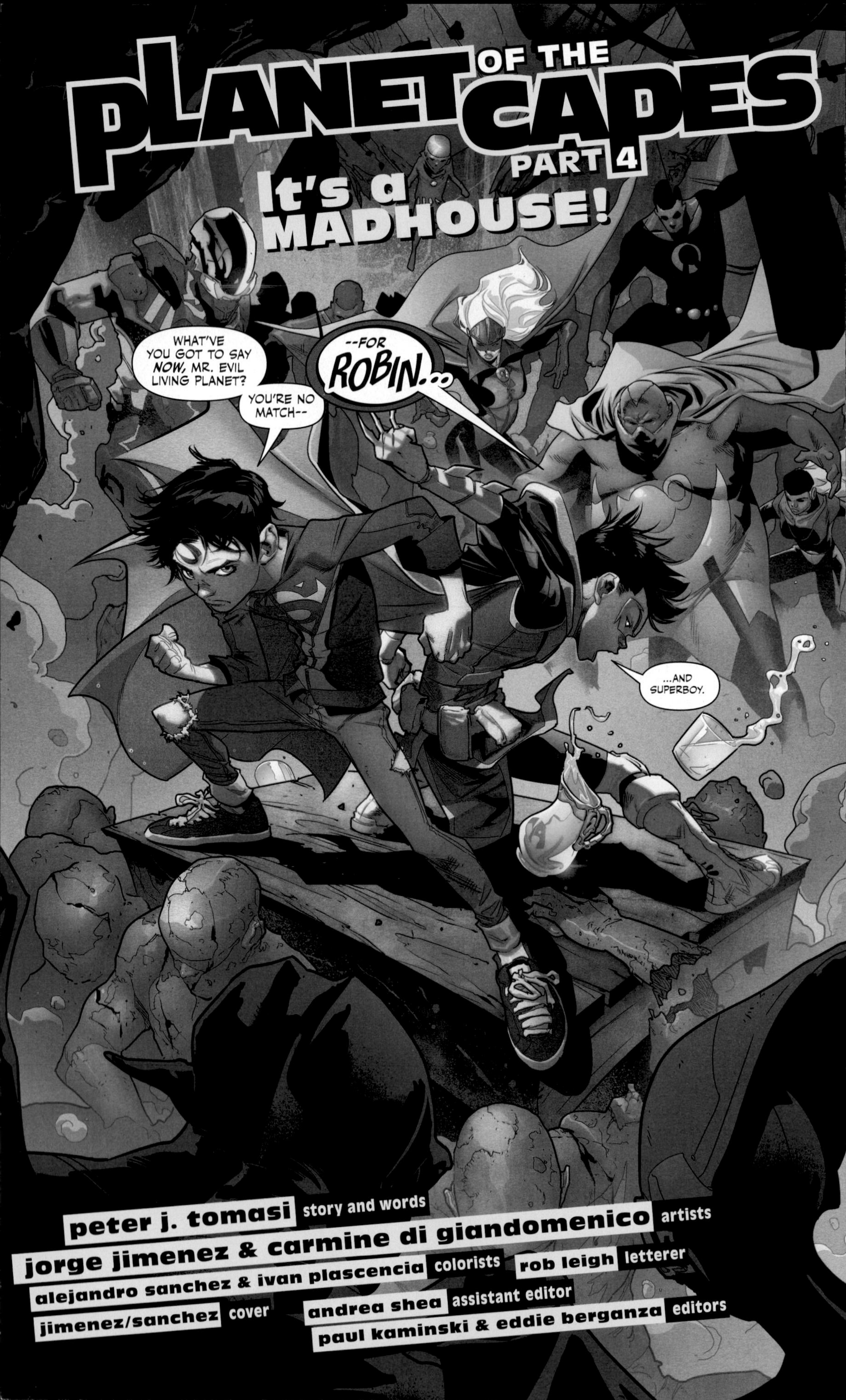
PLANET OF THE CAPES
PART 4
It's a MADHOUSE!
WHAT'VE YOU GOT TO SAY NOW, MR. EVIL LIVING PLANET?
YOU'RE NO MATCH--
--FOR ROBIN...
...AND SUPERBOY.
peter j. tomasi story and words
jorge jimenez & carmine di giandomenico artists
alejandro sanchez & ivan plascencia colorists
rob leigh letterer
jimenez/sanchez cover
andrea shea assistant editor
paul kaminski & eddie berganza editors

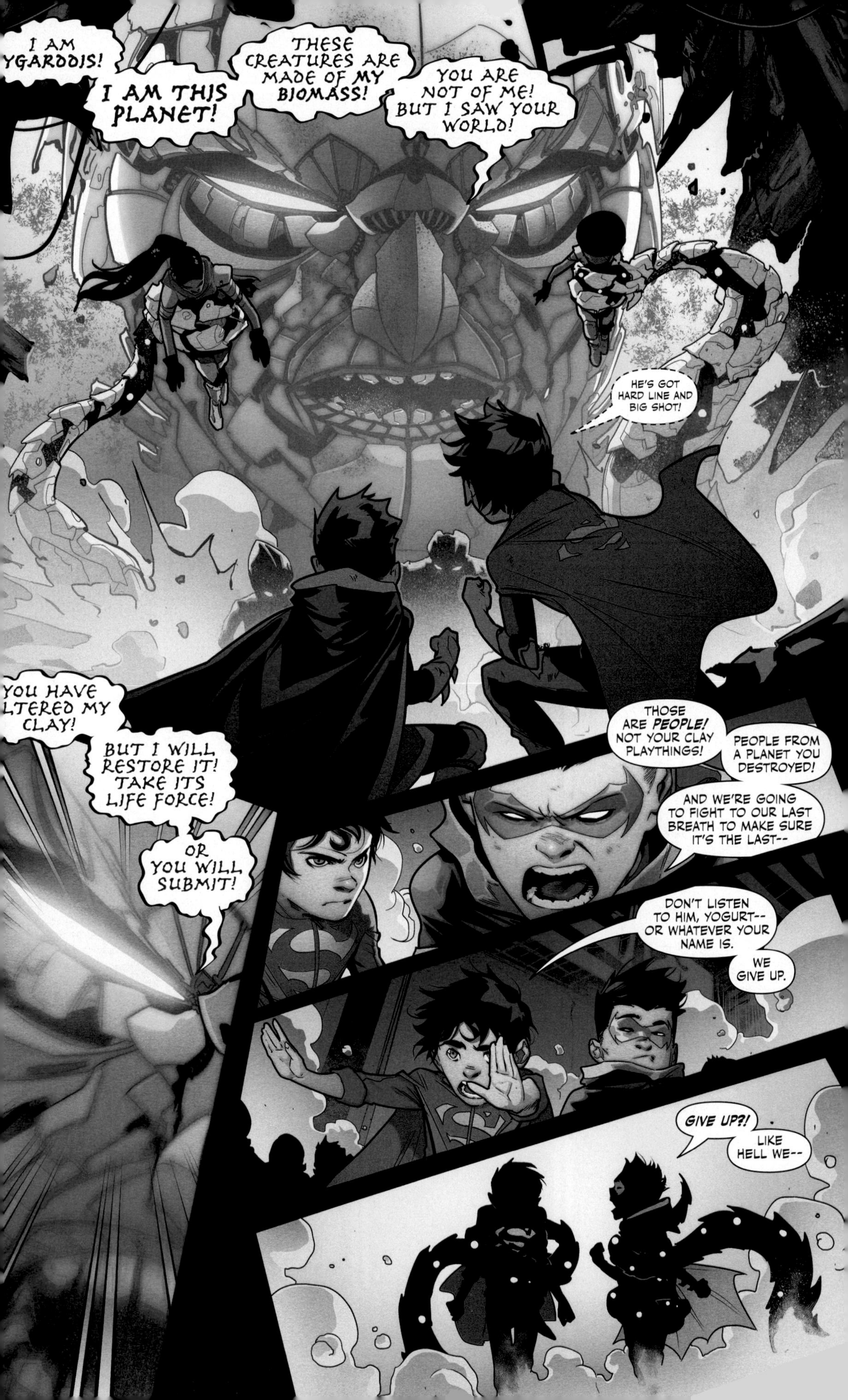
I AM YGARDDIS!
I AM THIS PLANET!
THESE CREATURES ARE MADE OF MY BIOMASS!
YOU ARE NOT OF ME! BUT I SAW YOUR WORLD!
HE'S GOT HARD LINE AND BIG SHOT!
YOU HAVE LTERED MY CLAY!
BUT I WILL RESTORE IT! TAKE ITS LIFE FORCE!
OR YOU WILL SUBMIT!
THOSE ARE PEOPLE! NOT YOUR CLAY PLAYTHINGS!
PEOPLE FROM A PLANET YOU DESTROYED!
AND WE'RE GOING TO FIGHT TO OUR LAST BREATH TO MAKE SURE IT'S THE LAST--
DON'T LISTEN TO HIM, YOGURT-- OR WHATEVER YOUR NAME IS.
WE GIVE UP.
GIVE UP?!
LIKE HELL WE--

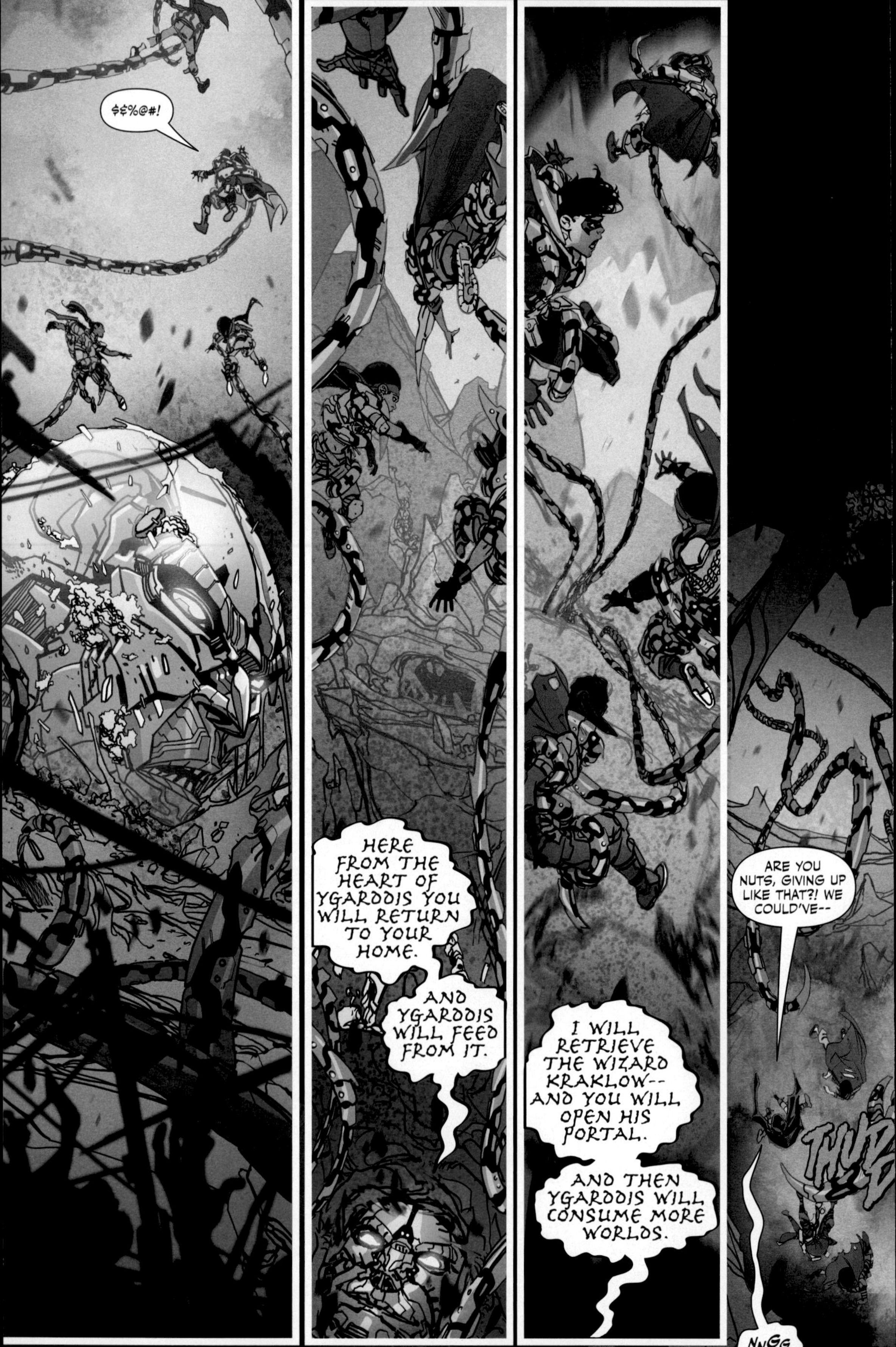
$¢%@#!
HERE FROM THE HEART OF YGARDDIS YOU WILL RETURN TO YOUR HOME.
AND YGARDDIS WILL FEED FROM IT.
I WILL RETRIEVE THE WIZARD KRAKLOW-- AND YOU WILL OPEN HIS PORTAL.
AND THEN YGARDDIS WILL CONSUME MORE WORLDS.
ARE YOU NUTS, GIVING UP LIKE THAT?! WE COULD'VE--
NNGG

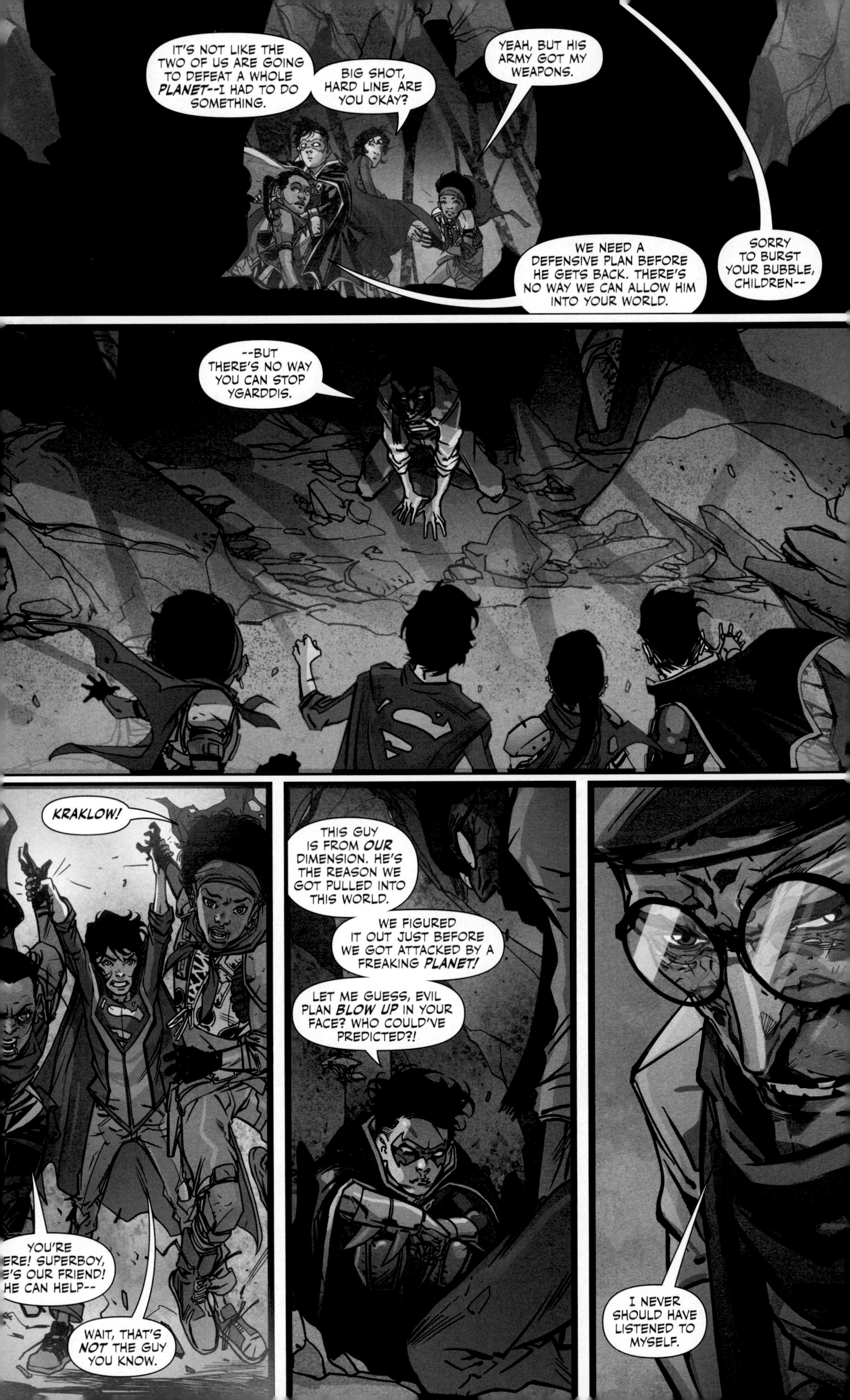
IT'S NOT LIKE THE TWO OF US ARE GOING TO DEFEAT A WHOLE *PLANET*--I HAD TO DO SOMETHING.
BIG SHOT, HARD LINE, ARE YOU OKAY?
YEAH, BUT HIS ARMY GOT MY WEAPONS.
WE NEED A DEFENSIVE PLAN BEFORE HE GETS BACK. THERE'S NO WAY WE CAN ALLOW HIM INTO YOUR WORLD.
SORRY TO BURST YOUR BUBBLE, CHILDREN--
--BUT THERE'S NO WAY YOU CAN STOP YGARDDIS.
KRAKLOW!
YOU'RE ERE! SUPERBOY, E'S OUR FRIEND! HE CAN HELP--
WAIT, THAT'S *NOT* THE GUY YOU KNOW.
THIS GUY IS FROM *OUR* DIMENSION. HE'S THE REASON WE GOT PULLED INTO THIS WORLD.
WE FIGURED IT OUT JUST BEFORE WE GOT ATTACKED BY A FREAKING *PLANET!*
LET ME GUESS, EVIL PLAN *BLOW UP* IN YOUR FACE? WHO COULD'VE PREDICTED?!
I NEVER SHOULD HAVE LISTENED TO MYSELF.

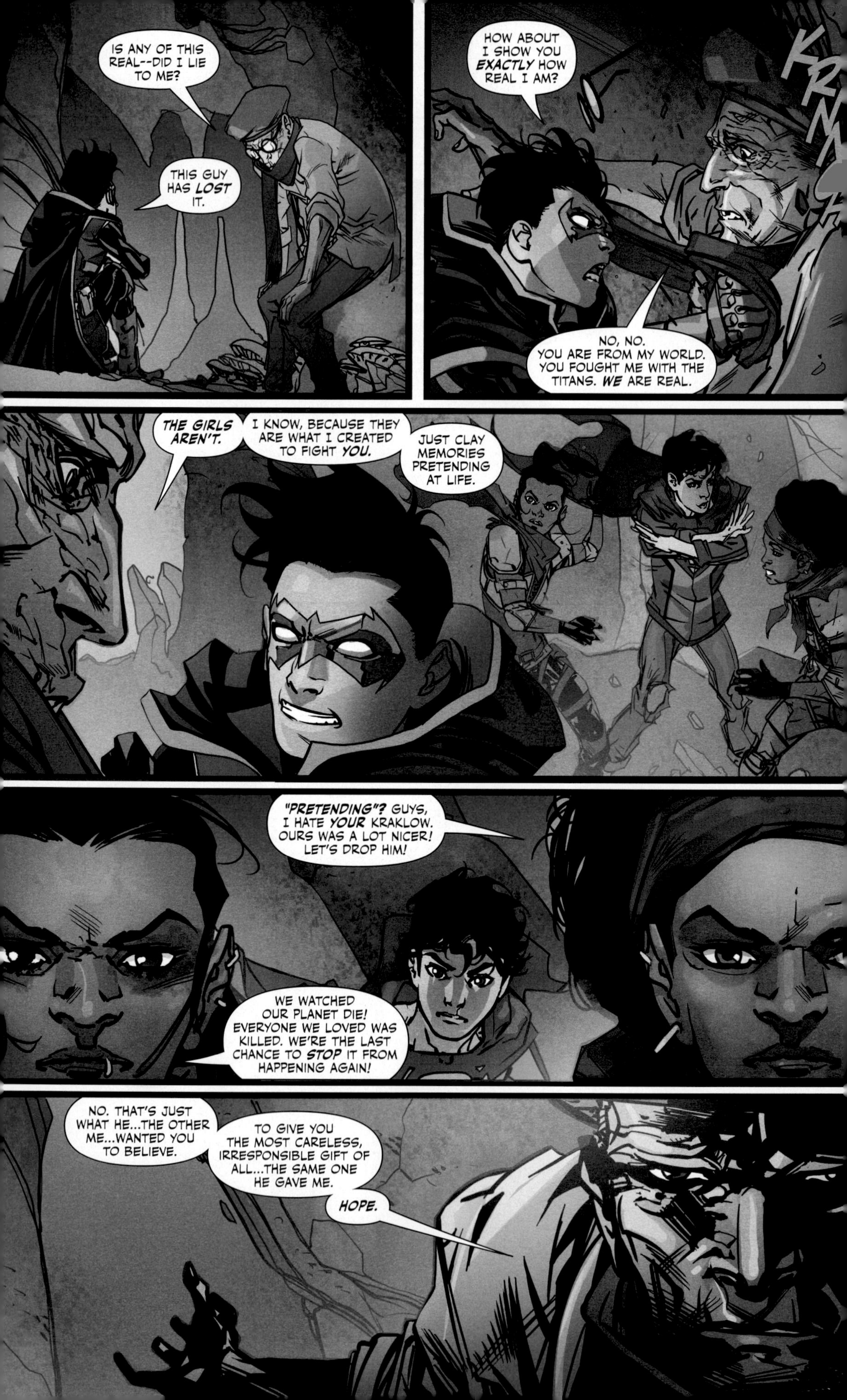
IS ANY OF THIS REAL--DID I LIE TO ME?
THIS GUY HAS LOST IT.
HOW ABOUT I SHOW YOU EXACTLY HOW REAL I AM?
NO, NO. YOU ARE FROM MY WORLD. YOU FOUGHT ME WITH THE TITANS. WE ARE REAL.
THE GIRLS AREN'T.
I KNOW, BECAUSE THEY ARE WHAT I CREATED TO FIGHT YOU.
JUST CLAY MEMORIES PRETENDING AT LIFE.
"PRETENDING"? GUYS, I HATE YOUR KRAKLOW. OURS WAS A LOT NICER! LET'S DROP HIM!
WE WATCHED OUR PLANET DIE! EVERYONE WE LOVED WAS KILLED. WE'RE THE LAST CHANCE TO STOP IT FROM HAPPENING AGAIN!
NO. THAT'S JUST WHAT HE...THE OTHER ME...WANTED YOU TO BELIEVE.
TO GIVE YOU THE MOST CARELESS, IRRESPONSIBLE GIFT OF ALL...THE SAME ONE HE GAVE ME.
HOPE.

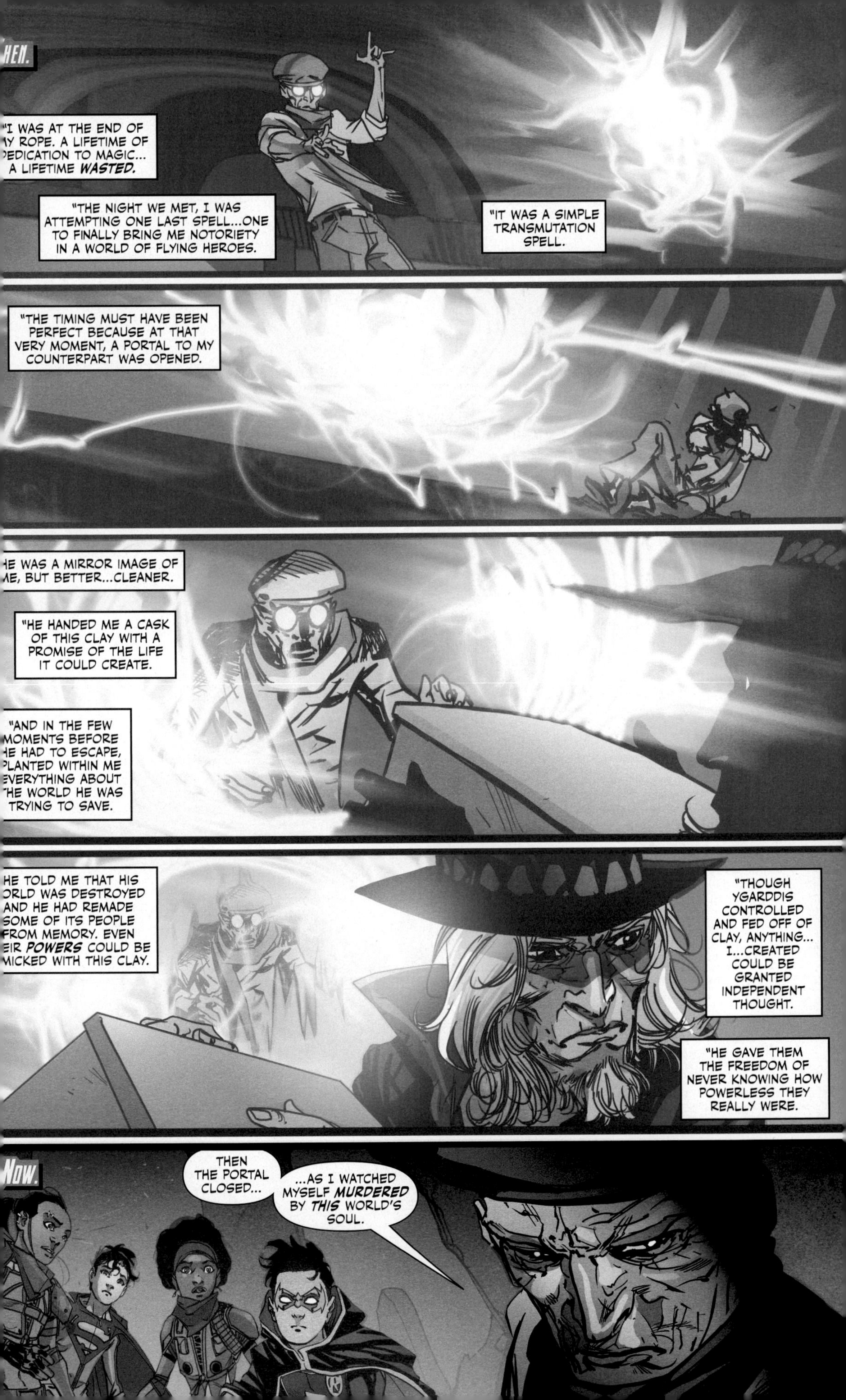
HEN.
"I WAS AT THE END OF
IY ROPE. A LIFETIME OF
DEDICATION TO MAGIC...
A LIFETIME WASTED.
"THE NIGHT WE MET, I WAS ATTEMPTING ONE LAST SPELL...ONE TO FINALLY BRING ME NOTORIETY IN A WORLD OF FLYING HEROES.
"IT WAS A SIMPLE TRANSMUTATION SPELL.
"THE TIMING MUST HAVE BEEN PERFECT BECAUSE AT THAT VERY MOMENT, A PORTAL TO MY COUNTERPART WAS OPENED.
HE WAS A MIRROR IMAGE OF ME, BUT BETTER...CLEANER.
"HE HANDED ME A CASK OF THIS CLAY WITH A PROMISE OF THE LIFE IT COULD CREATE.
"AND IN THE FEW MOMENTS BEFORE HE HAD TO ESCAPE, PLANTED WITHIN ME EVERYTHING ABOUT THE WORLD HE WAS TRYING TO SAVE.
HE TOLD ME THAT HIS ORLD WAS DESTROYED AND HE HAD REMADE SOME OF ITS PEOPLE FROM MEMORY. EVEN EIR POWERS COULD BE MICKED WITH THIS CLAY.
"THOUGH YGARDDIS CONTROLLED AND FED OFF OF CLAY, ANYTHING... I...CREATED COULD BE GRANTED INDEPENDENT THOUGHT.
"HE GAVE THEM THE FREEDOM OF NEVER KNOWING HOW POWERLESS THEY REALLY WERE.
NOW.
THEN THE PORTAL CLOSED...
...AS I WATCHED MYSELF MURDERED BY THIS WORLD'S SOUL.

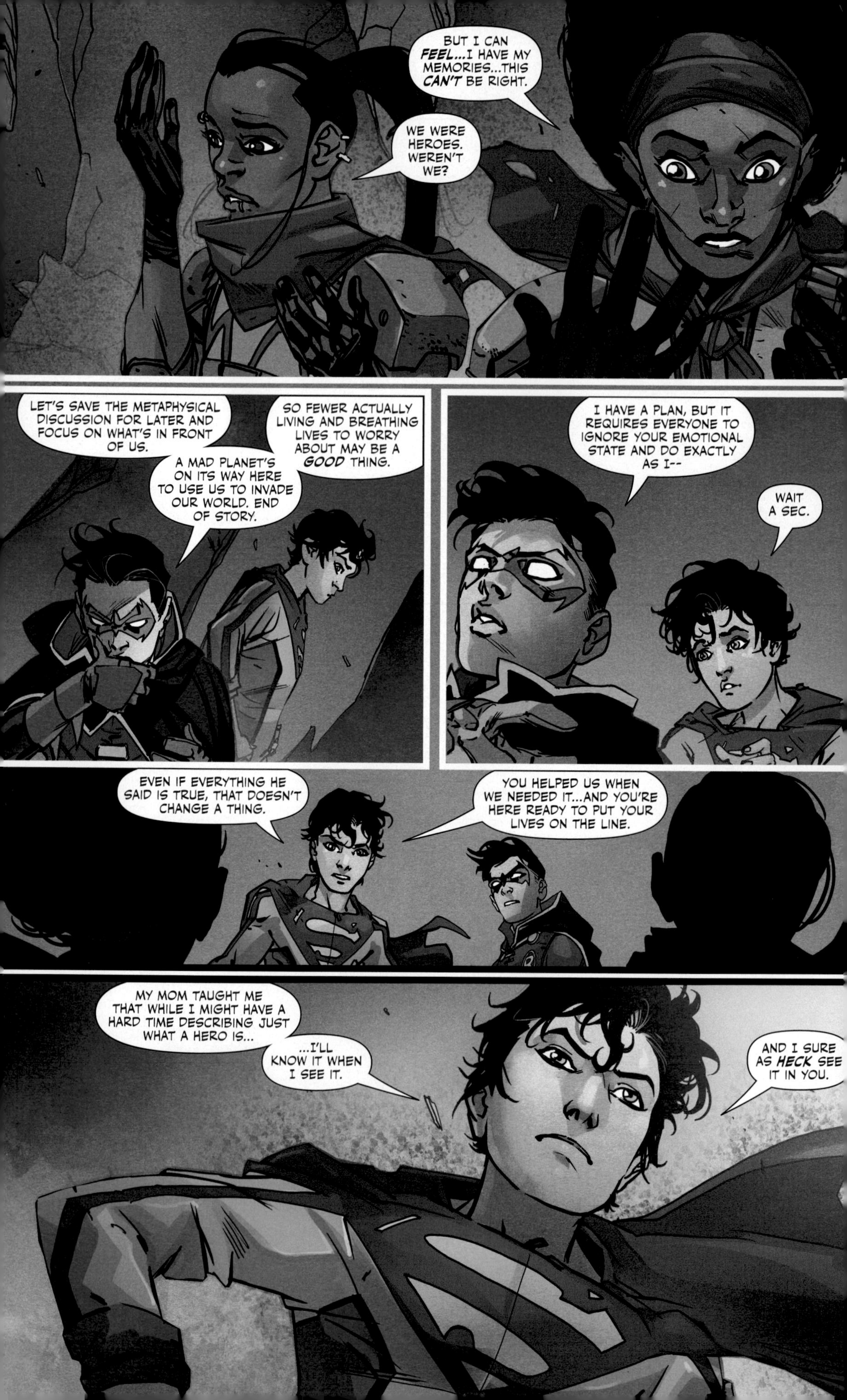
BUT I CAN FEEL...I HAVE MY MEMORIES...THIS CAN'T BE RIGHT.
WE WERE HEROES. WEREN'T WE?
LET'S SAVE THE METAPHYSICAL DISCUSSION FOR LATER AND FOCUS ON WHAT'S IN FRONT OF US.
A MAD PLANET'S ON ITS WAY HERE TO USE US TO INVADE OUR WORLD. END OF STORY.
SO FEWER ACTUALLY LIVING AND BREATHING LIVES TO WORRY ABOUT MAY BE A GOOD THING.
I HAVE A PLAN, BUT IT REQUIRES EVERYONE TO IGNORE YOUR EMOTIONAL STATE AND DO EXACTLY AS I--
WAIT A SEC.
EVEN IF EVERYTHING HE SAID IS TRUE, THAT DOESN'T CHANGE A THING.
YOU HELPED US WHEN WE NEEDED IT...AND YOU'RE HERE READY TO PUT YOUR LIVES ON THE LINE.
MY MOM TAUGHT ME THAT WHILE I MIGHT HAVE A HARD TIME DESCRIBING JUST WHAT A HERO IS...
...I'LL KNOW IT WHEN I SEE IT.
AND I SURE AS HECK SEE IT IN YOU.

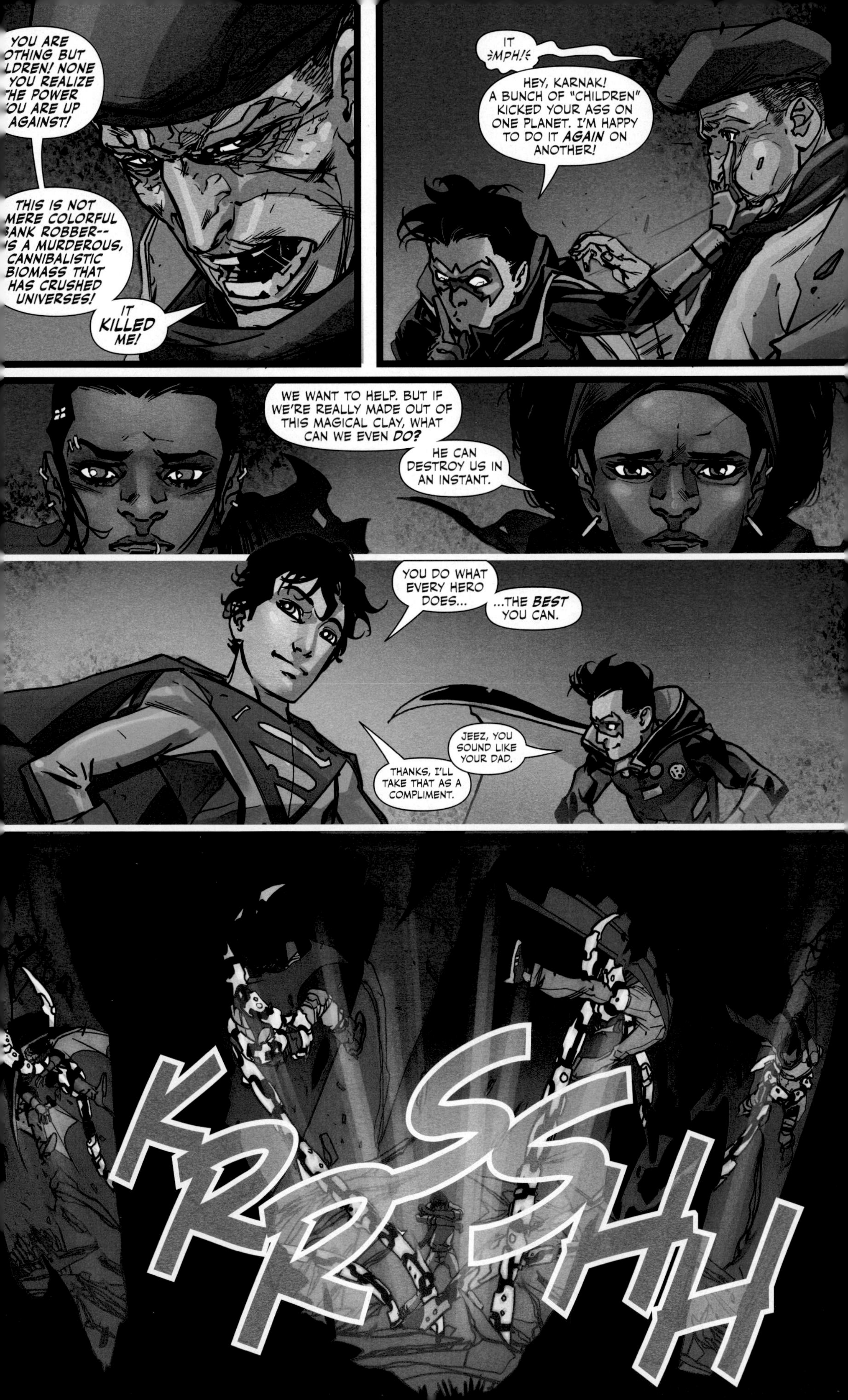
YOU ARE
OTHING BUT
LDREN! NONE
YOU REALIZE
THE POWER
YOU ARE UP
AGAINST!
THIS IS NOT
MERE COLORFUL
BANK ROBBER--
'S A MURDEROUS,
CANNIBALISTIC
BIOMASS THAT
HAS CRUSHED
UNIVERSES!
IT KILLED ME!
IT
MPH!
HEY, KARNAK! A BUNCH OF "CHILDREN" KICKED YOUR ASS ON ONE PLANET. I'M HAPPY TO DO IT AGAIN ON ANOTHER!
WE WANT TO HELP. BUT IF WE'RE REALLY MADE OUT OF THIS MAGICAL CLAY, WHAT CAN WE EVEN DO?
HE CAN DESTROY US IN AN INSTANT.
YOU DO WHAT EVERY HERO DOES...
...THE BEST YOU CAN.
JEEZ, YOU SOUND LIKE YOUR DAD.
THANKS, I'LL TAKE THAT AS A COMPLIMENT.
KRSSSHH

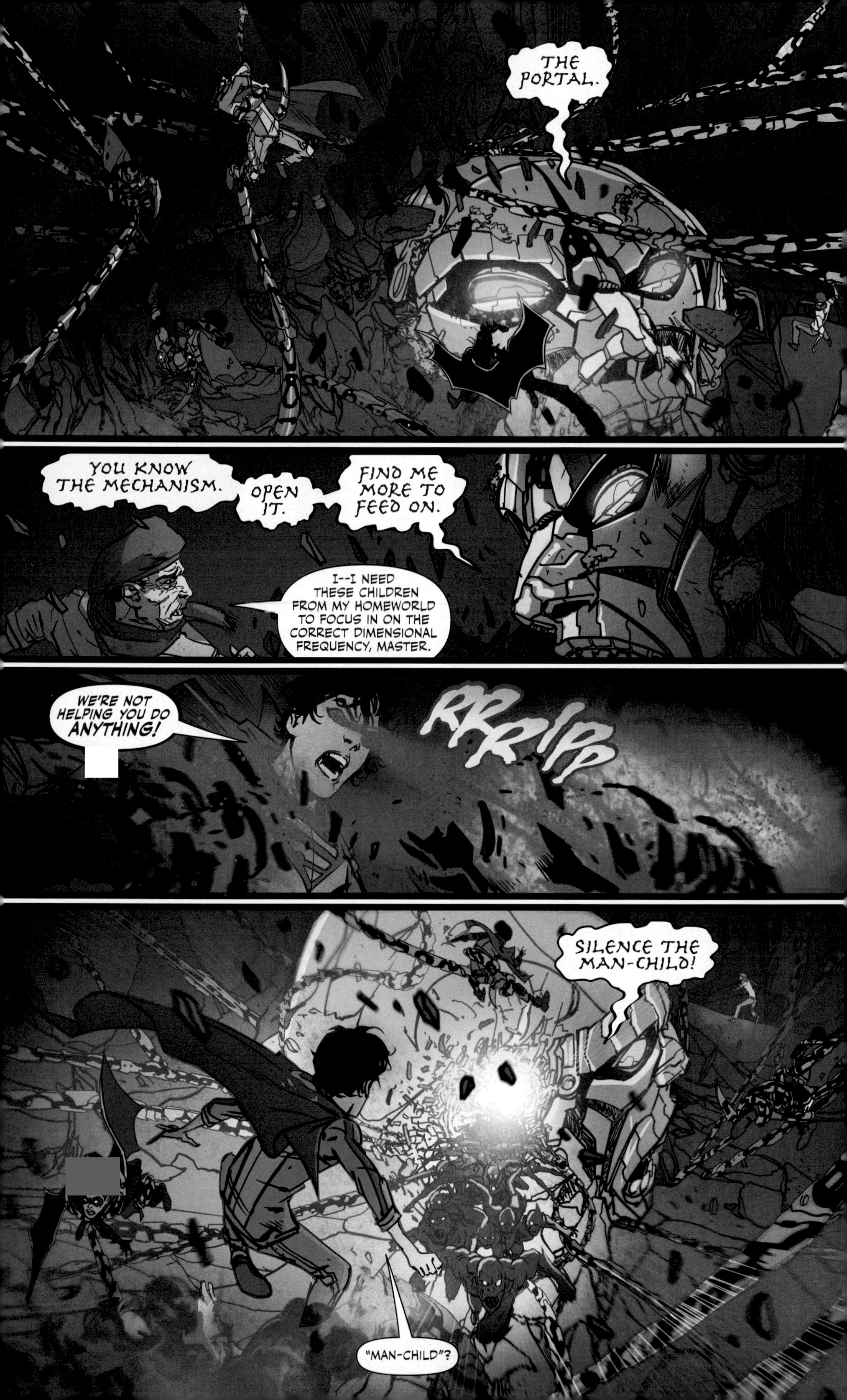
THE PORTAL.
YOU KNOW THE MECHANISM.
OPEN IT.
FIND ME MORE TO FEED ON.
I--I NEED THESE CHILDREN FROM MY HOMEWORLD TO FOCUS IN ON THE CORRECT DIMENSIONAL FREQUENCY, MASTER.
WE'RE NOT HELPING YOU DO ANYTHING!
RRRIPP
SILENCE THE MAN-CHILD!
"MAN-CHILD"?

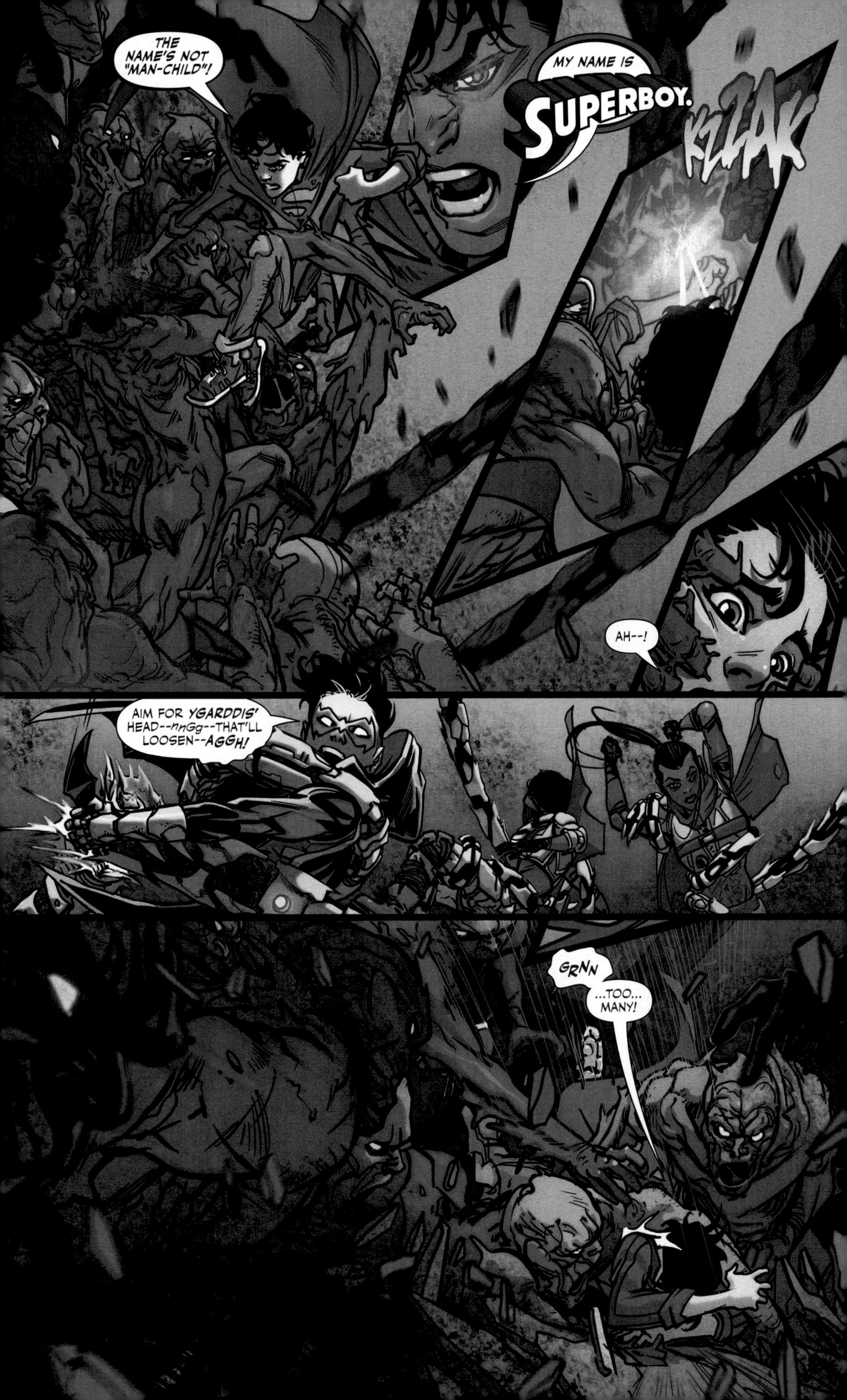
THE NAME'S NOT "MAN-CHILD"!
MY NAME IS
SUPERBOY.
KZZAK
AH--!
AIM FOR YGARDDIS' HEAD--nnGg--THAT'LL LOOSEN--AGGH!
GRNN
...TOO... MANY!

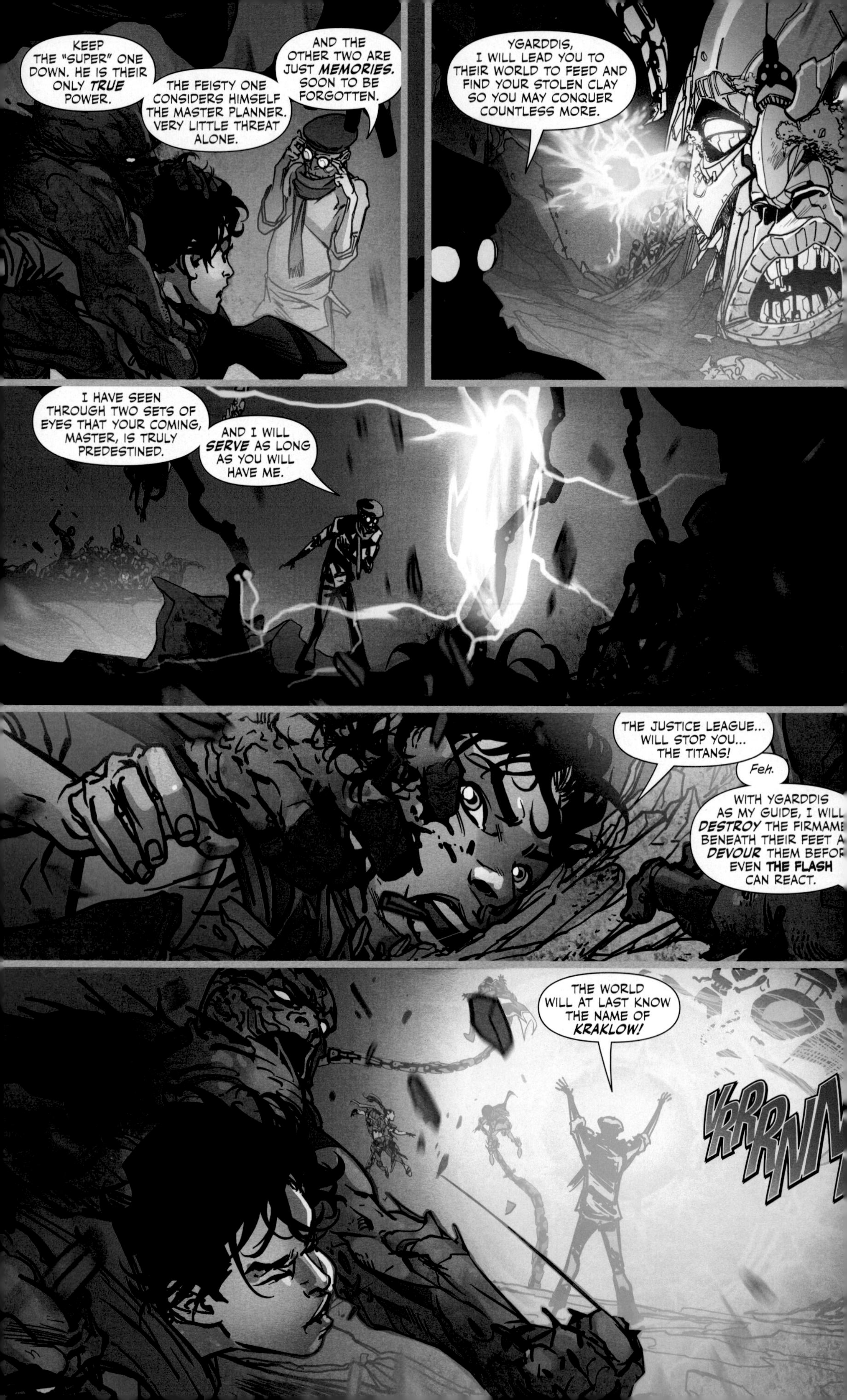
KEEP THE "SUPER" ONE DOWN. HE IS THEIR ONLY *TRUE* POWER.
THE FEISTY ONE CONSIDERS HIMSELF THE MASTER PLANNER. VERY LITTLE THREAT ALONE.
AND THE OTHER TWO ARE JUST *MEMORIES.* SOON TO BE FORGOTTEN.
YGARDDIS, I WILL LEAD YOU TO THEIR WORLD TO FEED AND FIND YOUR STOLEN CLAY SO YOU MAY CONQUER COUNTLESS MORE.
I HAVE SEEN THROUGH TWO SETS OF EYES THAT YOUR COMING, MASTER, IS TRULY PREDESTINED.
AND I WILL *SERVE* AS LONG AS YOU WILL HAVE ME.
THE JUSTICE LEAGUE... WILL STOP YOU... THE TITANS!
Feh.
WITH YGARDDIS AS MY GUIDE, I WILL *DESTROY* THE FIRMAME BENEATH THEIR FEET A *DEVOUR* THEM BEFOR EVEN **THE FLASH** CAN REACT.
THE WORLD WILL AT LAST KNOW THE NAME OF *KRAKLOW!*
VRRRNN

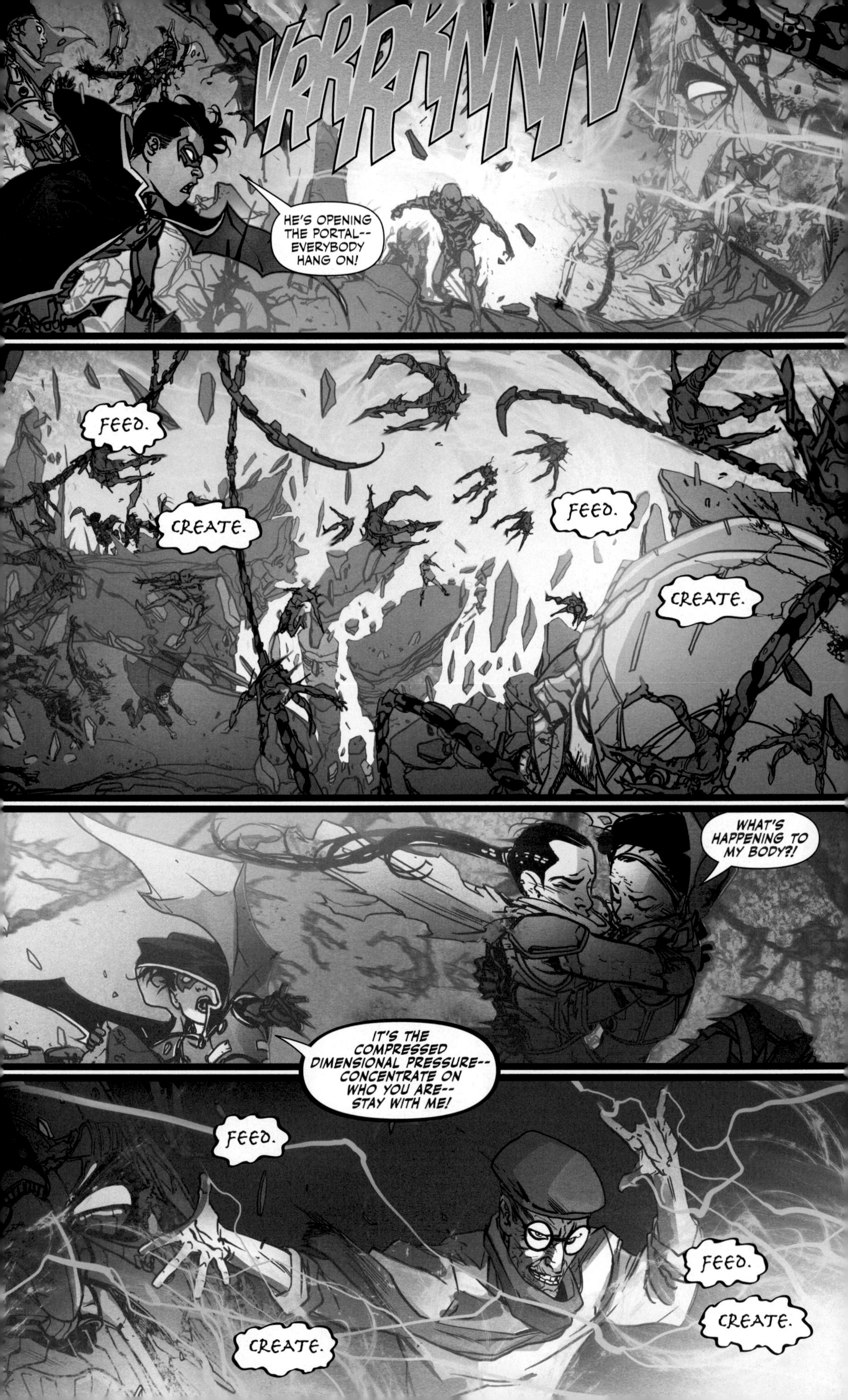
VRRRKVVVVV
HE'S OPENING THE PORTAL-- EVERYBODY HANG ON!
FEED.
CREATE.
FEED.
CREATE.
WHAT'S HAPPENING TO MY BODY?!
IT'S THE COMPRESSED DIMENSIONAL PRESSURE-- CONCENTRATE ON WHO YOU ARE-- STAY WITH ME!
FEED.
FEED.
CREATE.
CREATE.

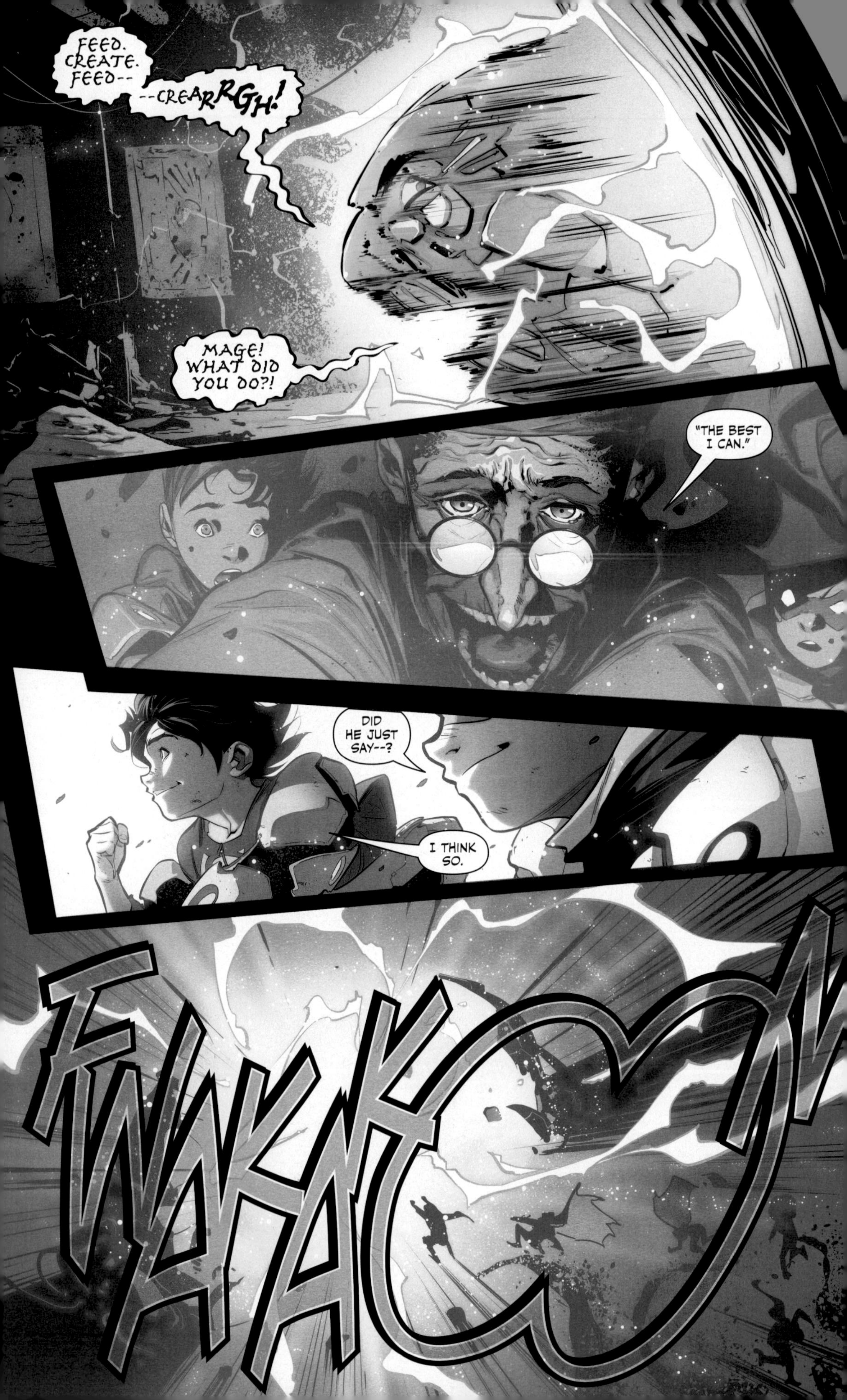
FEED. CREATE. FEED--
--CREARRGH!
MAGE! WHAT DID YOU DO?!
"THE BEST I CAN."
DID HE JUST SAY--?
I THINK SO.

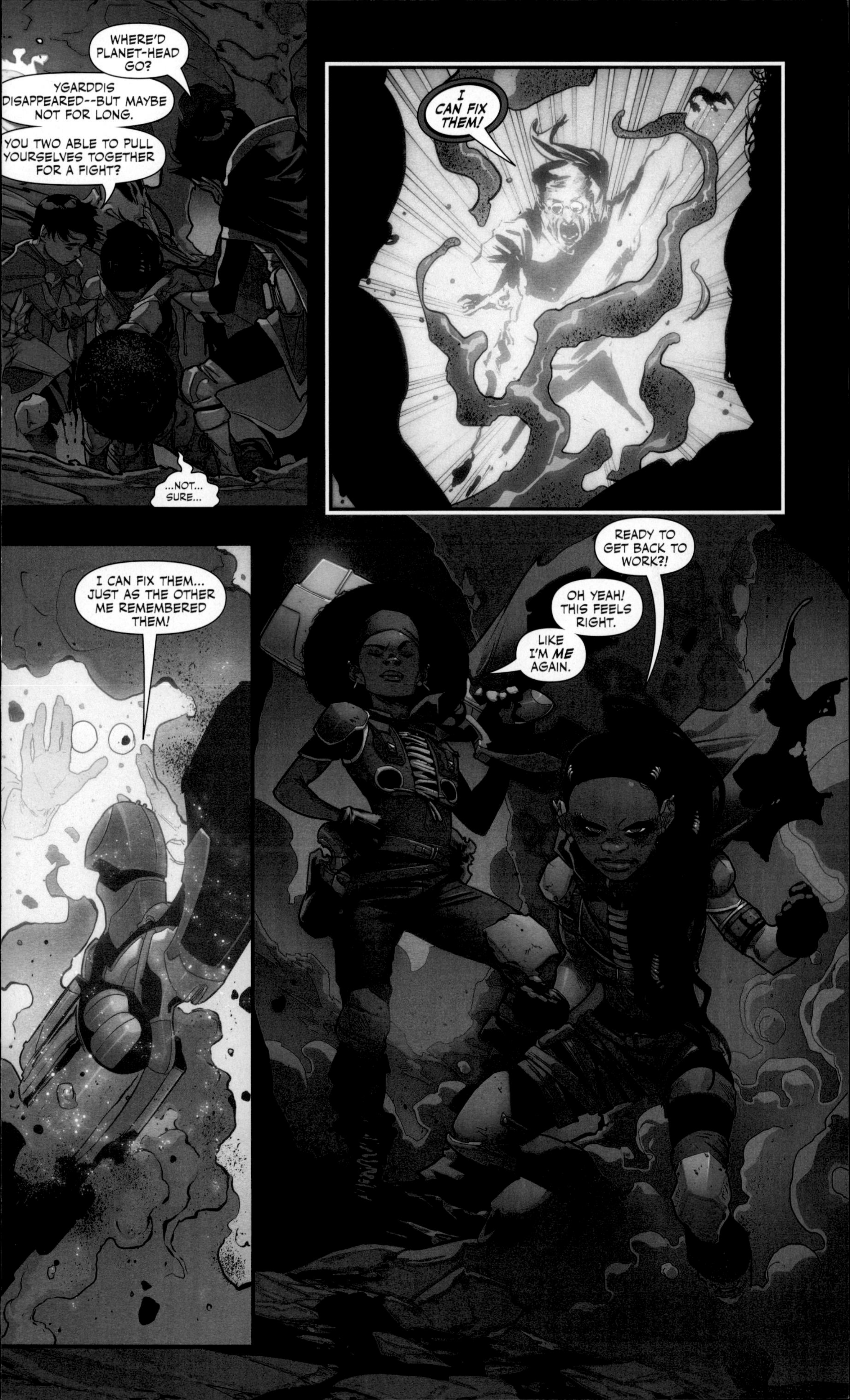
WHERE'D PLANET-HEAD GO?
YGARDDIS DISAPPEARED--BUT MAYBE NOT FOR LONG.
YOU TWO ABLE TO PULL YOURSELVES TOGETHER FOR A FIGHT?
...NOT... SURE...
I CAN FIX THEM!
I CAN FIX THEM... JUST AS THE OTHER ME REMEMBERED THEM!
READY TO GET BACK TO WORK?!
OH YEAH! THIS FEELS RIGHT.
LIKE I'M *ME* AGAIN.

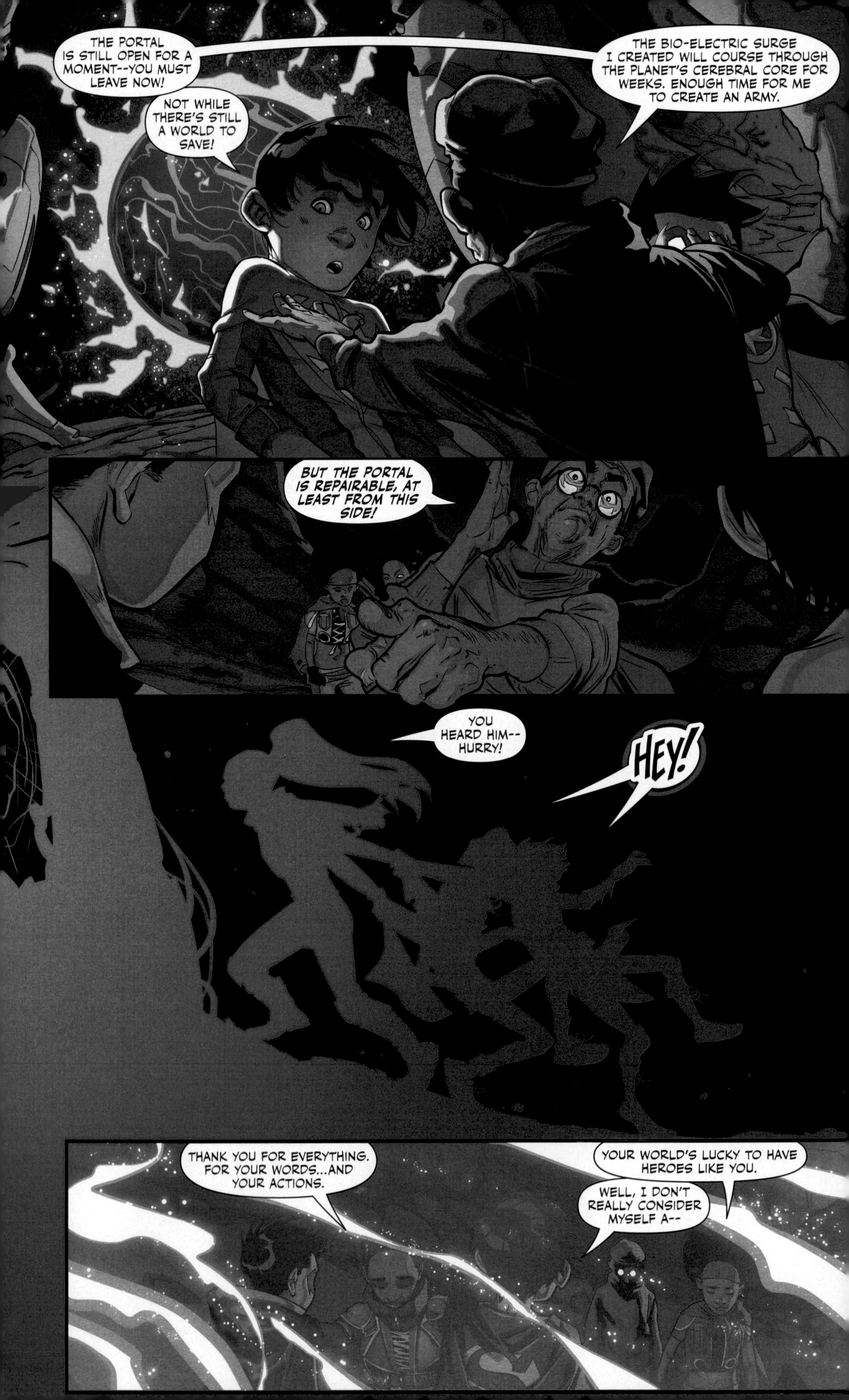

THE PORTAL IS STILL OPEN FOR A MOMENT--YOU MUST LEAVE NOW!
THE BIO-ELECTRIC SURGE I CREATED WILL COURSE THROUGH THE PLANET'S CEREBRAL CORE FOR WEEKS. ENOUGH TIME FOR ME TO CREATE AN ARMY.
NOT WHILE THERE'S STILL A WORLD TO SAVE!
BUT THE PORTAL IS REPAIRABLE, AT LEAST FROM THIS SIDE!
YOU HEARD HIM--HURRY!
HEY!
THANK YOU FOR EVERYTHING. FOR YOUR WORDS...AND YOUR ACTIONS.
YOUR WORLD'S LUCKY TO HAVE HEROES LIKE YOU.
WELL, I DON'T REALLY CONSIDER MYSELF A--

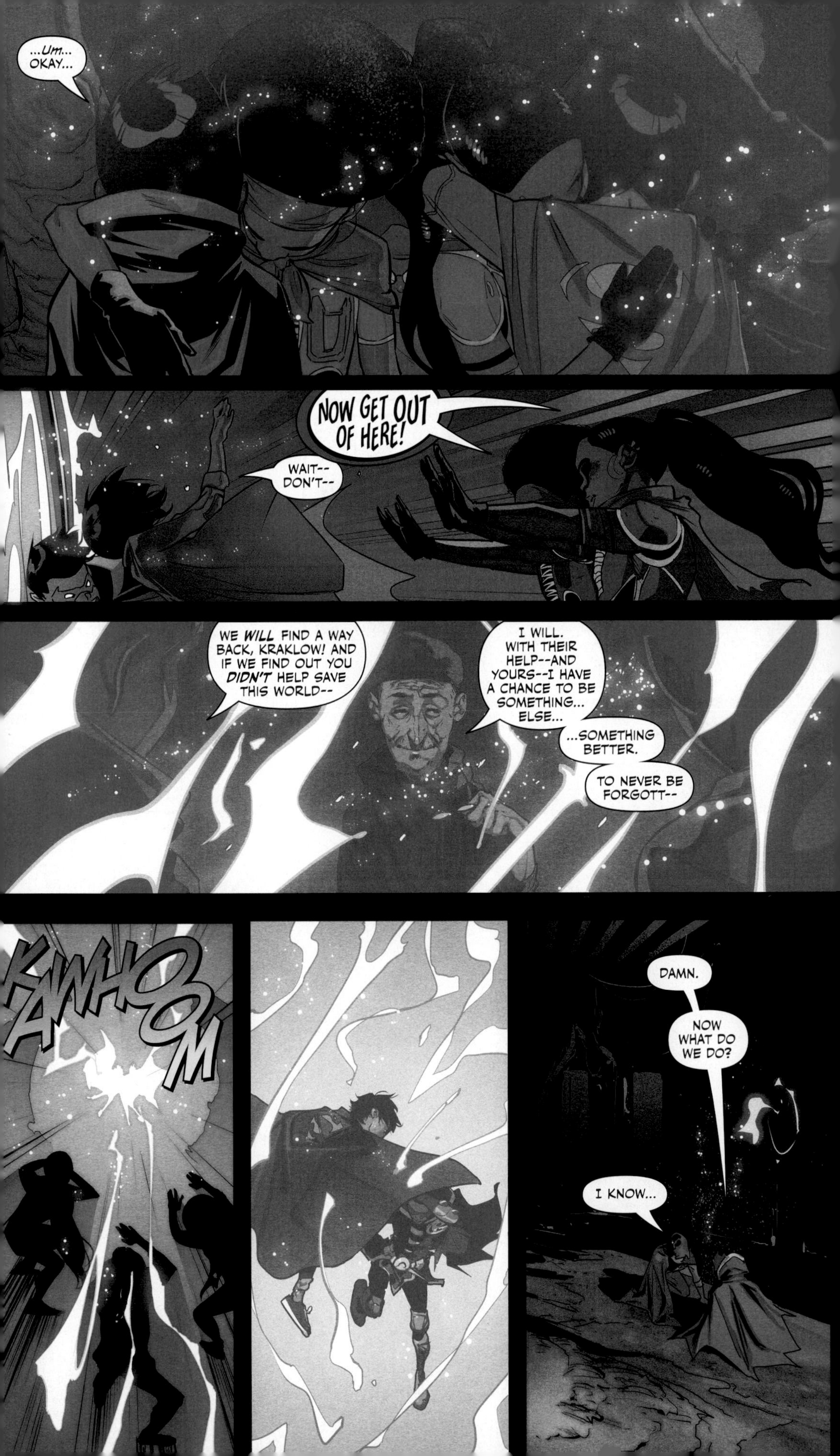

...Um... OKAY...
NOW GET OUT OF HERE!
WAIT-- DON'T--
WE WILL FIND A WAY BACK, KRAKLOW! AND IF WE FIND OUT YOU DIDN'T HELP SAVE THIS WORLD--
I WILL. WITH THEIR HELP--AND YOURS--I HAVE A CHANCE TO BE SOMETHING... ELSE...
...SOMETHING BETTER.
TO NEVER BE FORGOTT--
KAWHOOM
DAMN.
NOW WHAT DO WE DO?
I KNOW...

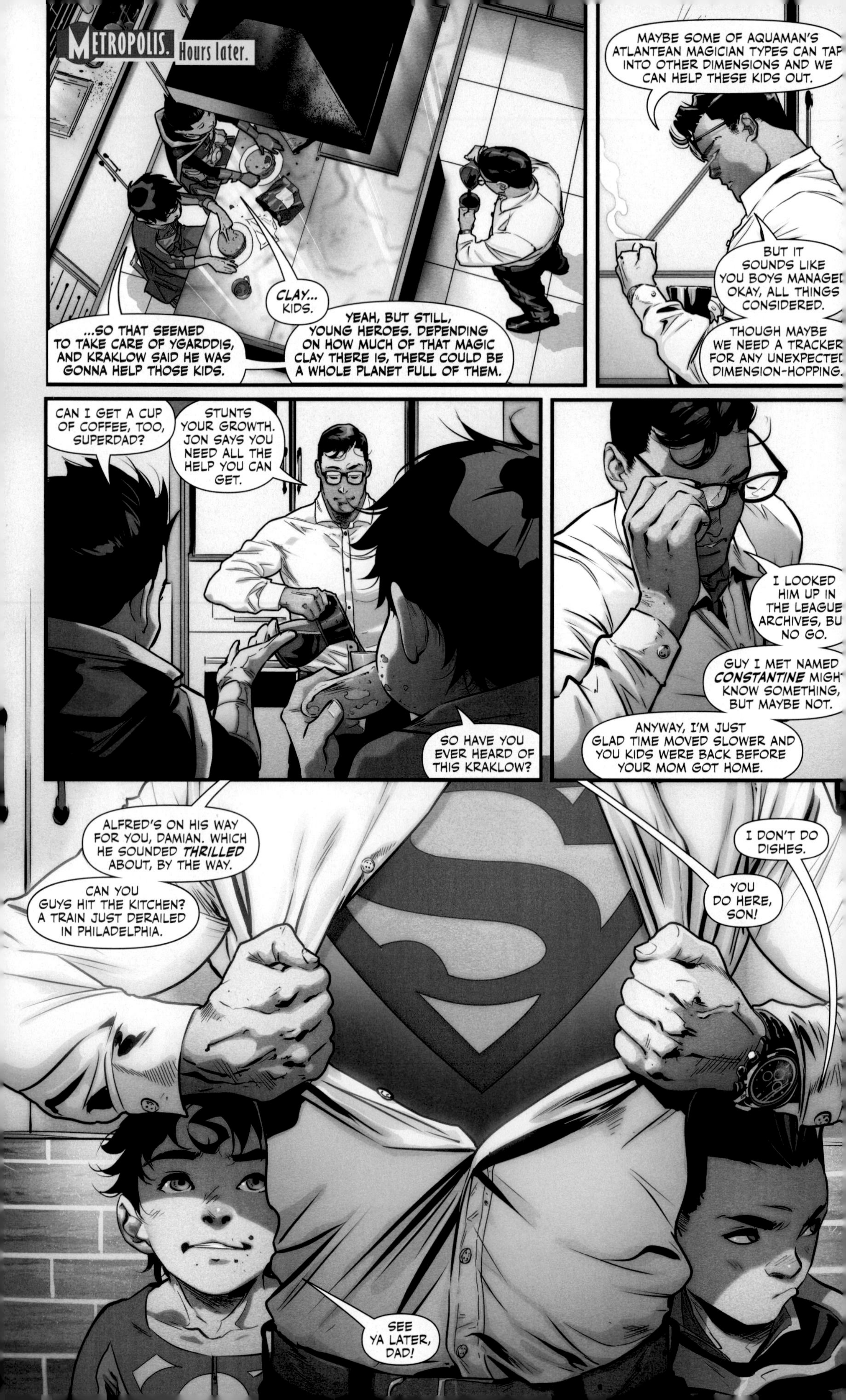
METROPOLIS. Hours later.
...SO THAT SEEMED TO TAKE CARE OF YGARDDIS, AND KRAKLOW SAID HE WAS GONNA HELP THOSE KIDS.
CLAY... KIDS.
YEAH, BUT STILL, YOUNG HEROES. DEPENDING ON HOW MUCH OF THAT MAGIC CLAY THERE IS, THERE COULD BE A WHOLE PLANET FULL OF THEM.
MAYBE SOME OF AQUAMAN'S ATLANTEAN MAGICIAN TYPES CAN TAP INTO OTHER DIMENSIONS AND WE CAN HELP THESE KIDS OUT.
BUT IT SOUNDS LIKE YOU BOYS MANAGED OKAY, ALL THINGS CONSIDERED.
THOUGH MAYBE WE NEED A TRACKER FOR ANY UNEXPECTED DIMENSION-HOPPING.
CAN I GET A CUP OF COFFEE, TOO, SUPERDAD?
STUNTS YOUR GROWTH. JON SAYS YOU NEED ALL THE HELP YOU CAN GET.
SO HAVE YOU EVER HEARD OF THIS KRAKLOW?
I LOOKED HIM UP IN THE LEAGUE ARCHIVES, BUT NO GO.
GUY I MET NAMED *CONSTANTINE* MIGHT KNOW SOMETHING, BUT MAYBE NOT.
ANYWAY, I'M JUST GLAD TIME MOVED SLOWER AND YOU KIDS WERE BACK BEFORE YOUR MOM GOT HOME.
ALFRED'S ON HIS WAY FOR YOU, DAMIAN. WHICH HE SOUNDED *THRILLED* ABOUT, BY THE WAY.
CAN YOU GUYS HIT THE KITCHEN? A TRAIN JUST DERAILED IN PHILADELPHIA.
I DON'T DO DISHES.
YOU DO HERE, SON!
SEE YA LATER, DAD!

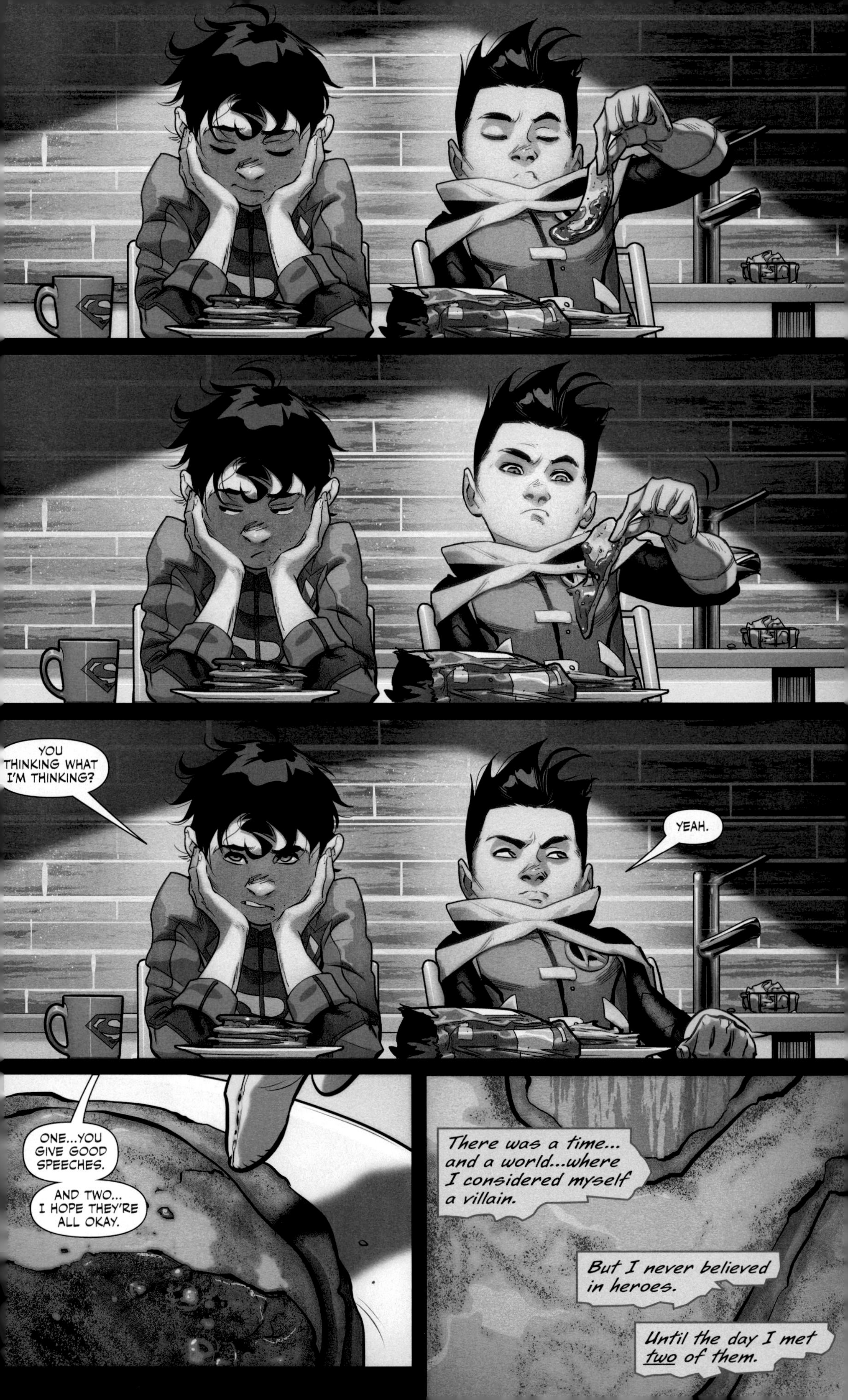

YOU THINKING WHAT I'M THINKING?
YEAH.
ONE...YOU GIVE GOOD SPEECHES.
AND TWO... I HOPE THEY'RE ALL OKAY.
There was a time... and a world...where I considered myself a villain.
But I never believed in heroes.
Until the day I met two of them.

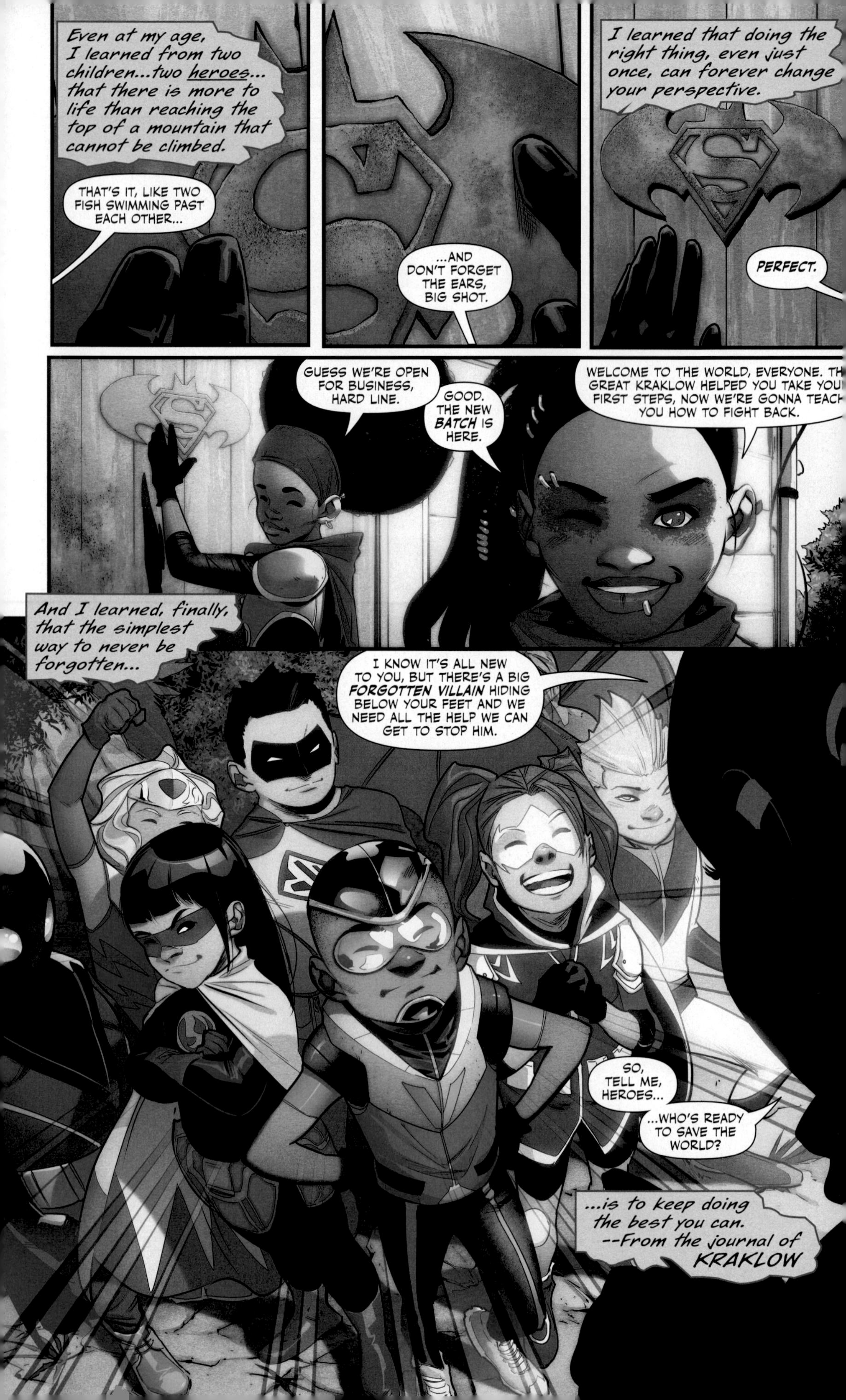
Even at my age, I learned from two children...two heroes... that there is more to life than reaching the top of a mountain that cannot be climbed.
THAT'S IT, LIKE TWO FISH SWIMMING PAST EACH OTHER...
...AND DON'T FORGET THE EARS, BIG SHOT.
I learned that doing the right thing, even just once, can forever change your perspective.
PERFECT.
GUESS WE'RE OPEN FOR BUSINESS, HARD LINE.
GOOD. THE NEW BATCH IS HERE.
WELCOME TO THE WORLD, EVERYONE. TH GREAT KRAKLOW HELPED YOU TAKE YOU FIRST STEPS, NOW WE'RE GONNA TEACH YOU HOW TO FIGHT BACK.
And I learned, finally, that the simplest way to never be forgotten...
I KNOW IT'S ALL NEW TO YOU, BUT THERE'S A BIG FORGOTTEN VILLAIN HIDING BELOW YOUR FEET AND WE NEED ALL THE HELP WE CAN GET TO STOP HIM.
SO, TELL ME, HEROES...
...WHO'S READY TO SAVE THE WORLD?
...is to keep doing the best you can.
--From the journal of KRAKLOW

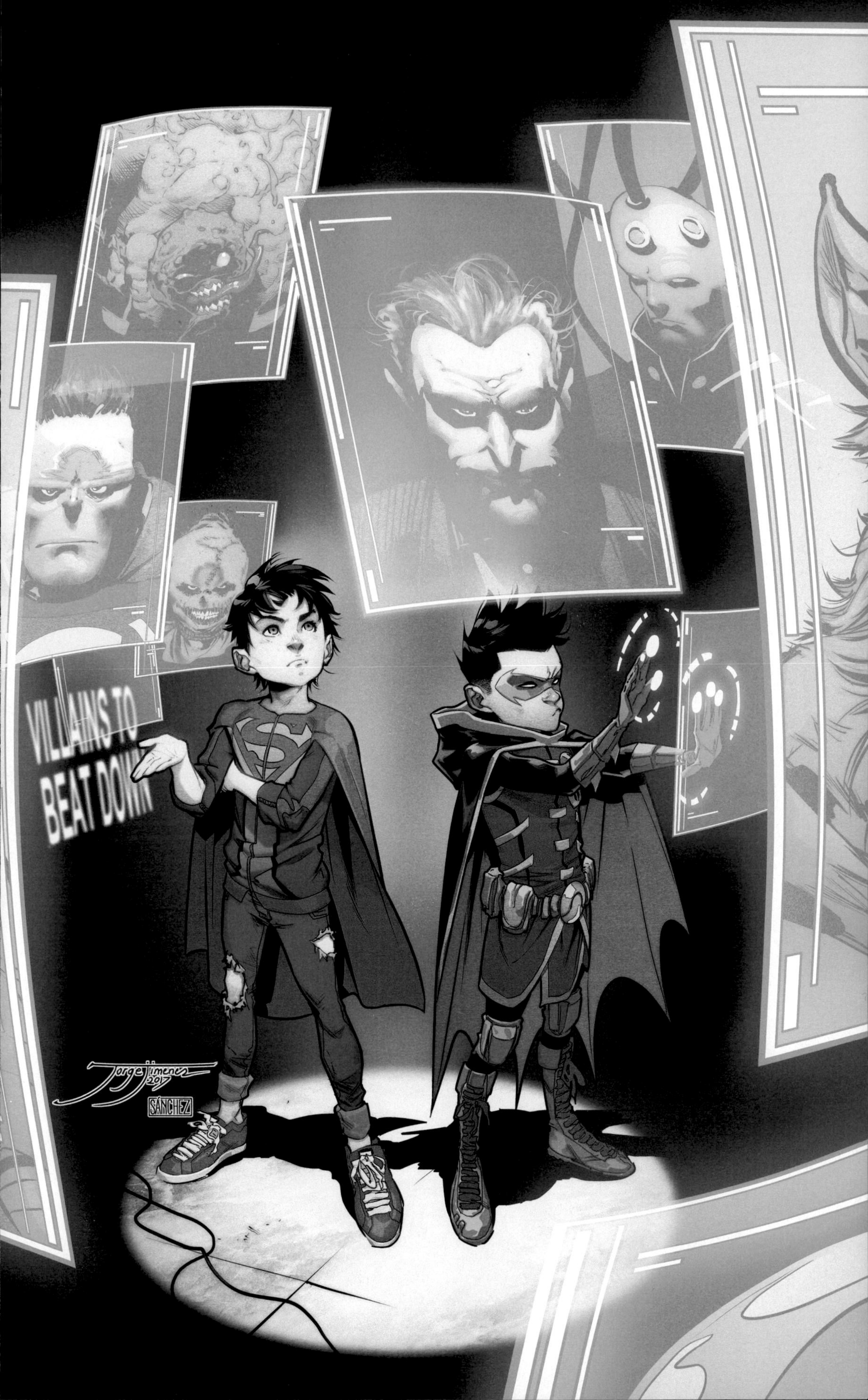
VILLAINS TO BEAT DOWN
Jorge Jimenez 2017
SÁNCHEZ

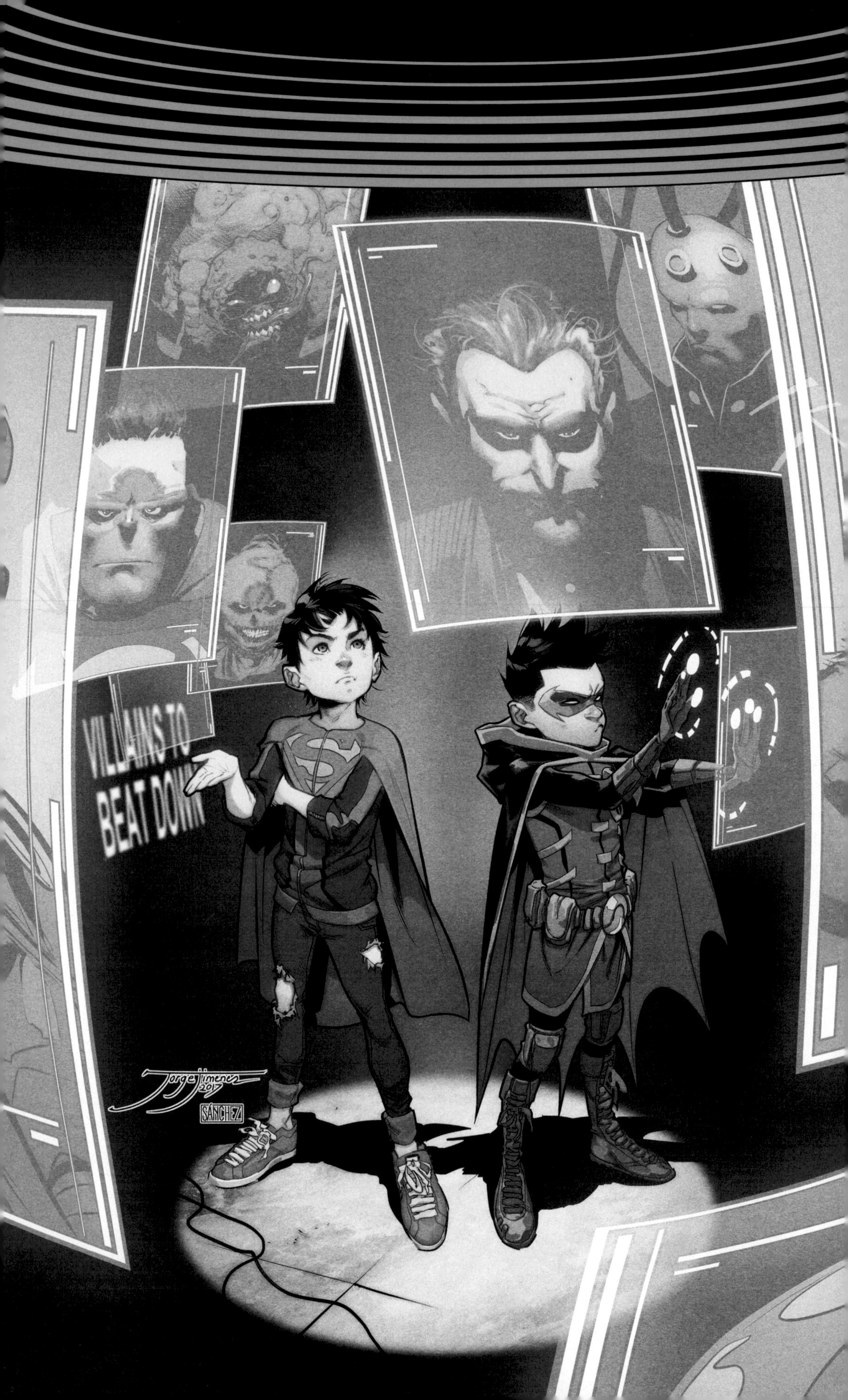
VILLAINS TO
BEAT DOWN
Jorge Jimenez 2017
SÁNCHEZ

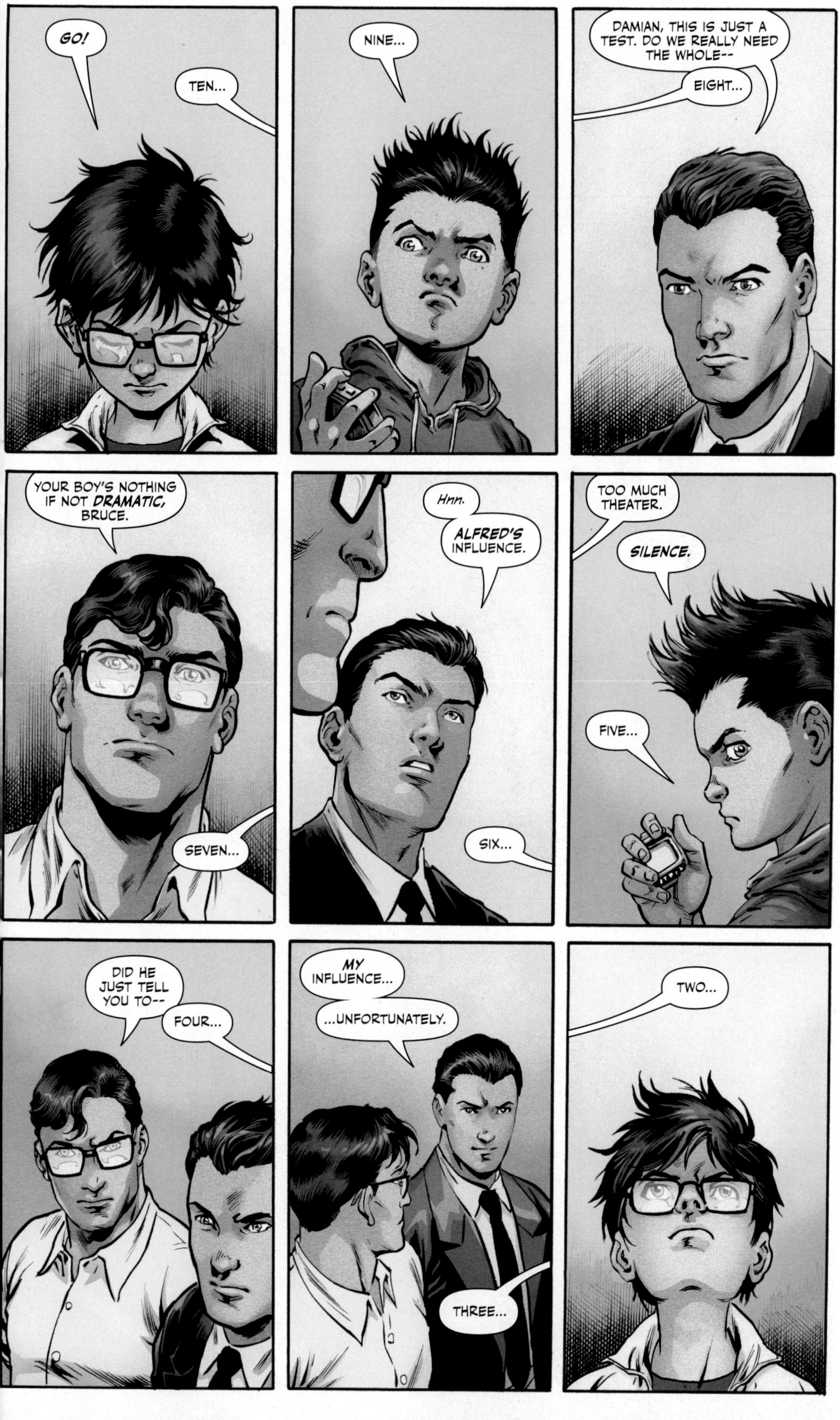
GO!
TEN...
NINE...
DAMIAN, THIS IS JUST A TEST. DO WE REALLY NEED THE WHOLE--
EIGHT...
YOUR BOY'S NOTHING IF NOT DRAMATIC, BRUCE.
SEVEN...
Hnn.
ALFRED'S INFLUENCE.
SIX...
TOO MUCH THEATER.
SILENCE.
FIVE...
DID HE JUST TELL YOU TO--
FOUR...
MY INFLUENCE...
...UNFORTUNATELY.
THREE...
TWO...

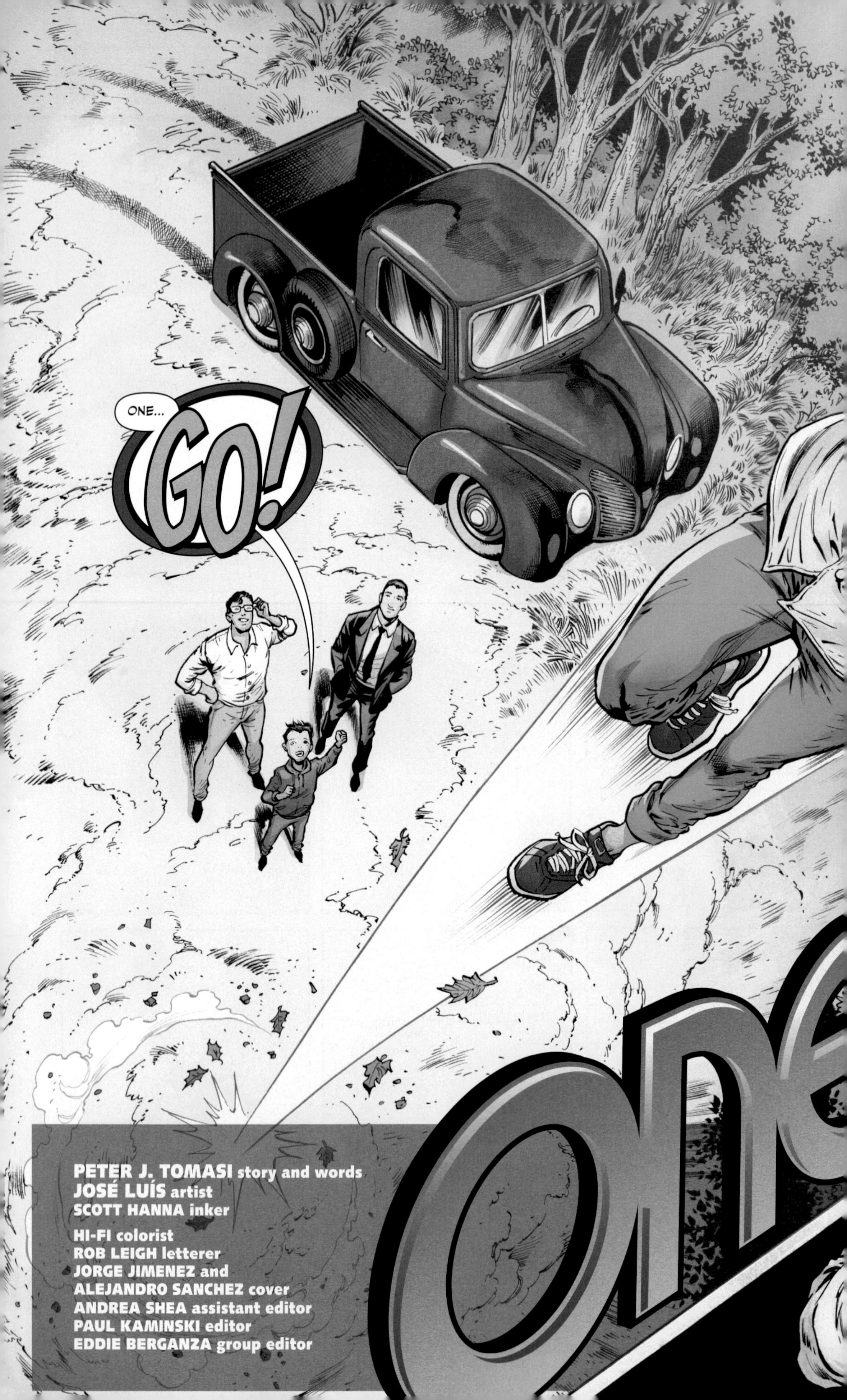
ONE...
GO!
one
PETER J. TOMASI story and words
JOSÉ LUÍS artist
SCOTT HANNA inker
HI-FI colorist
ROB LEIGH letterer
JORGE JIMENEZ and
ALEJANDRO SANCHEZ cover
ANDREA SHEA assistant editor
PAUL KAMINSKI editor
EDDIE BERGANZA group editor

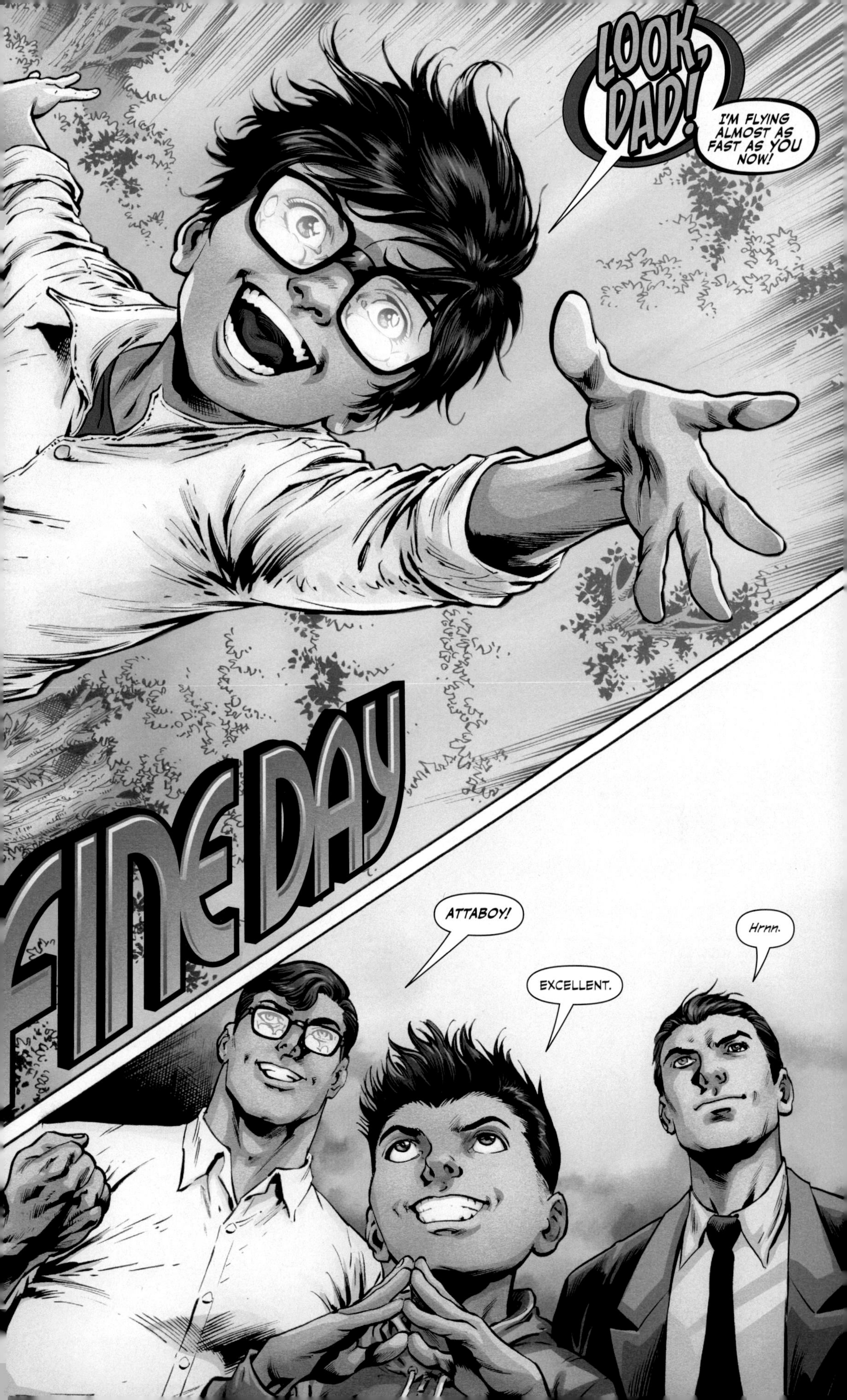
LOOK, DAD!
I'M FLYING ALMOST AS FAST AS YOU NOW!
FINE DAY
ATTABOY!
EXCELLENT.
Hrnn.

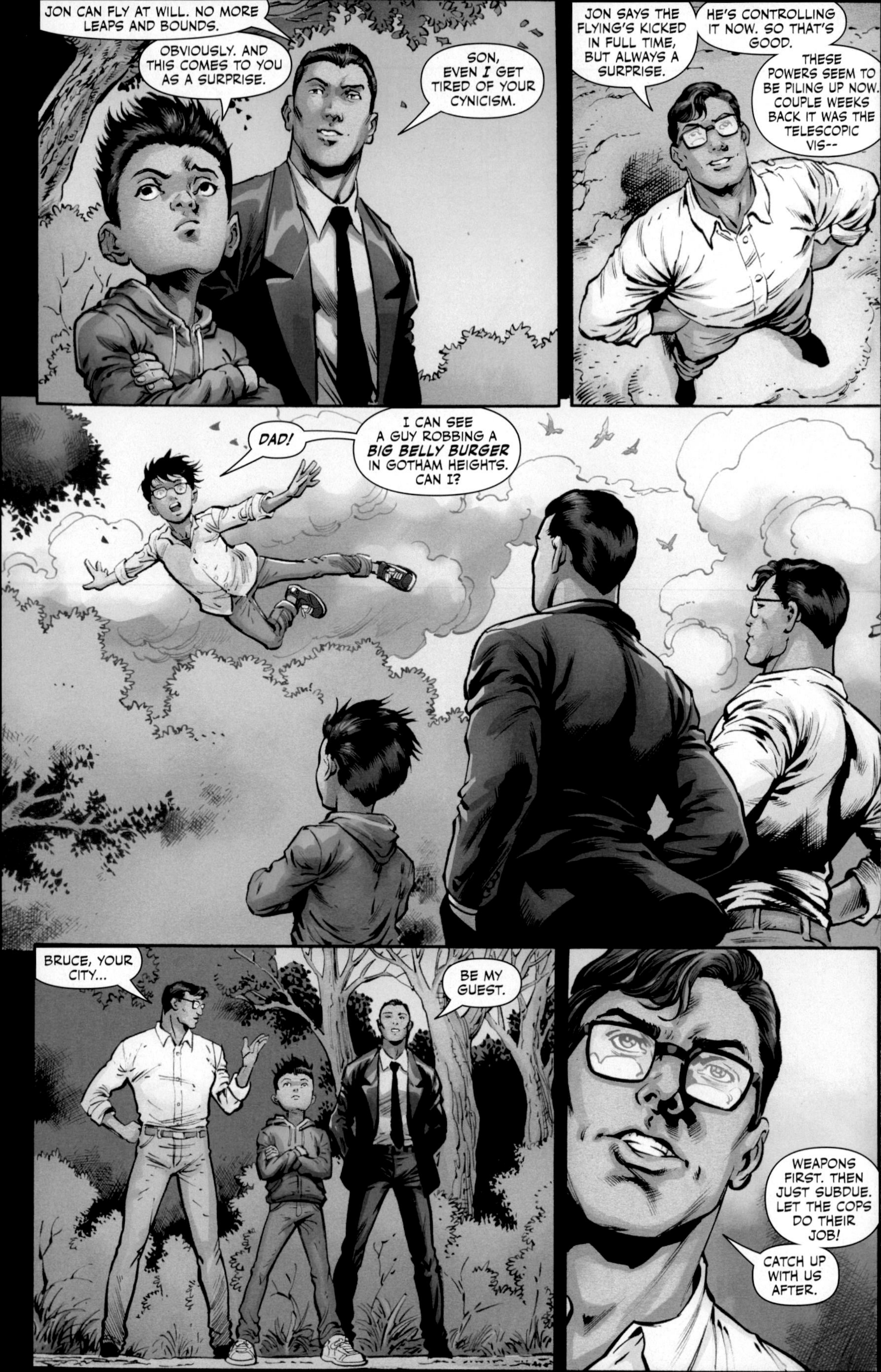
JON CAN FLY AT WILL. NO MORE LEAPS AND BOUNDS.
OBVIOUSLY. AND THIS COMES TO YOU AS A SURPRISE.
SON, EVEN *I* GET TIRED OF YOUR CYNICISM.
JON SAYS THE FLYING'S KICKED IN FULL TIME, BUT ALWAYS A SURPRISE.
HE'S CONTROLLING IT NOW. SO THAT'S GOOD.
THESE POWERS SEEM TO BE PILING UP NOW. COUPLE WEEKS BACK IT WAS THE TELESCOPIC VIS--
DAD!
I CAN SEE A GUY ROBBING A ***BIG BELLY BURGER*** IN GOTHAM HEIGHTS. CAN I?
BRUCE, YOUR CITY...
BE MY GUEST.
WEAPONS FIRST. THEN JUST SUBDUE. LET THE COPS DO THEIR JOB!
CATCH UP WITH US AFTER.

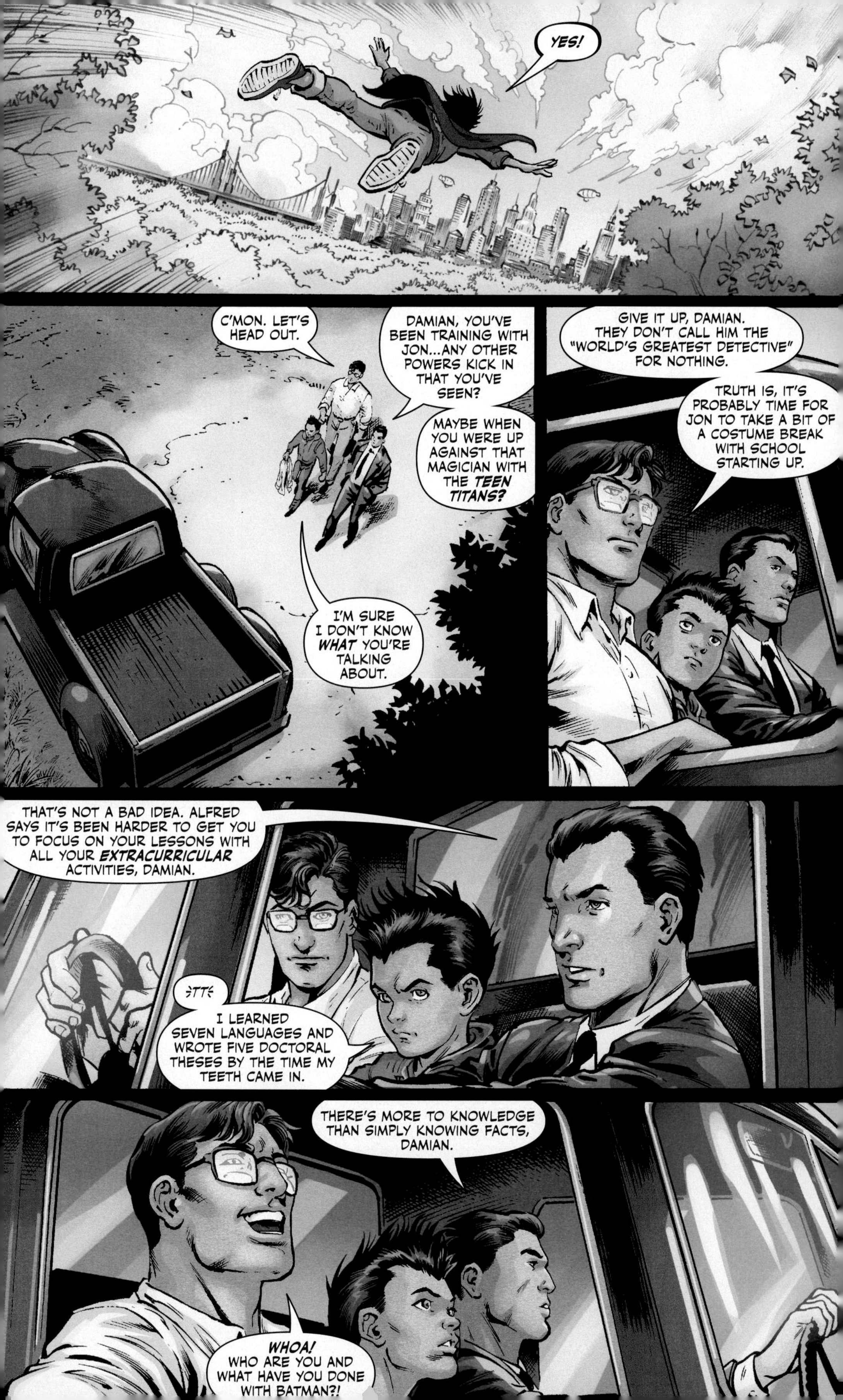
YES!
C'MON. LET'S HEAD OUT.
DAMIAN, YOU'VE BEEN TRAINING WITH JON...ANY OTHER POWERS KICK IN THAT YOU'VE SEEN?
MAYBE WHEN YOU WERE UP AGAINST THAT MAGICIAN WITH THE *TEEN TITANS?*
I'M SURE I DON'T KNOW *WHAT* YOU'RE TALKING ABOUT.
GIVE IT UP, DAMIAN. THEY DON'T CALL HIM THE "WORLD'S GREATEST DETECTIVE" FOR NOTHING.
TRUTH IS, IT'S PROBABLY TIME FOR JON TO TAKE A BIT OF A COSTUME BREAK WITH SCHOOL STARTING UP.
THAT'S NOT A BAD IDEA. ALFRED SAYS IT'S BEEN HARDER TO GET YOU TO FOCUS ON YOUR LESSONS WITH ALL YOUR *EXTRACURRICULAR* ACTIVITIES, DAMIAN.
TT
I LEARNED SEVEN LANGUAGES AND WROTE FIVE DOCTORAL THESES BY THE TIME MY TEETH CAME IN.
THERE'S MORE TO KNOWLEDGE THAN SIMPLY KNOWING FACTS, DAMIAN.
WHOA! WHO ARE YOU AND WHAT HAVE YOU DONE WITH BATMAN?!

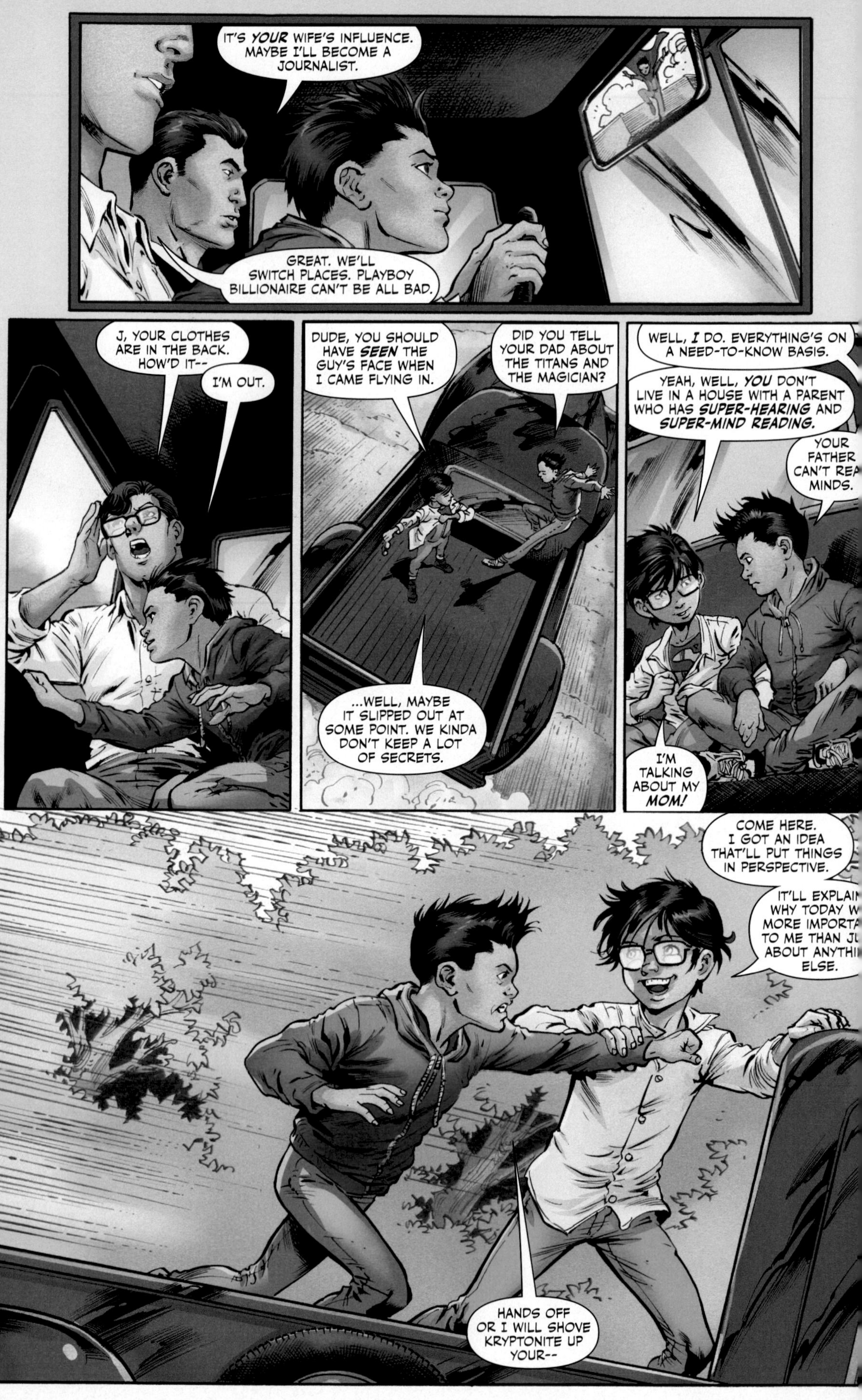

IT'S *YOUR* WIFE'S INFLUENCE. MAYBE I'LL BECOME A JOURNALIST.
GREAT. WE'LL SWITCH PLACES. PLAYBOY BILLIONAIRE CAN'T BE ALL BAD.
J, YOUR CLOTHES ARE IN THE BACK. HOW'D IT--
I'M OUT.
DUDE, YOU SHOULD HAVE *SEEN* THE GUY'S FACE WHEN I CAME FLYING IN.
DID YOU TELL YOUR DAD ABOUT THE TITANS AND THE MAGICIAN?
...WELL, MAYBE IT SLIPPED OUT AT SOME POINT. WE KINDA DON'T KEEP A LOT OF SECRETS.
WELL, *I* DO. EVERYTHING'S ON A NEED-TO-KNOW BASIS.
YEAH, WELL, *YOU* DON'T LIVE IN A HOUSE WITH A PARENT WHO HAS *SUPER-HEARING* AND *SUPER-MIND READING.*
YOUR FATHER CAN'T REA MINDS.
I'M TALKING ABOUT MY *MOM!*
COME HERE. I GOT AN IDEA THAT'LL PUT THINGS IN PERSPECTIVE.
IT'LL EXPLAI WHY TODAY W MORE IMPORTA TO ME THAN JU ABOUT ANYTHI ELSE.
HANDS OFF OR I WILL SHOVE KRYPTONITE UP YOUR--

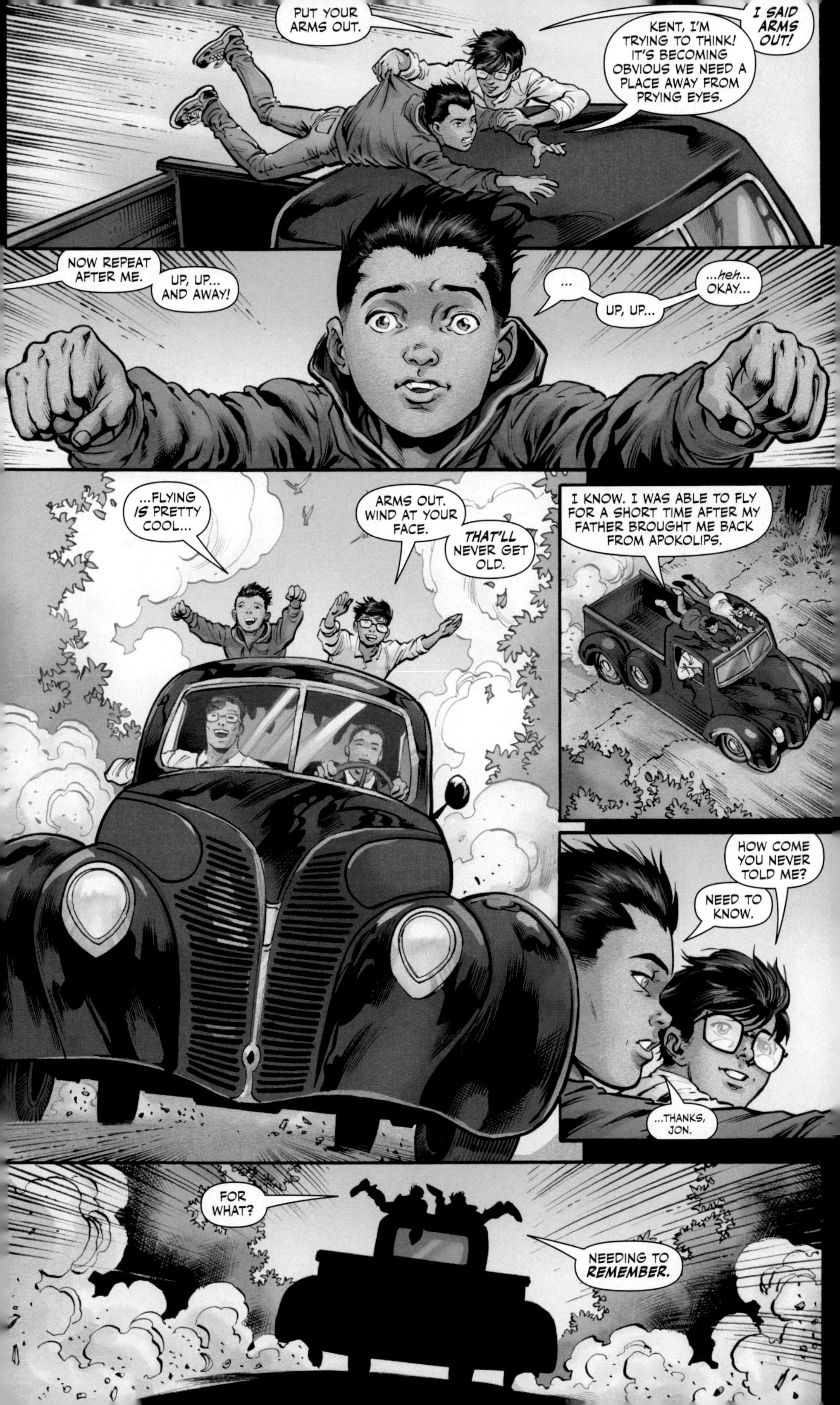
PUT YOUR ARMS OUT.
KENT, I'M TRYING TO THINK! IT'S BECOMING OBVIOUS WE NEED A PLACE AWAY FROM PRYING EYES.
I SAID ARMS OUT!
NOW REPEAT AFTER ME.
UP, UP... AND AWAY!
...
UP, UP...
...heh... OKAY...
...FLYING IS PRETTY COOL...
ARMS OUT. WIND AT YOUR FACE.
THAT'LL NEVER GET OLD.
I KNOW. I WAS ABLE TO FLY FOR A SHORT TIME AFTER MY FATHER BROUGHT ME BACK FROM APOKOLIPS.
HOW COME YOU NEVER TOLD ME?
NEED TO KNOW.
...THANKS, JON.
FOR WHAT?
NEEDING TO REMEMBER.

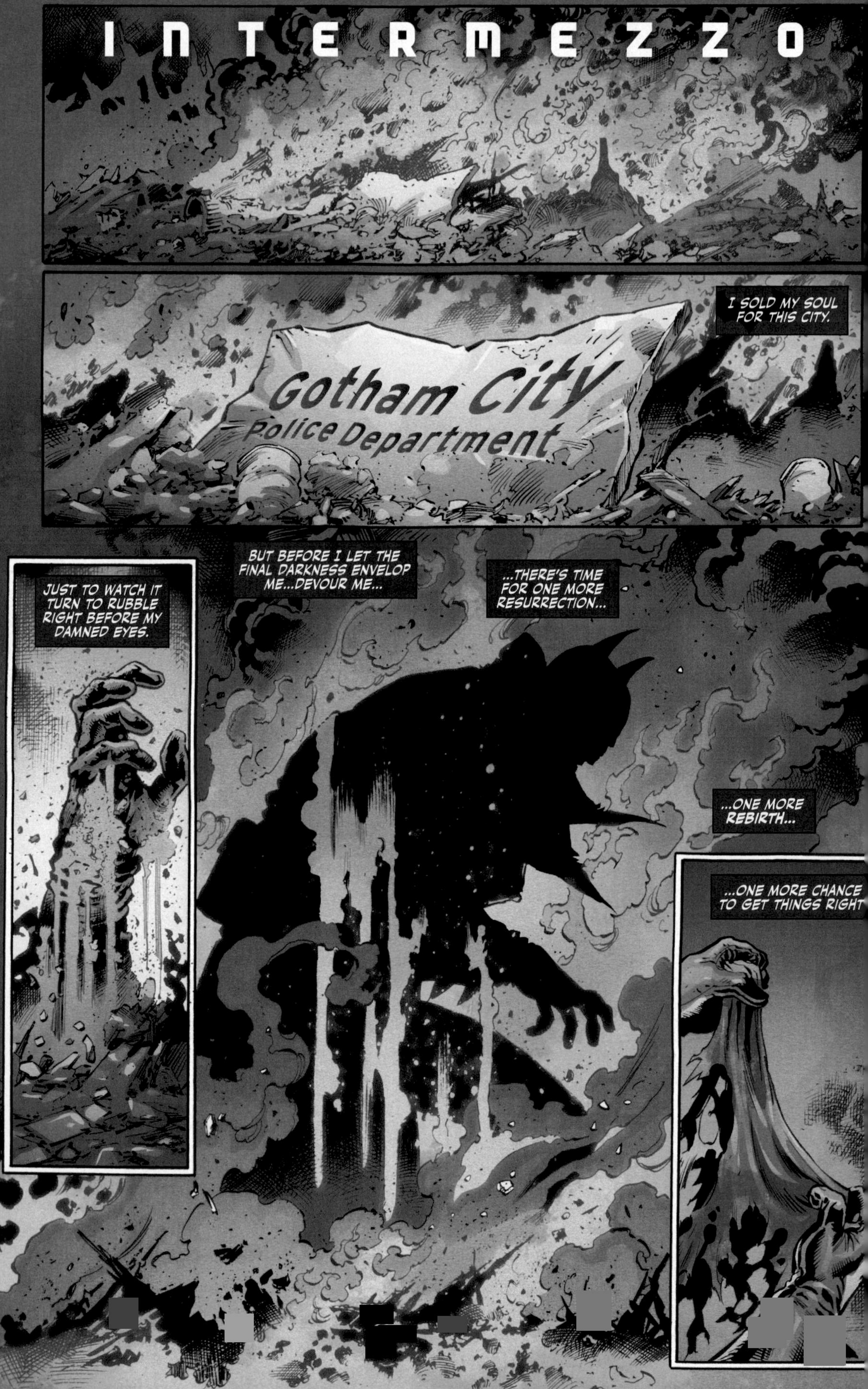
INTERMEZZO
Gotham City
Police Department
I SOLD MY SOUL FOR THIS CITY.
JUST TO WATCH IT TURN TO RUBBLE RIGHT BEFORE MY DAMNED EYES.
BUT BEFORE I LET THE FINAL DARKNESS ENVELOP ME...DEVOUR ME...
...THERE'S TIME FOR ONE MORE RESURRECTION...
...ONE MORE REBIRTH...
...ONE MORE CHANCE TO GET THINGS RIGHT

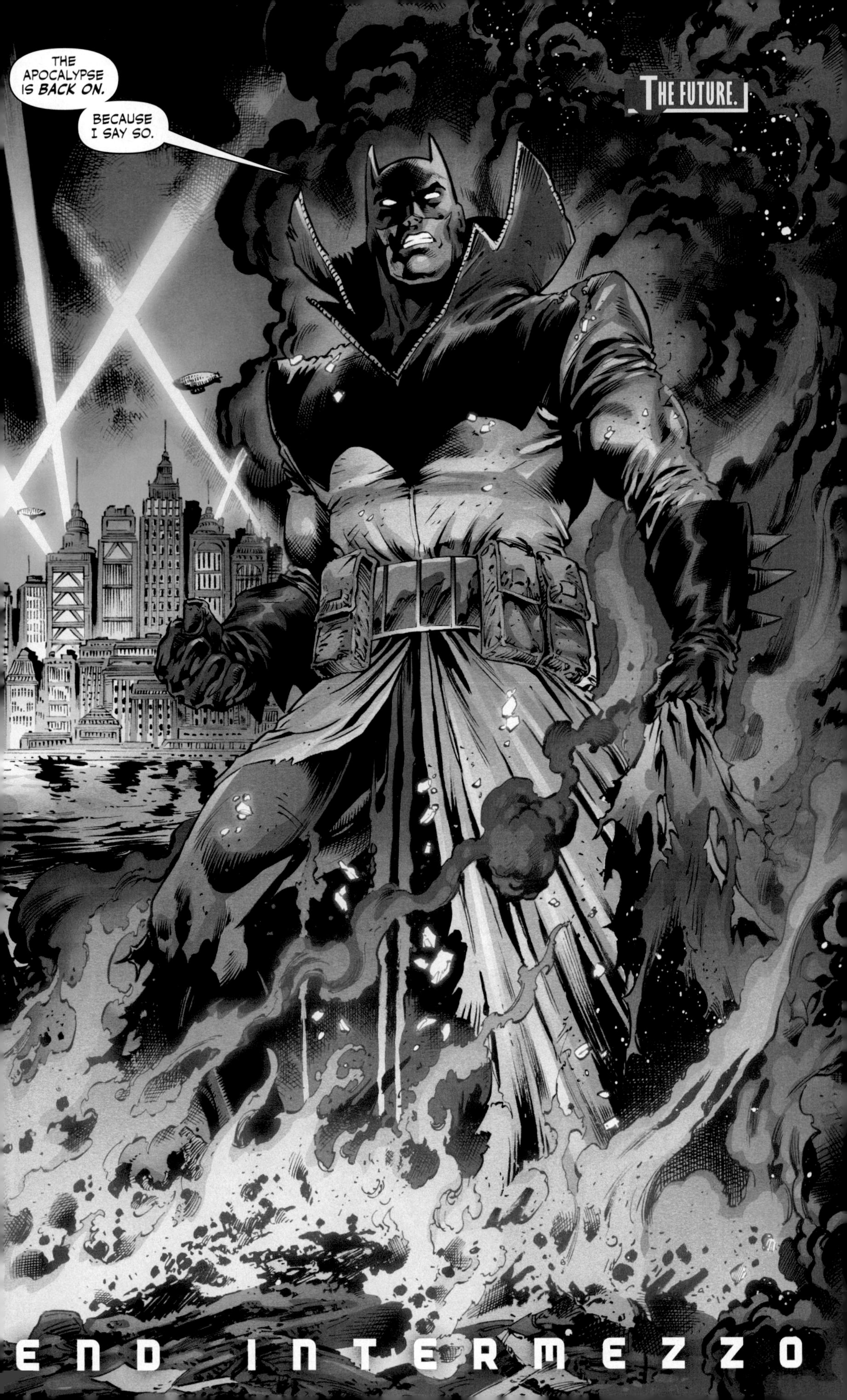
THE APOCALYPSE IS BACK ON.
BECAUSE I SAY SO.
THE FUTURE.
END INTERMEZZO

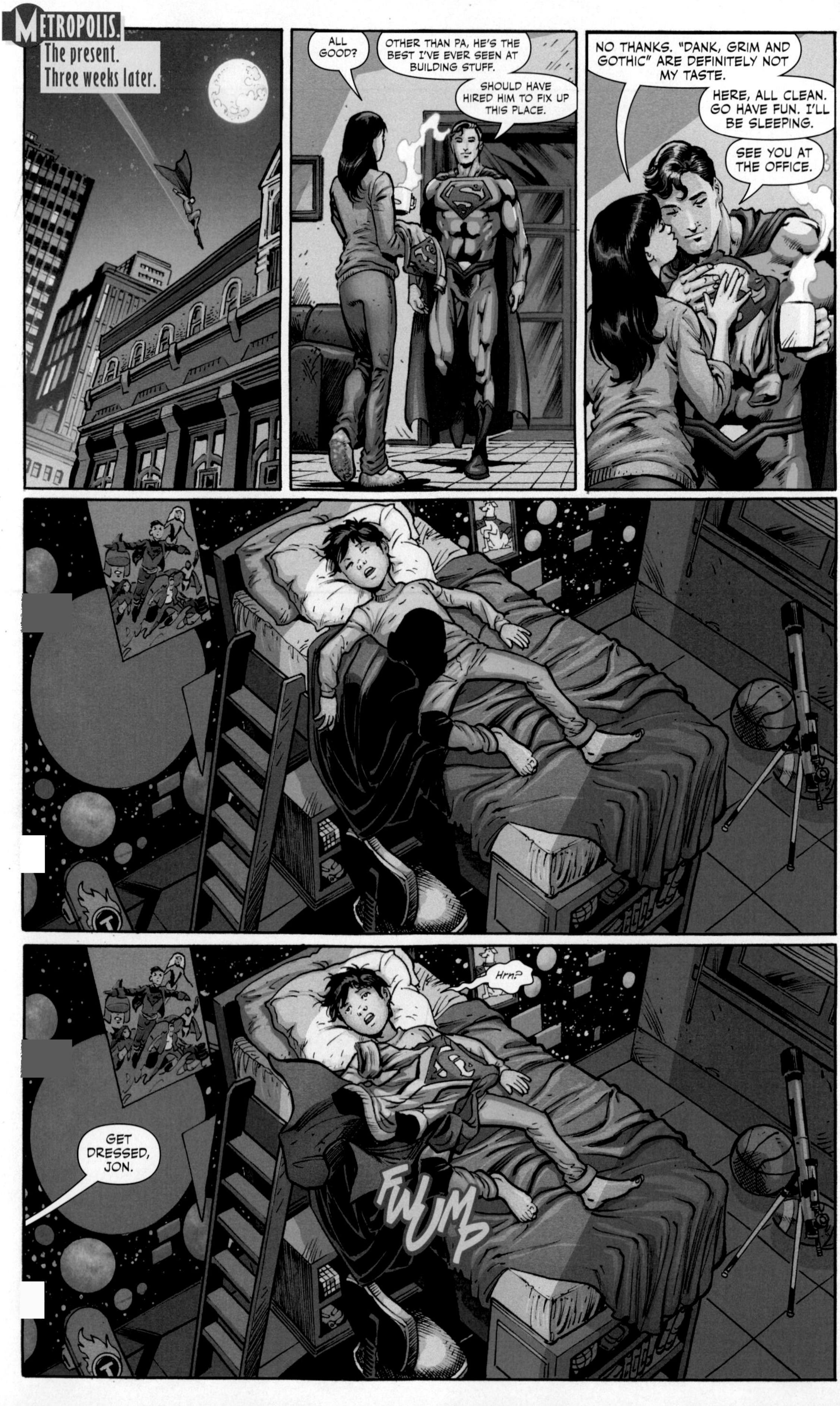
METROPOLIS.
The present.
Three weeks later.
ALL GOOD?
OTHER THAN PA, HE'S THE BEST I'VE EVER SEEN AT BUILDING STUFF.
SHOULD HAVE HIRED HIM TO FIX UP THIS PLACE.
NO THANKS. "DANK, GRIM AND GOTHIC" ARE DEFINITELY NOT MY TASTE.
HERE, ALL CLEAN. GO HAVE FUN. I'LL BE SLEEPING.
SEE YOU AT THE OFFICE.
Hrn?
GET DRESSED, JON.
FWUMP

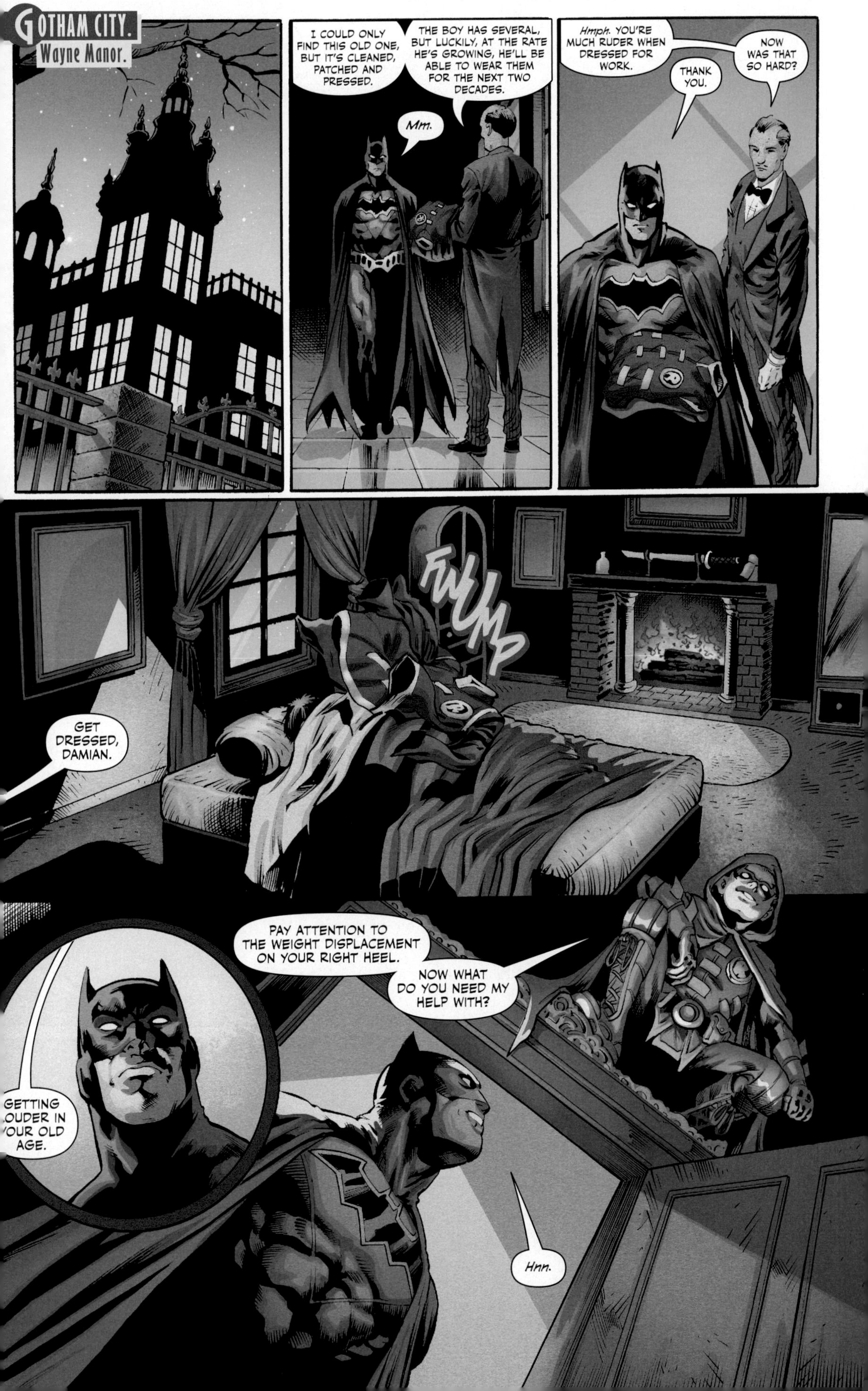
GOTHAM CITY.
Wayne Manor.
I COULD ONLY FIND THIS OLD ONE, BUT IT'S CLEANED, PATCHED AND PRESSED.
THE BOY HAS SEVERAL, BUT LUCKILY, AT THE RATE HE'S GROWING, HE'LL BE ABLE TO WEAR THEM FOR THE NEXT TWO DECADES.
Mm.
Hmph. YOU'RE MUCH RUDER WHEN DRESSED FOR WORK.
THANK YOU.
NOW WAS THAT SO HARD?
FWUMP
GET DRESSED, DAMIAN.
PAY ATTENTION TO THE WEIGHT DISPLACEMENT ON YOUR RIGHT HEEL.
NOW WHAT DO YOU NEED MY HELP WITH?
GETTING LOUDER IN YOUR OLD AGE.
Hnn.

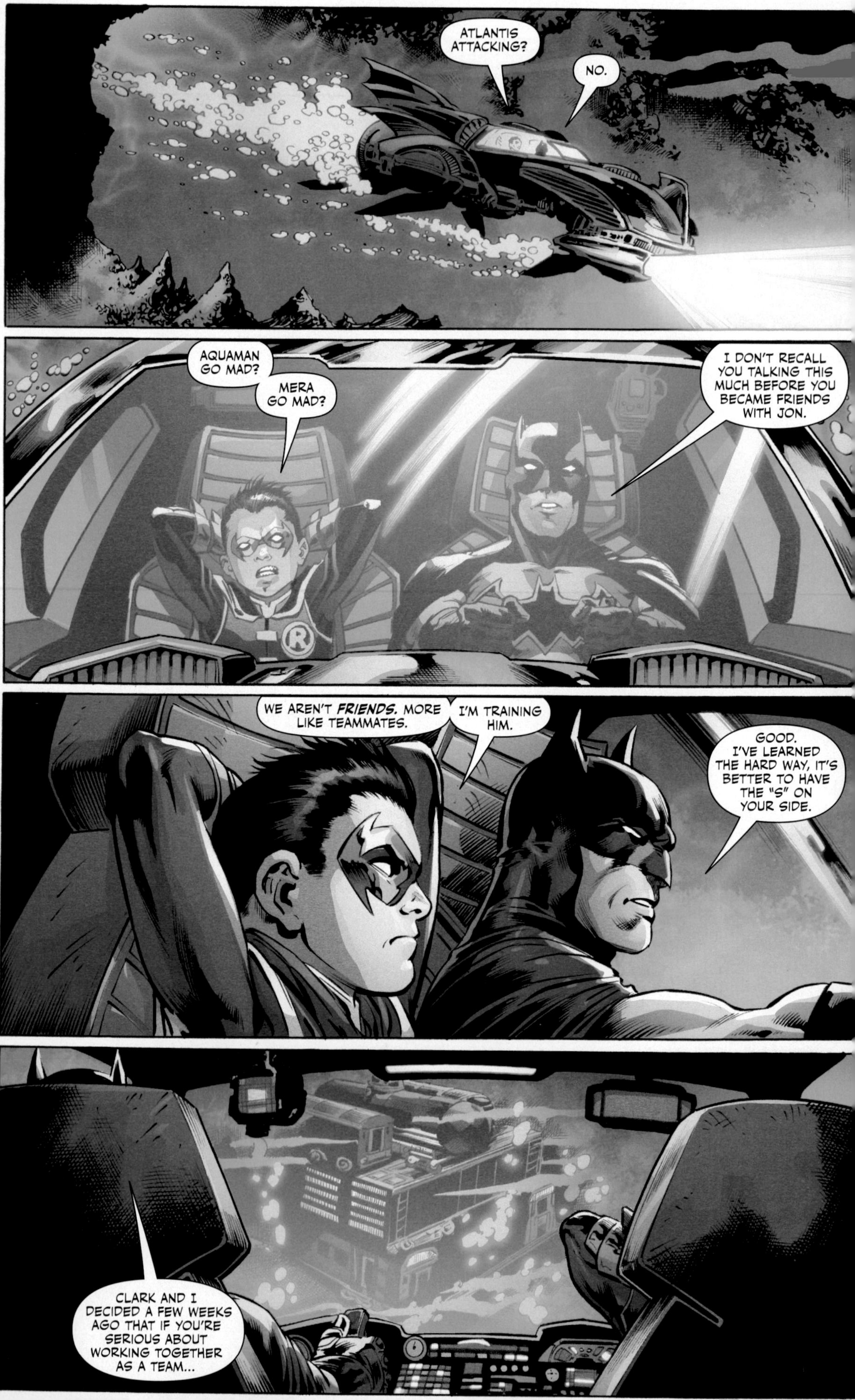
ATLANTIS ATTACKING?
NO.
AQUAMAN GO MAD?
MERA GO MAD?
I DON'T RECALL YOU TALKING THIS MUCH BEFORE YOU BECAME FRIENDS WITH JON.
WE AREN'T *FRIENDS.* MORE LIKE TEAMMATES.
I'M TRAINING HIM.
GOOD. I'VE LEARNED THE HARD WAY, IT'S BETTER TO HAVE THE "S" ON YOUR SIDE.
CLARK AND I DECIDED A FEW WEEKS AGO THAT IF YOU'RE SERIOUS ABOUT WORKING TOGETHER AS A TEAM...

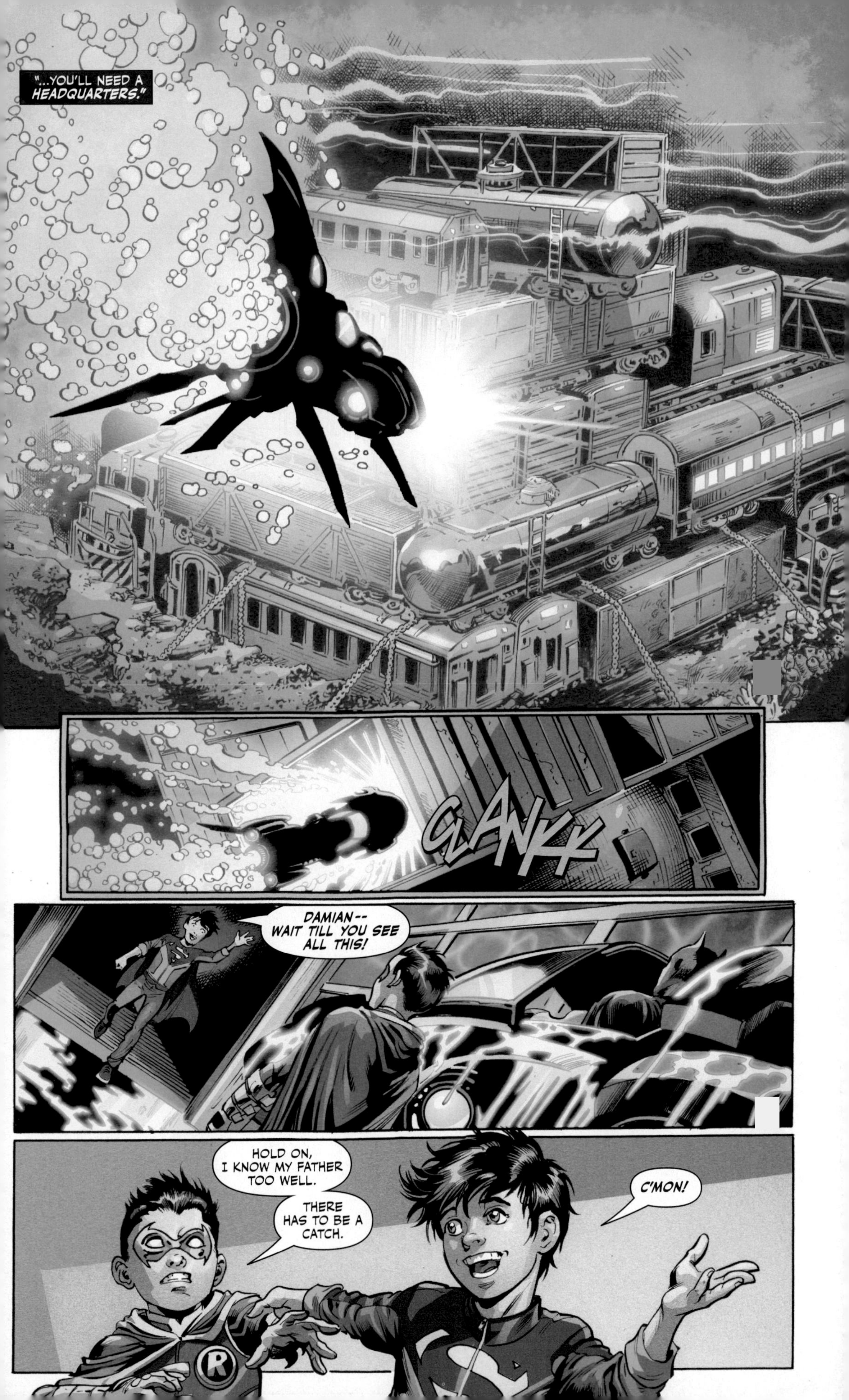
"...YOU'LL NEED A HEADQUARTERS."
CLANKK
DAMIAN-- WAIT TILL YOU SEE ALL THIS!
HOLD ON, I KNOW MY FATHER TOO WELL.
THERE HAS TO BE A CATCH.
C'MON!

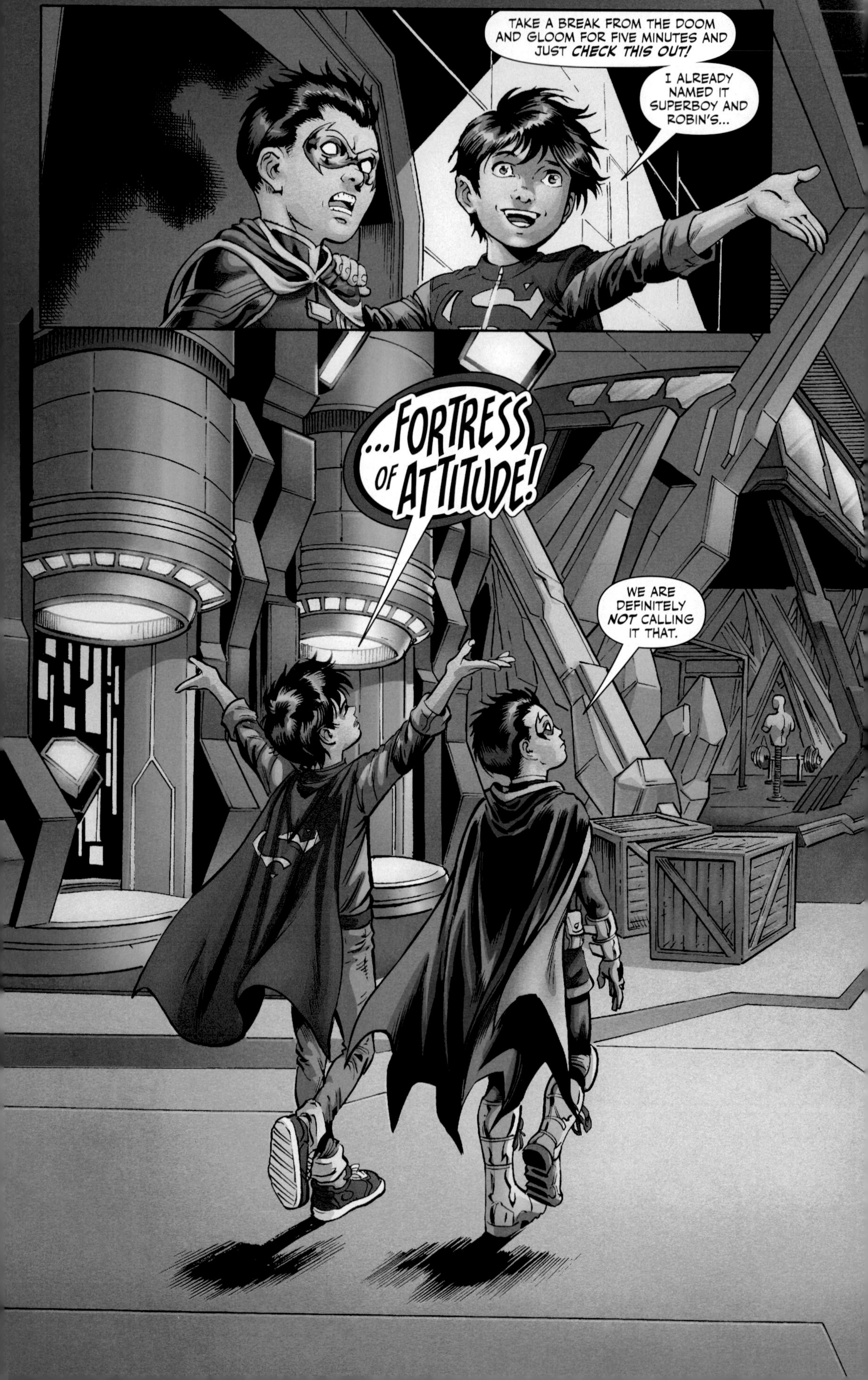
TAKE A BREAK FROM THE DOOM AND GLOOM FOR FIVE MINUTES AND JUST CHECK THIS OUT!
I ALREADY NAMED IT SUPERBOY AND ROBIN'S...
...FORTRESS OF ATTITUDE!
WE ARE DEFINITELY NOT CALLING IT THAT.

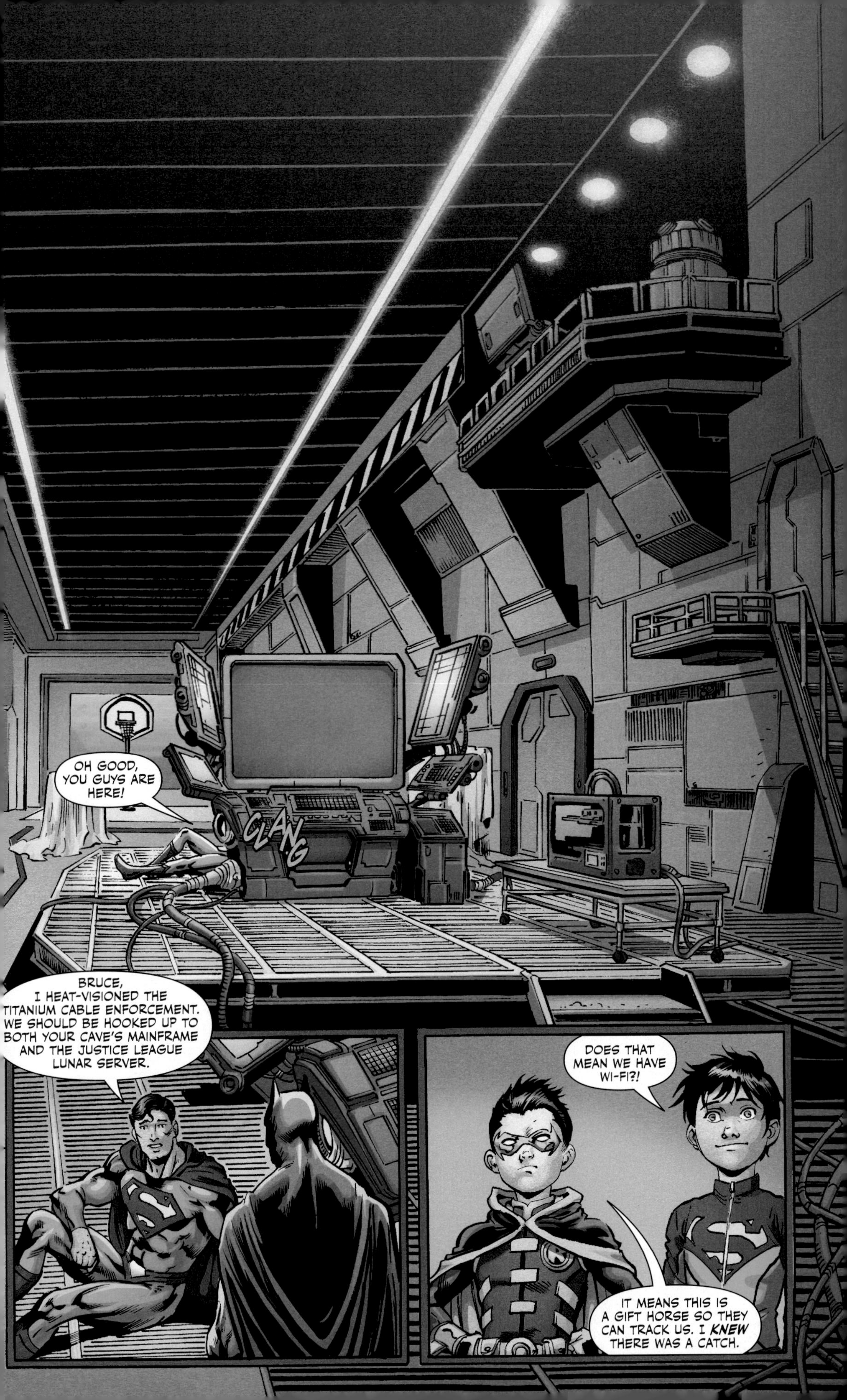
OH GOOD, YOU GUYS ARE HERE!
CLANG
BRUCE, I HEAT-VISIONED THE TITANIUM CABLE ENFORCEMENT. WE SHOULD BE HOOKED UP TO BOTH YOUR CAVE'S MAINFRAME AND THE JUSTICE LEAGUE LUNAR SERVER.
DOES THAT MEAN WE HAVE WI-FI?!
IT MEANS THIS IS A GIFT HORSE SO THEY CAN TRACK US. I *KNEW* THERE WAS A CATCH.

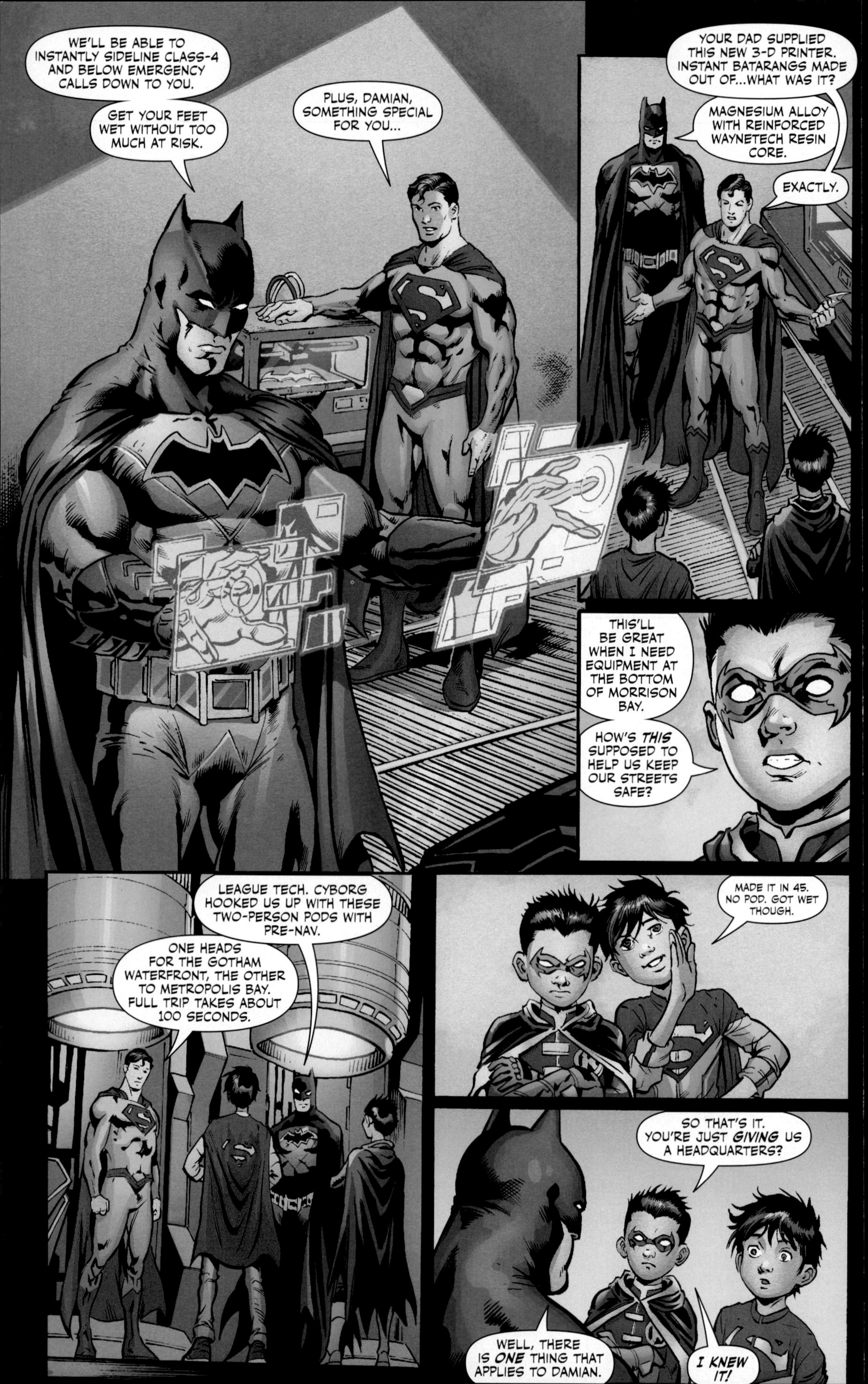
WE'LL BE ABLE TO INSTANTLY SIDELINE CLASS-4 AND BELOW EMERGENCY CALLS DOWN TO YOU.
GET YOUR FEET WET WITHOUT TOO MUCH AT RISK.
PLUS, DAMIAN, SOMETHING SPECIAL FOR YOU...
YOUR DAD SUPPLIED THIS NEW 3-D PRINTER. INSTANT BATARANGS MADE OUT OF...WHAT WAS IT?
MAGNESIUM ALLOY WITH REINFORCED WAYNETECH RESIN CORE.
EXACTLY.
THIS'LL BE GREAT WHEN I NEED EQUIPMENT AT THE BOTTOM OF MORRISON BAY.
HOW'S *THIS* SUPPOSED TO HELP US KEEP OUR STREETS SAFE?
LEAGUE TECH. CYBORG HOOKED US UP WITH THESE TWO-PERSON PODS WITH PRE-NAV.
ONE HEADS FOR THE GOTHAM WATERFRONT, THE OTHER TO METROPOLIS BAY. FULL TRIP TAKES ABOUT 100 SECONDS.
MADE IT IN 45. NO POD. GOT WET THOUGH.
SO THAT'S IT. YOU'RE JUST *GIVING* US A HEADQUARTERS?
WELL, THERE IS *ONE* THING THAT APPLIES TO DAMIAN.
I KNEW IT!

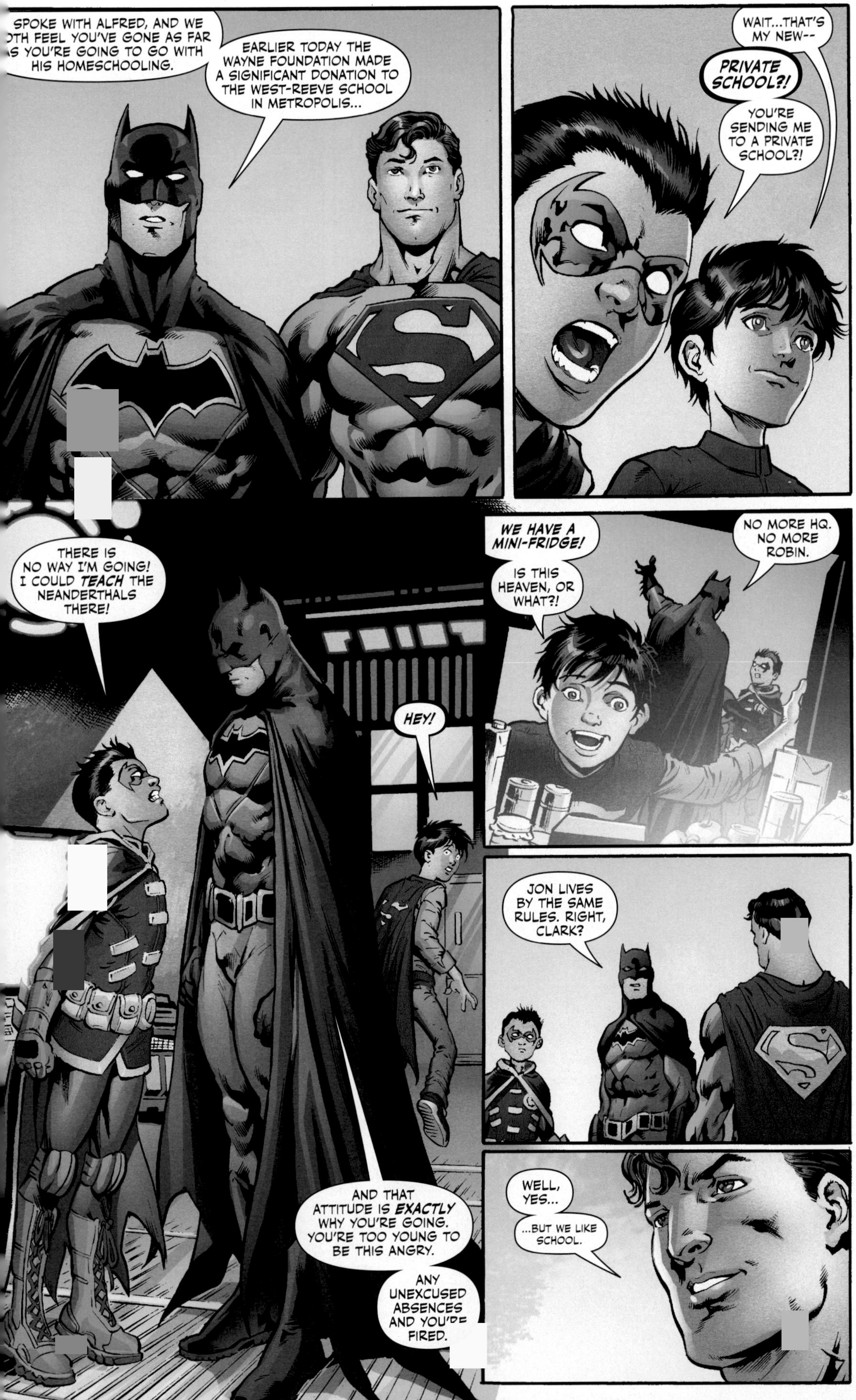
SPOKE WITH ALFRED, AND WE
OTH FEEL YOU'VE GONE AS FAR
S YOU'RE GOING TO GO WITH
HIS HOMESCHOOLING.
EARLIER TODAY THE WAYNE FOUNDATION MADE A SIGNIFICANT DONATION TO THE WEST-REEVE SCHOOL IN METROPOLIS...
WAIT...THAT'S MY NEW--
PRIVATE SCHOOL?!
YOU'RE SENDING ME TO A PRIVATE SCHOOL?!
THERE IS NO WAY I'M GOING! I COULD TEACH THE NEANDERTHALS THERE!
HEY!
AND THAT ATTITUDE IS EXACTLY WHY YOU'RE GOING. YOU'RE TOO YOUNG TO BE THIS ANGRY.
ANY UNEXCUSED ABSENCES AND YOU'RE FIRED.
WE HAVE A MINI-FRIDGE!
IS THIS HEAVEN, OR WHAT?!
NO MORE HQ. NO MORE ROBIN.
JON LIVES BY THE SAME RULES. RIGHT, CLARK?
WELL, YES...
...BUT WE LIKE SCHOOL.

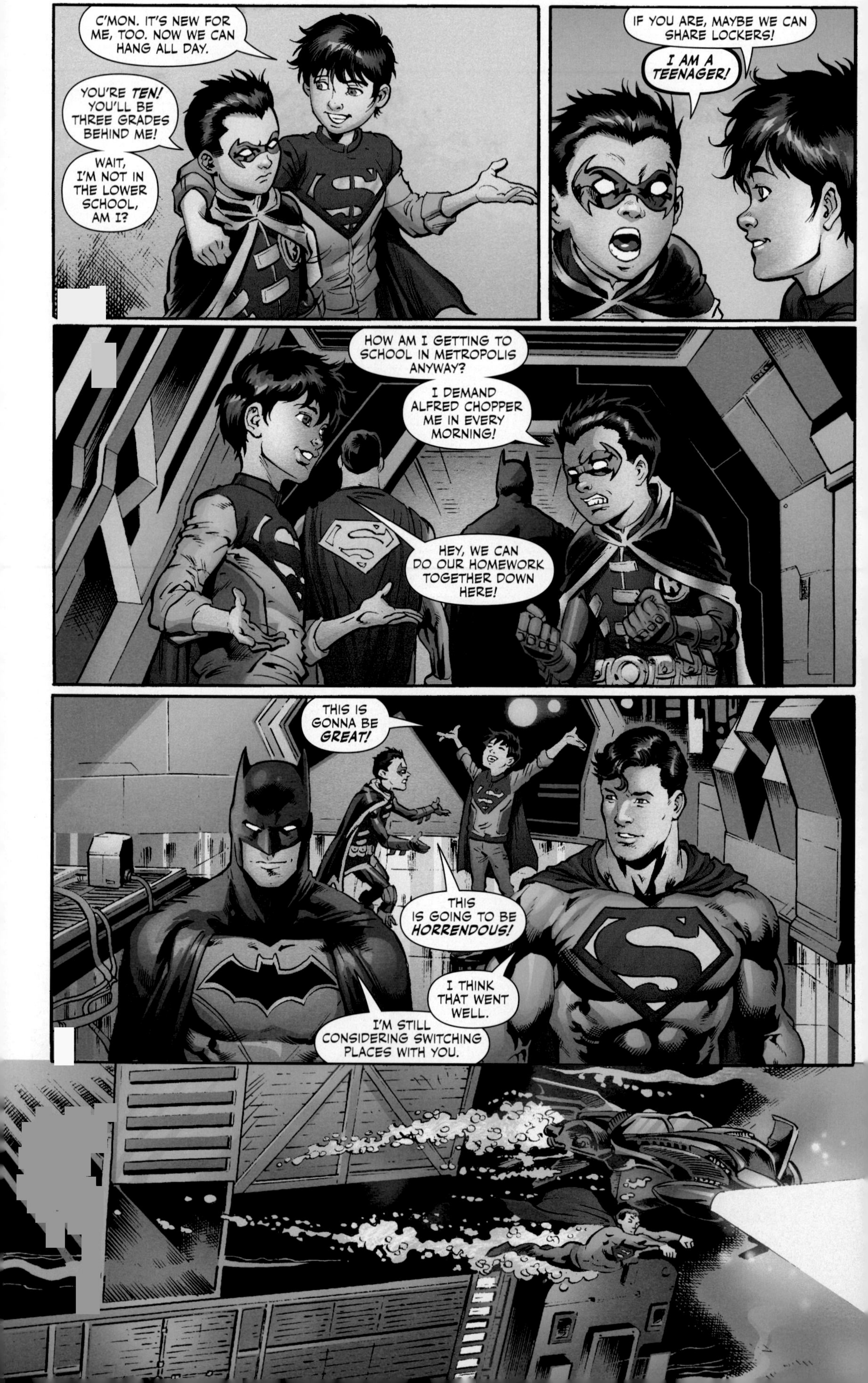
C'MON. IT'S NEW FOR ME, TOO. NOW WE CAN HANG ALL DAY.
YOU'RE *TEN!* YOU'LL BE THREE GRADES BEHIND ME!
WAIT, I'M NOT IN THE LOWER SCHOOL, AM I?
IF YOU ARE, MAYBE WE CAN SHARE LOCKERS!
I AM A TEENAGER!
HOW AM I GETTING TO SCHOOL IN METROPOLIS ANYWAY?
I DEMAND ALFRED CHOPPER ME IN EVERY MORNING!
HEY, WE CAN DO OUR HOMEWORK TOGETHER DOWN HERE!
THIS IS GONNA BE *GREAT!*
THIS IS GOING TO BE *HORRENDOUS!*
I THINK THAT WENT WELL.
I'M STILL CONSIDERING SWITCHING PLACES WITH YOU.

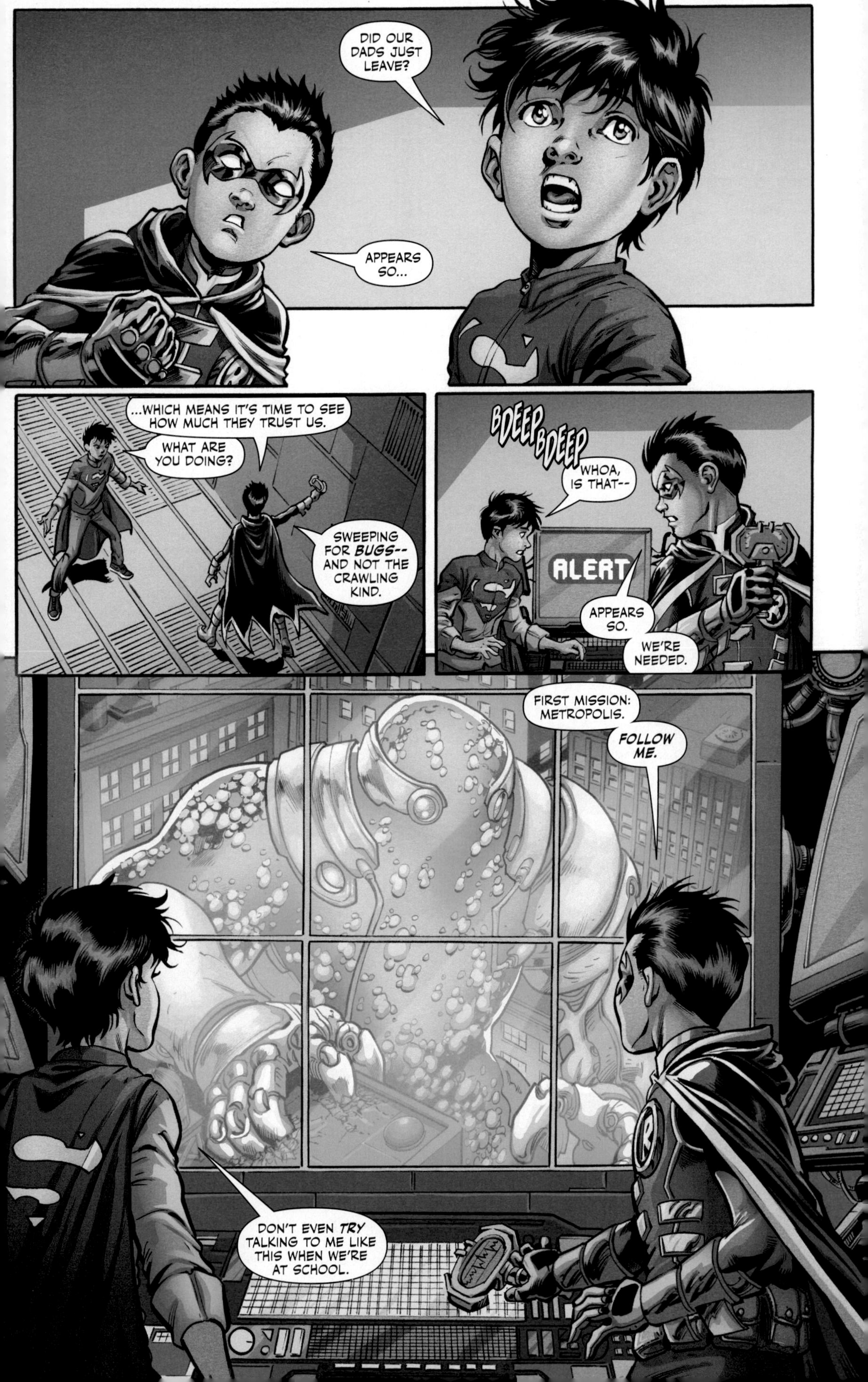
DID OUR DADS JUST LEAVE?
APPEARS SO...
...WHICH MEANS IT'S TIME TO SEE HOW MUCH THEY TRUST US.
WHAT ARE YOU DOING?
SWEEPING FOR BUGS-- AND NOT THE CRAWLING KIND.
BDEEP BDEEP
WHOA, IS THAT--
ALERT
APPEARS SO.
WE'RE NEEDED.
FIRST MISSION: METROPOLIS.
FOLLOW ME.
DON'T EVEN TRY TALKING TO ME LIKE THIS WHEN WE'RE AT SCHOOL.

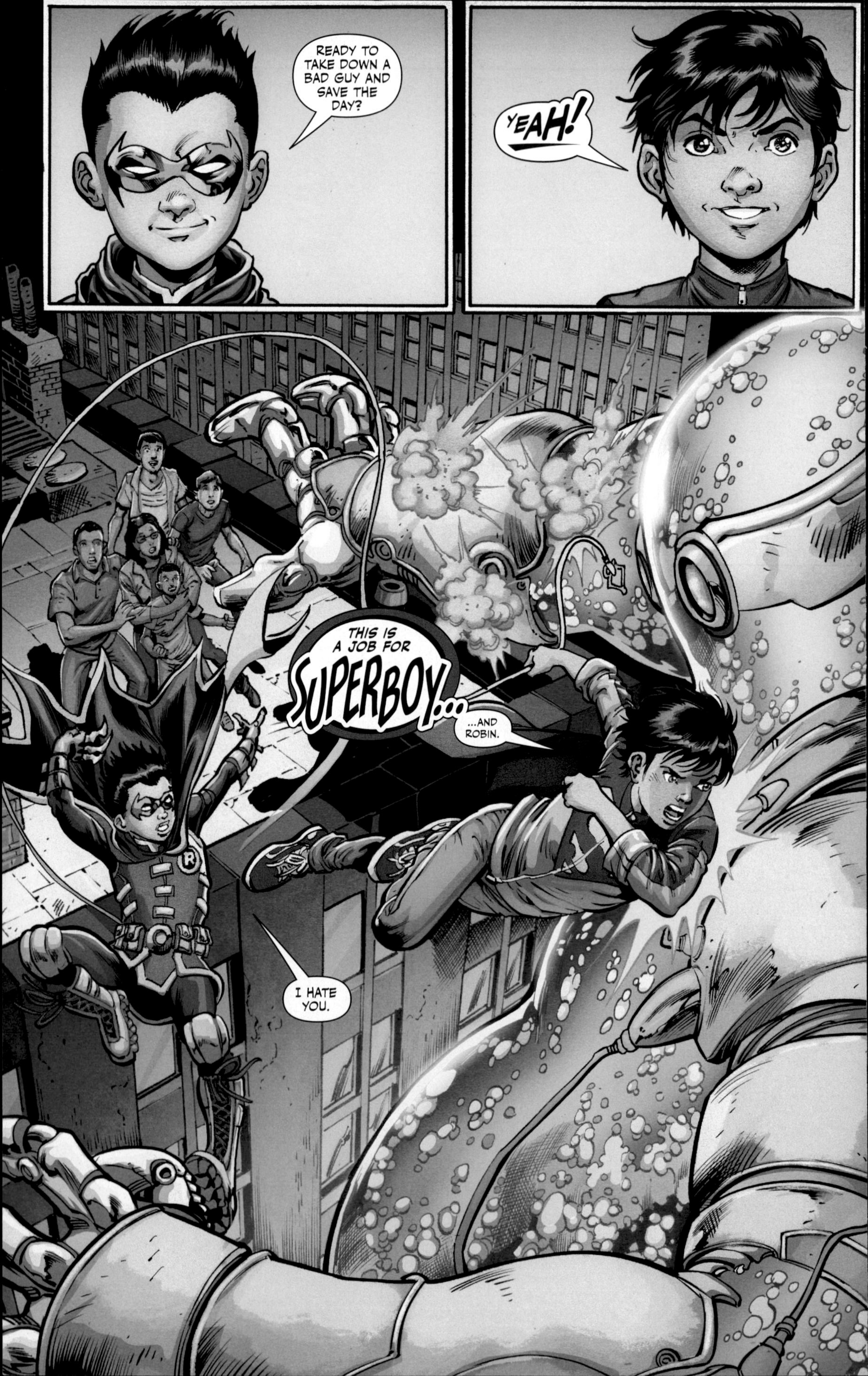

READY TO TAKE DOWN A BAD GUY AND SAVE THE DAY?
YEAH!
THIS IS A JOB FOR SUPERBOY...
...AND ROBIN.
I HATE YOU.

Super Sons

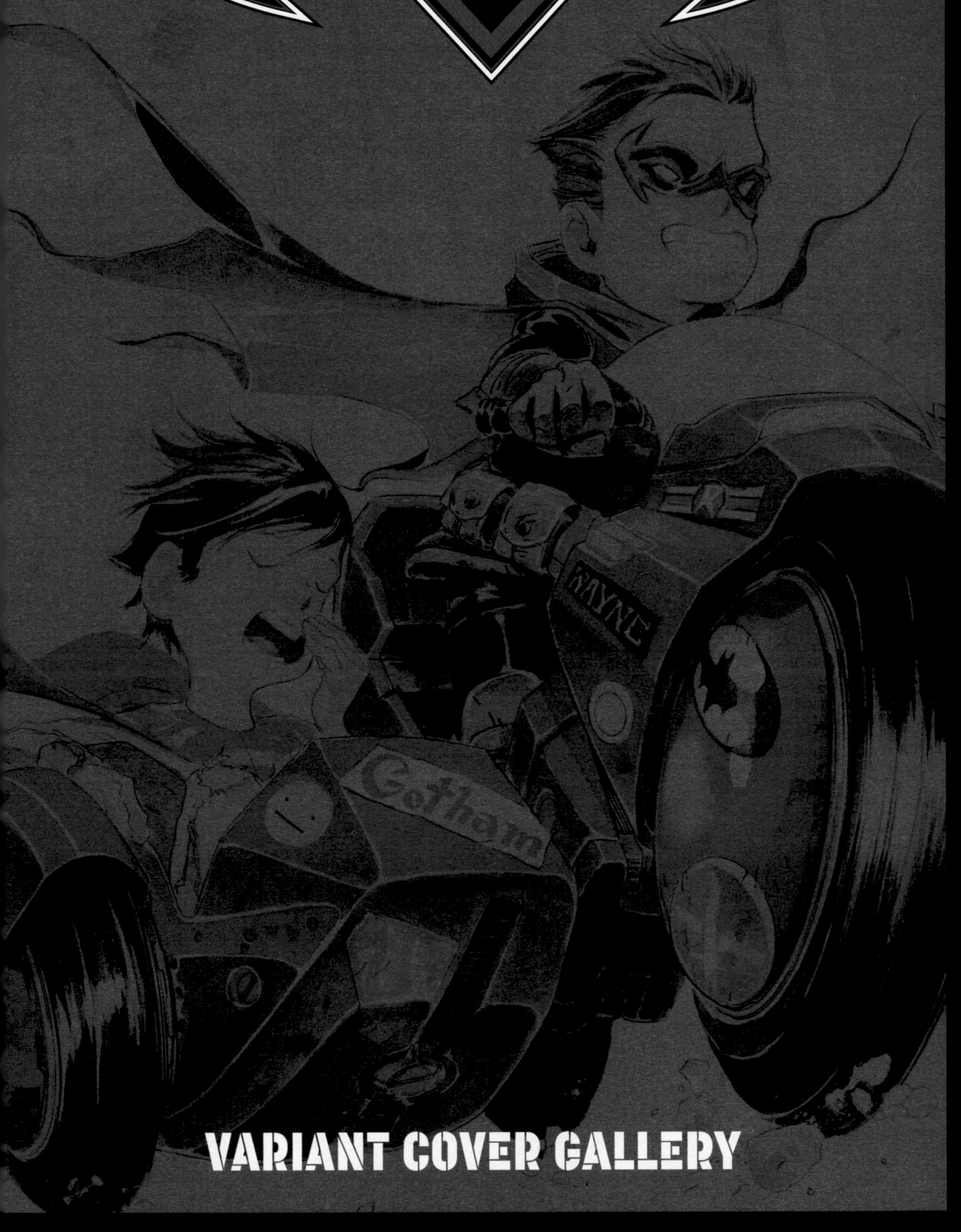
WAYNE
Gotham

VARIANT COVER GALLERY

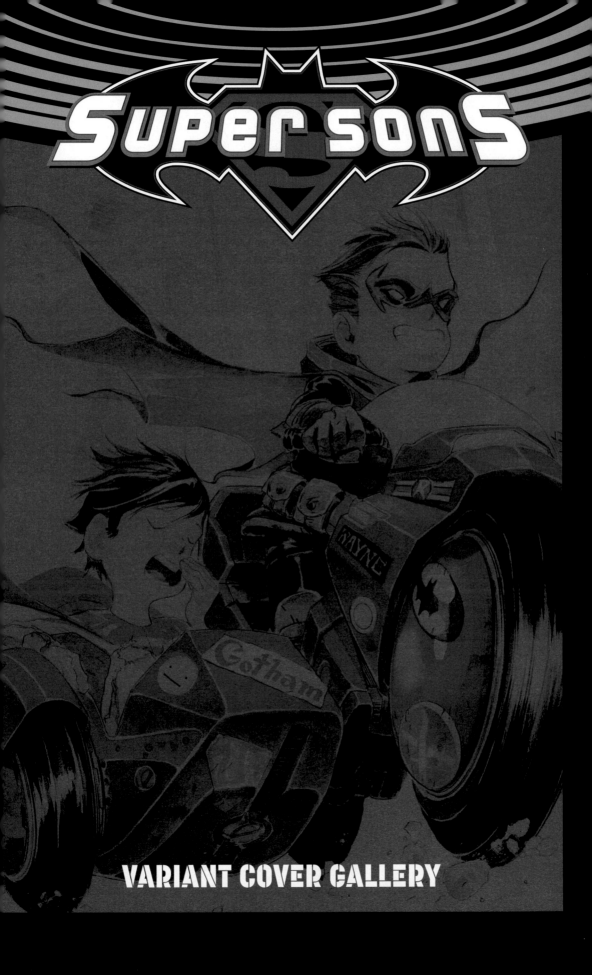

Variant cover art for SUPER SONS #6
by DUSTIN NGUYEN

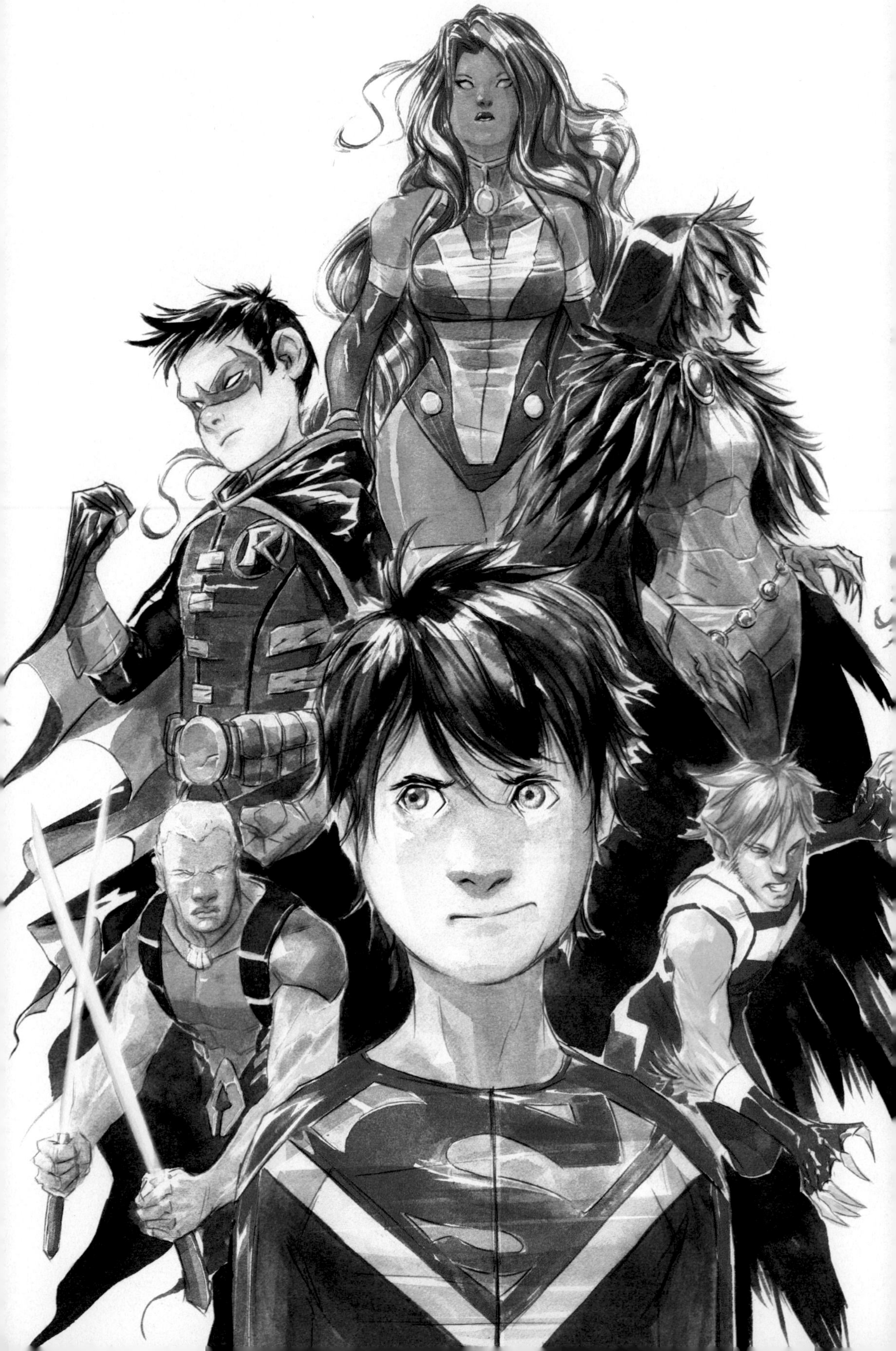

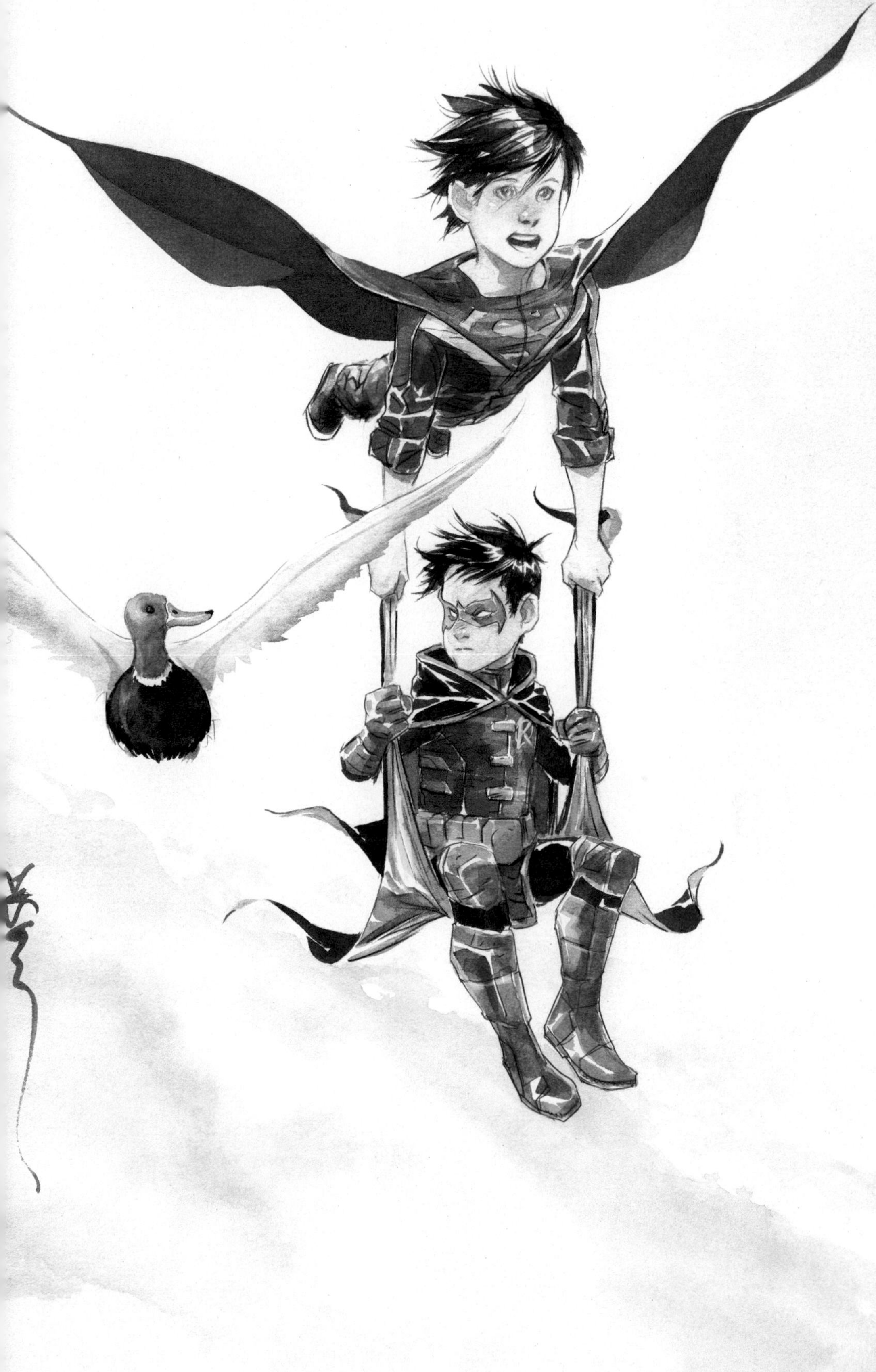

Variant cover art for SUPER SONS #7
by DUSTIN NGUYEN

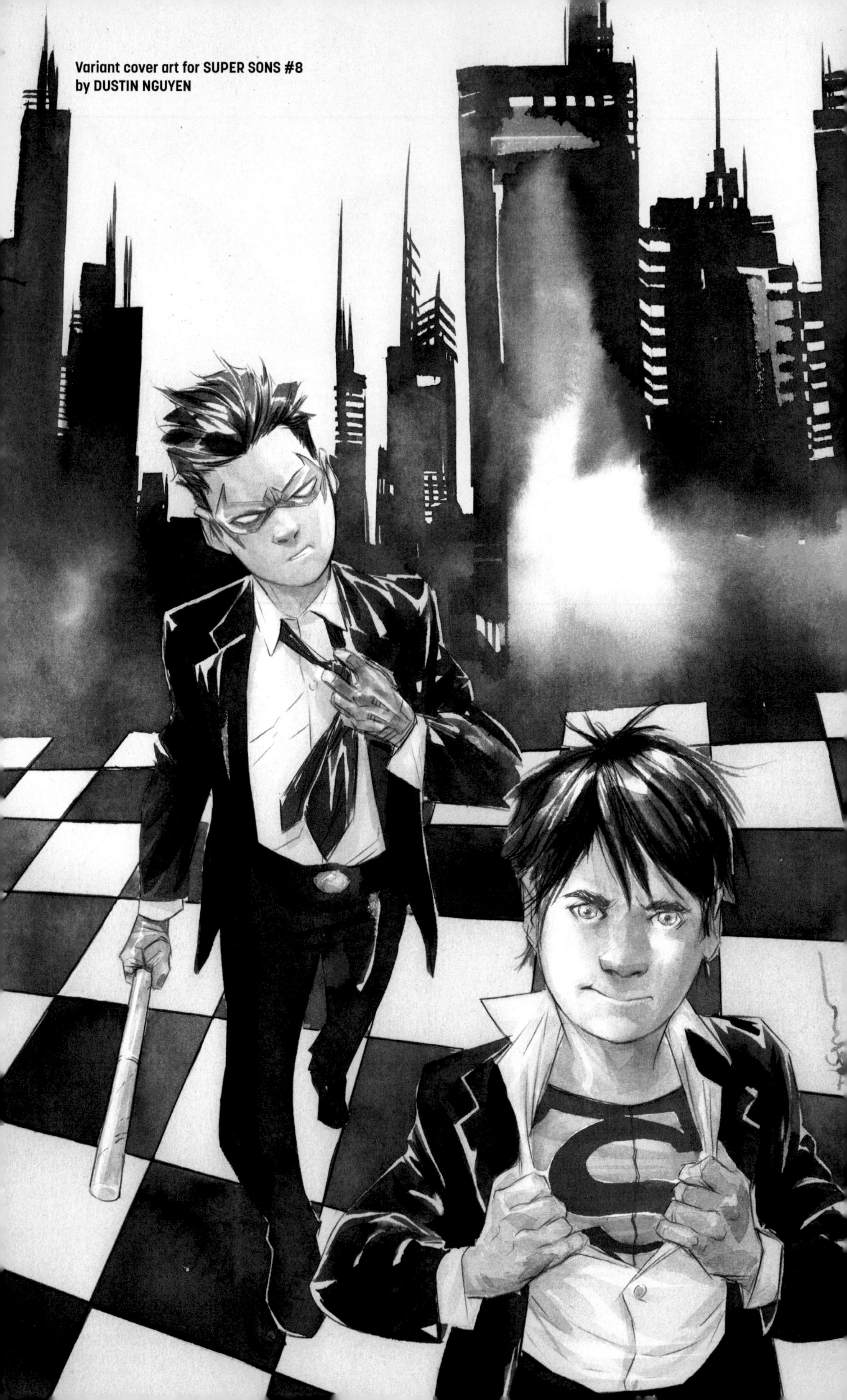

Variant cover art for SUPER SONS #8
by DUSTIN NGUYEN

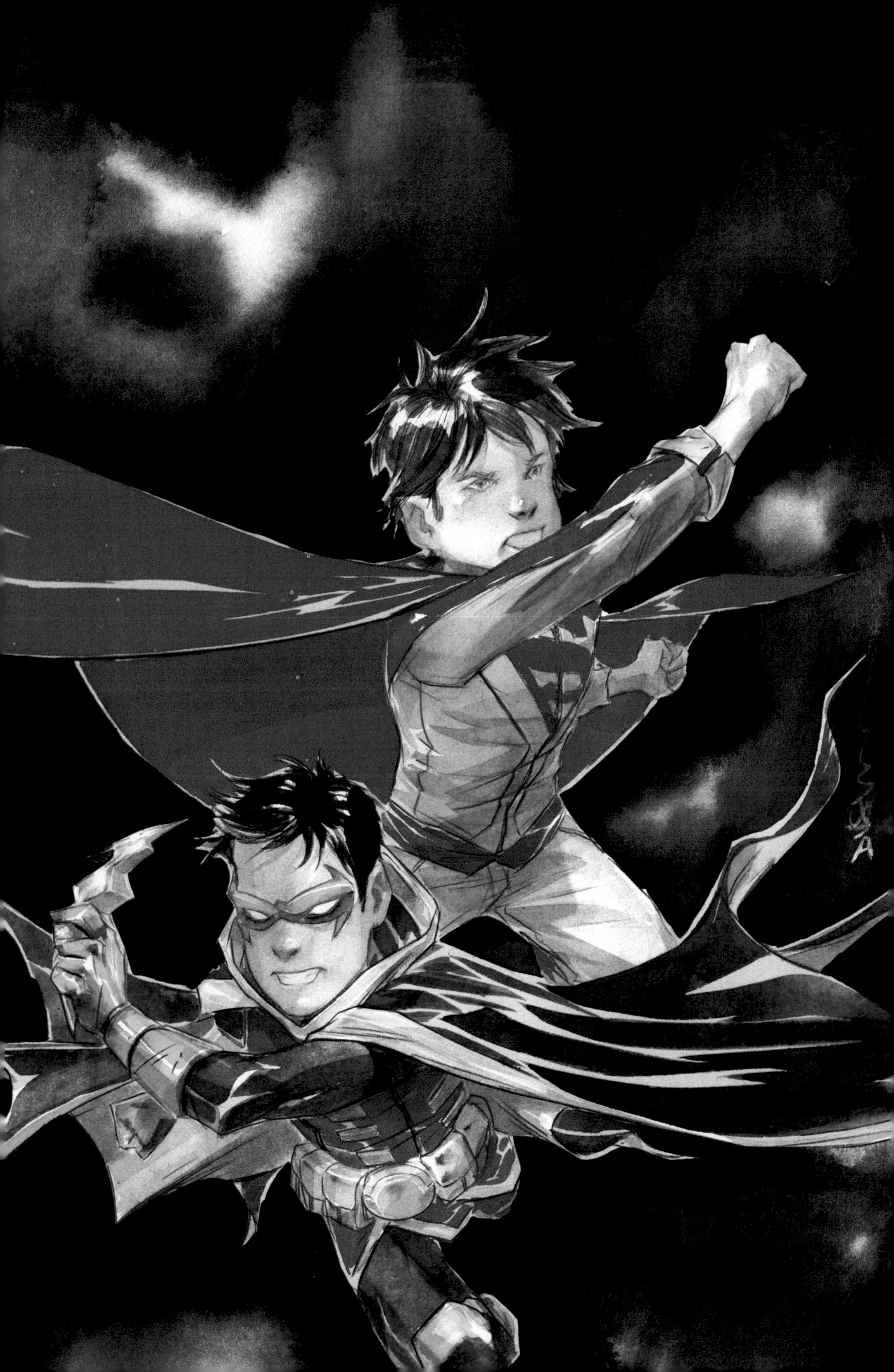

Variant cover art for SUPER SONS #9
by DUSTIN NGUYEN

Variant cover art for SUPER SONS #10
by DUSTIN NGUYEN

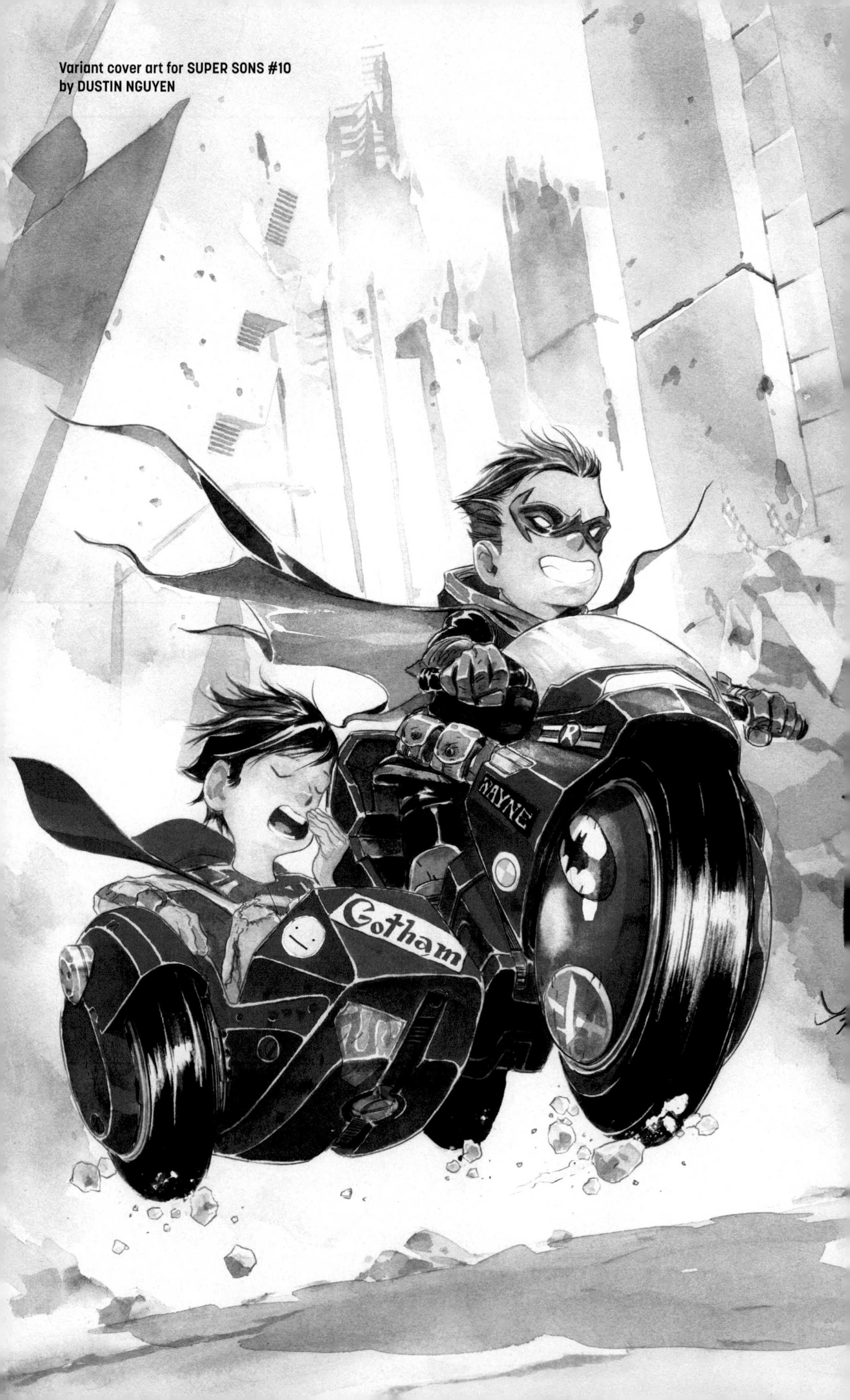

ALIEN DESIGN
BY JORGE JIMENEZ

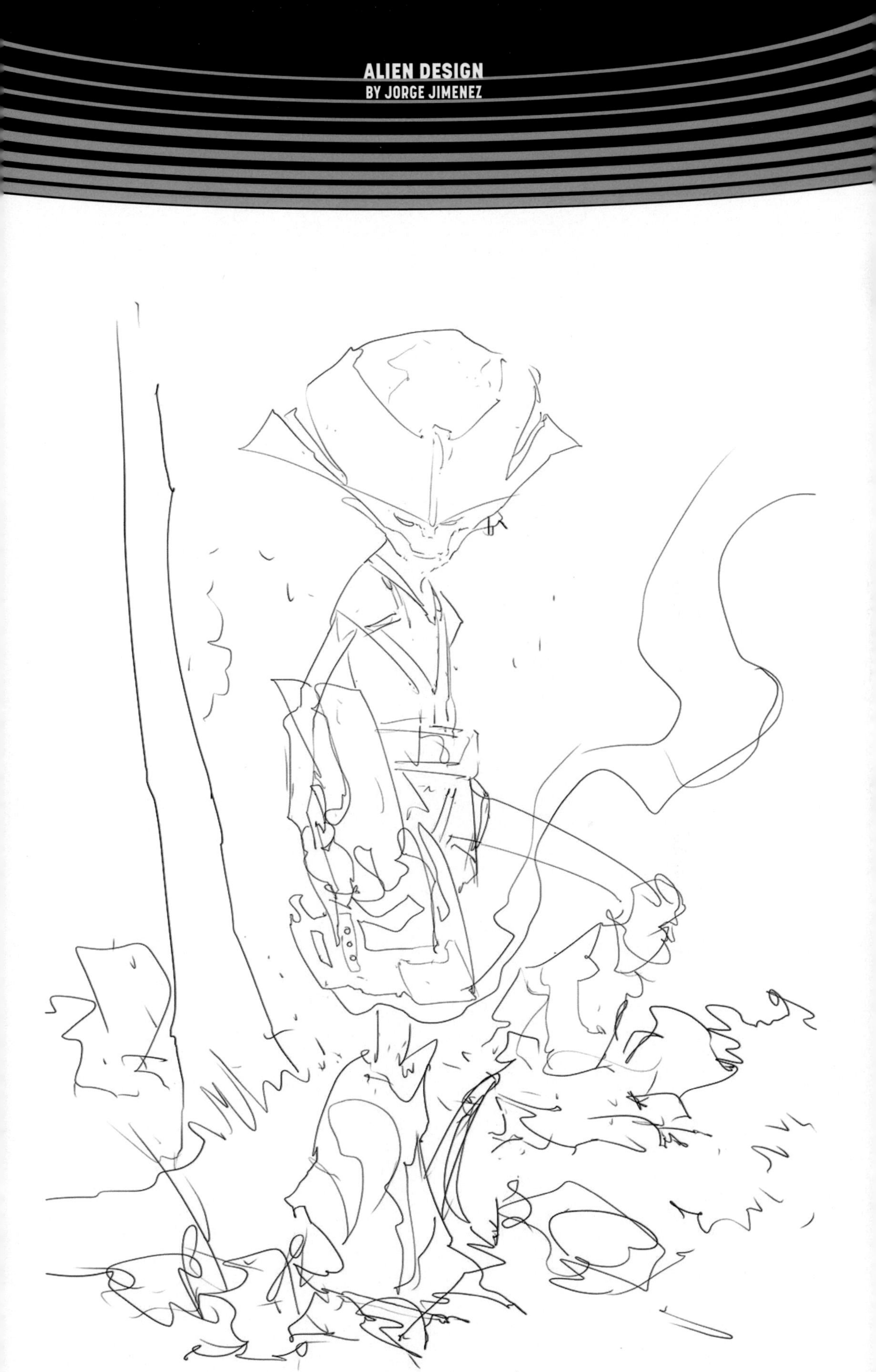

SUPER SONS #6 COVER SKETCHES
BY JORGE JIMENEZ

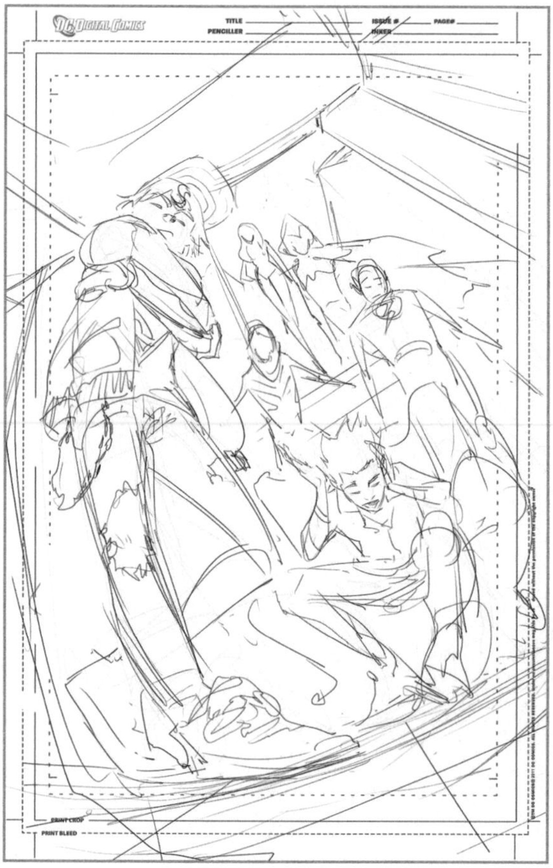
DC DIGITAL COMICS
TITLE
PENCILLER
ISSUE #
INKER
PAGE#
PRINT CROP
PRINT BLEED

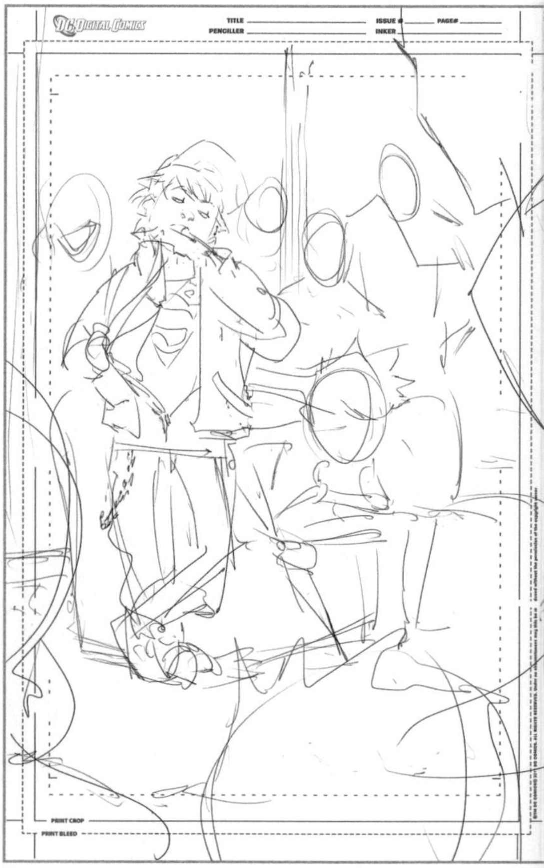
DC DIGITAL COMICS
TITLE
PENCILLER
ISSUE #
INKER
PAGE#
PRINT CROP
PRINT BLEED

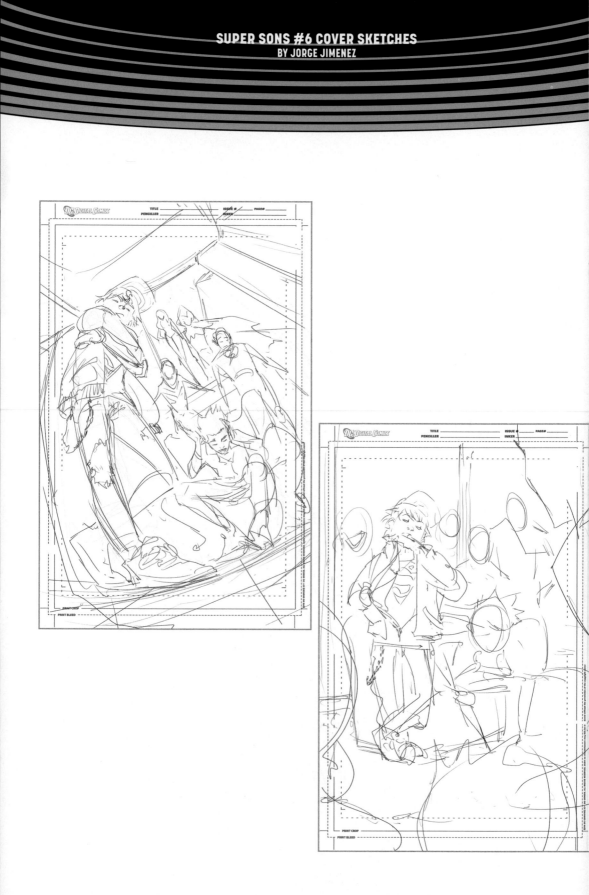

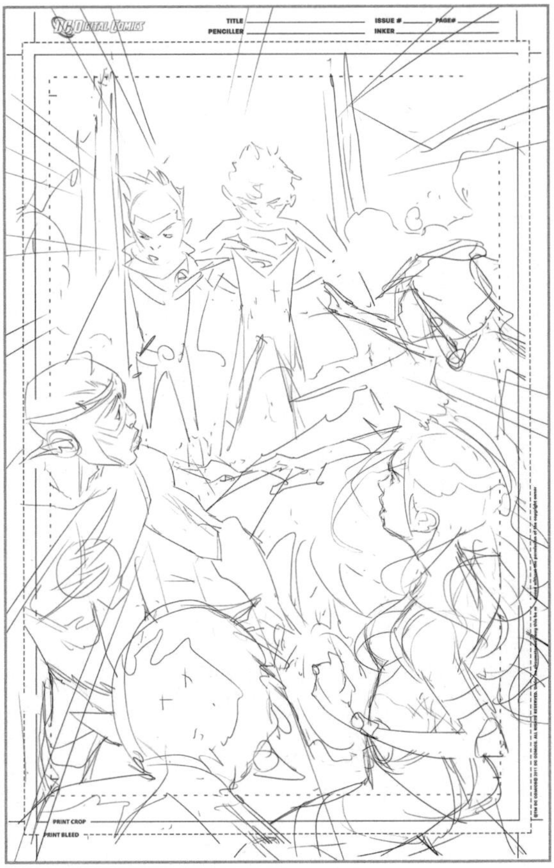
TITLE
PENCILLER
ISSUE #
PAGE#
INKER
PRINT CROP
PRINT BLEED

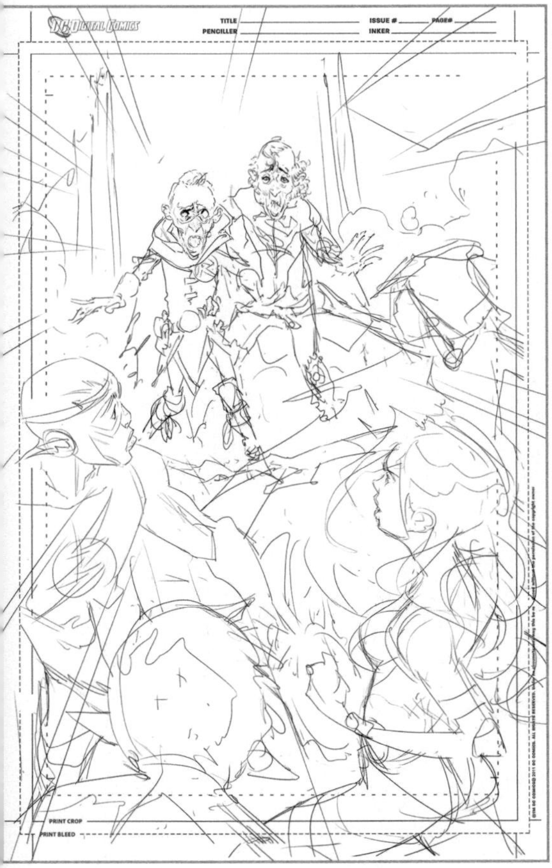
TITLE
PENCILLER
ISSUE #
PAGE#
INKER
PRINT CROP
PRINT BLEED

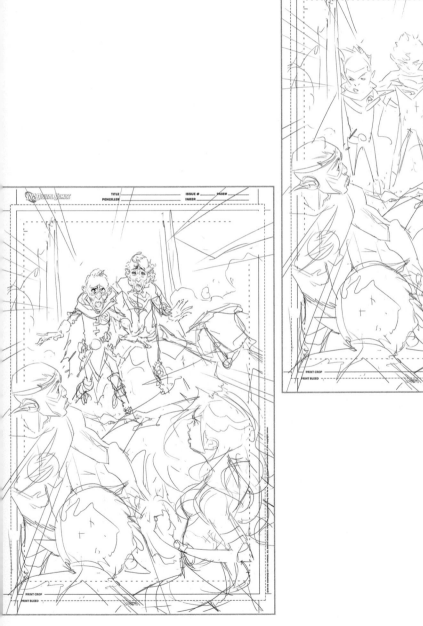

SUPER SONS #7 COVER SKETCH
BY JORGE JIMENEZ

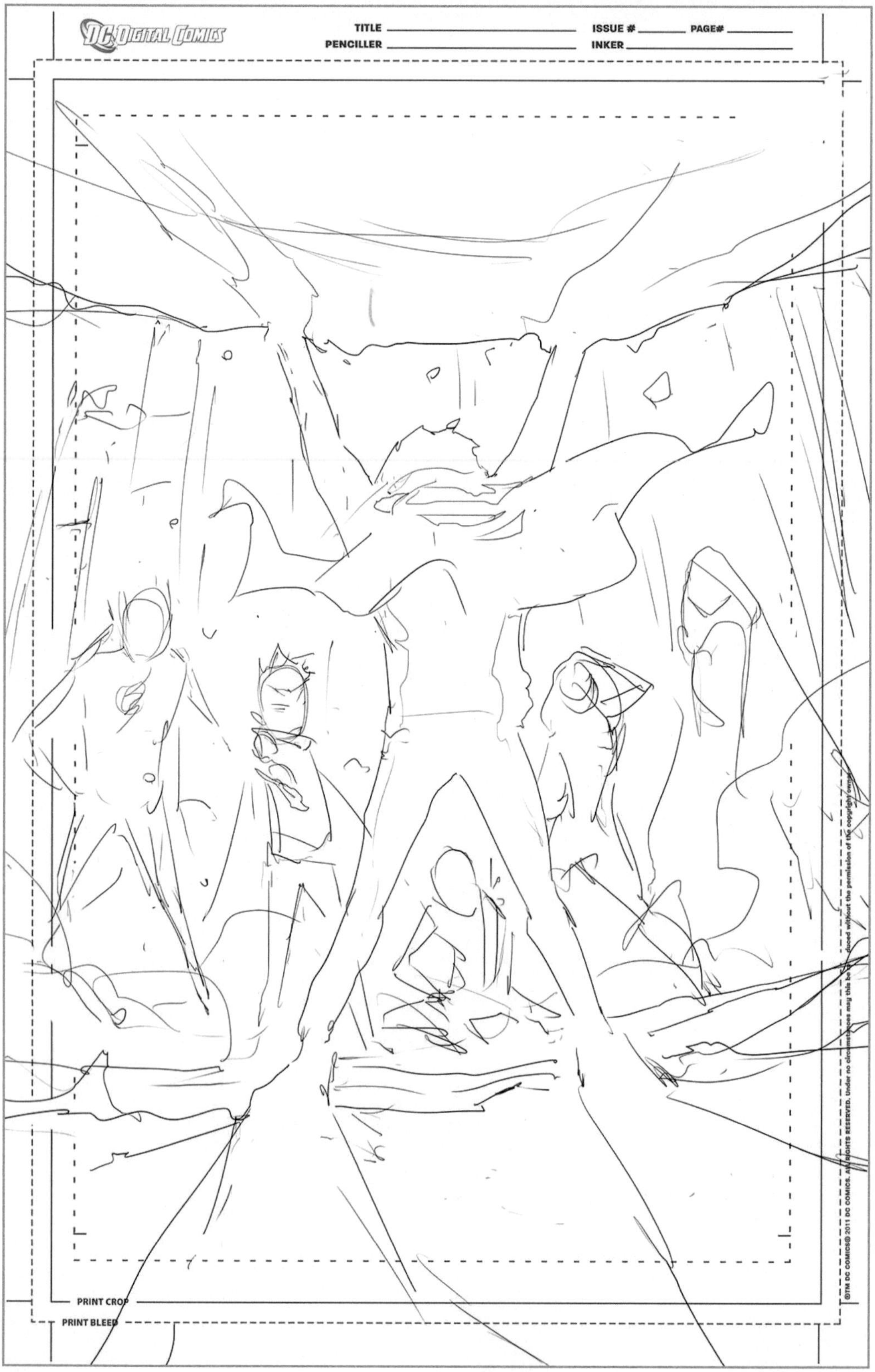
DC DIGITAL COMICS
TITLE
ISSUE #
PAGE#
PENCILLER
INKER
PRINT CROP
PRINT BLEED

SUPER SONS #8 COVER SKETCHES

BY JORGE JIMENEZ

ALIEN VEGETATION
Town
Celestial hole opening devic
space ships

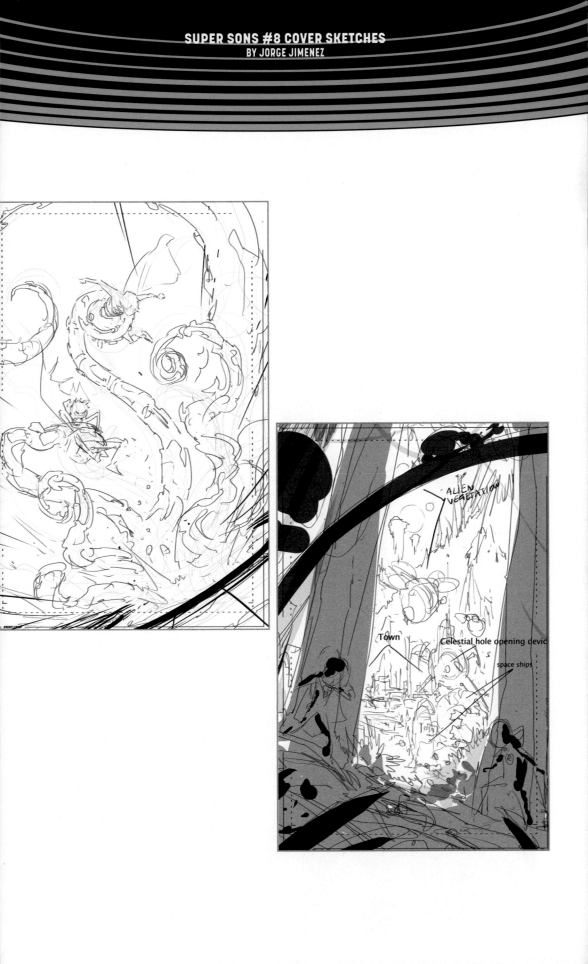

SUPER SONS #9 COVER SKETCHES
BY JORGE JIMENEZ

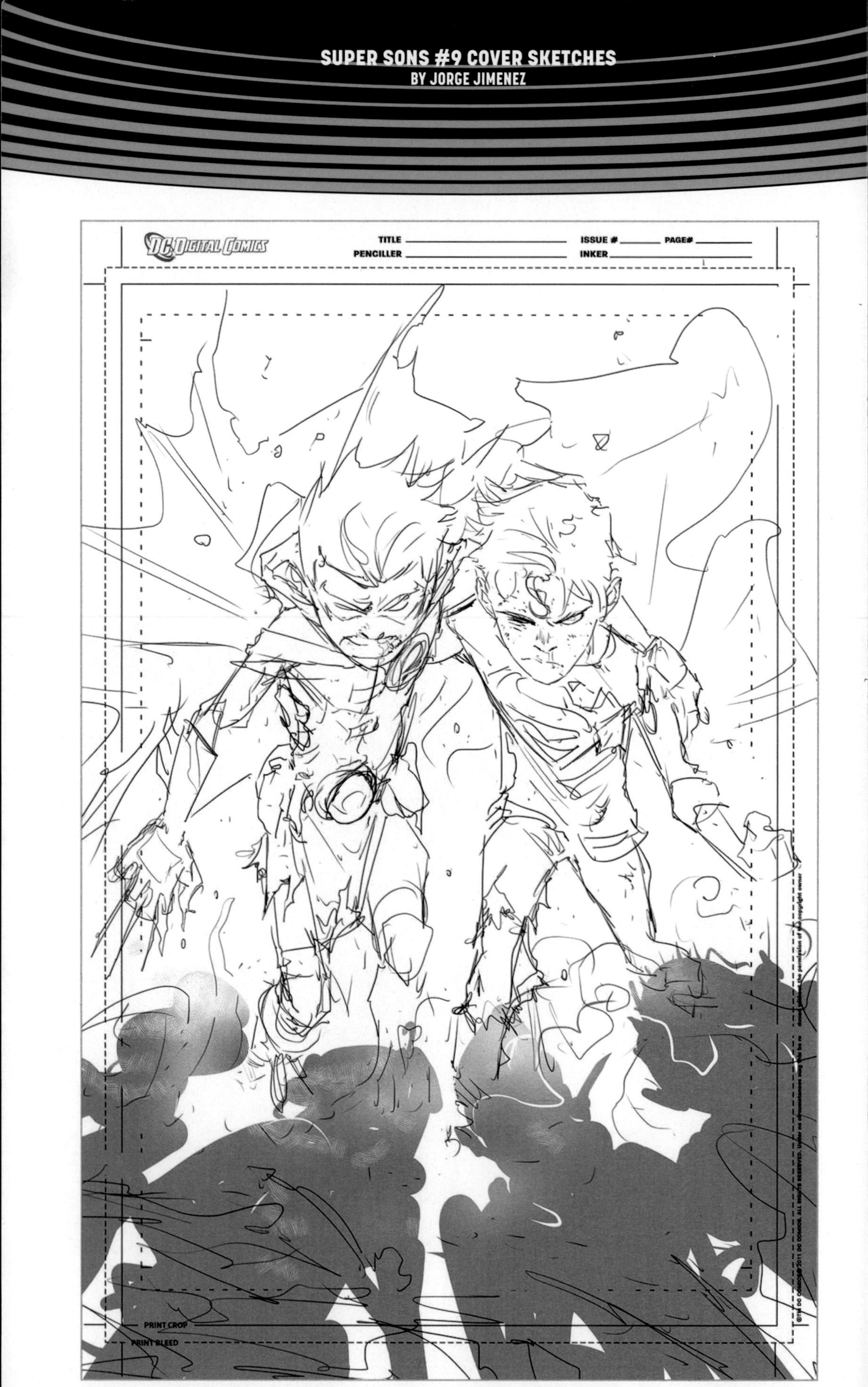
TITLE
ISSUE #
PAGE#
PENCILLER
INKER
PRINT CROP
PRINT BLEED

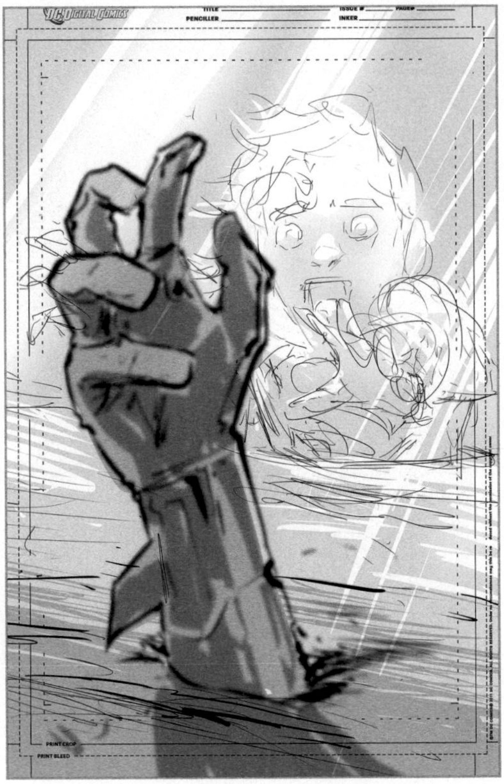
DC DIGITAL COMICS
TITLE
PENCILLER
ISSUE #
PAGE#
INKER
PRINT CROP
PRINT BLEED

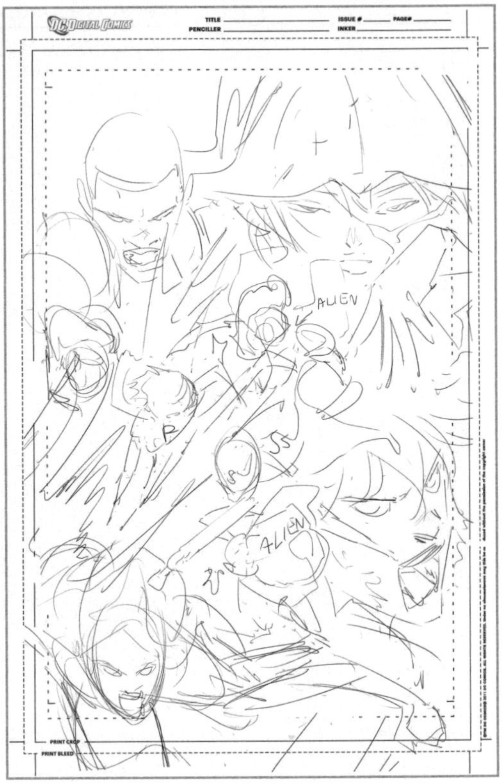
DC DIGITAL COMICS
TITLE
PENCILLER
ISSUE #
PAGE#
INKER
ALIEN
ALIEN
PRINT CROP
PRINT BLEED

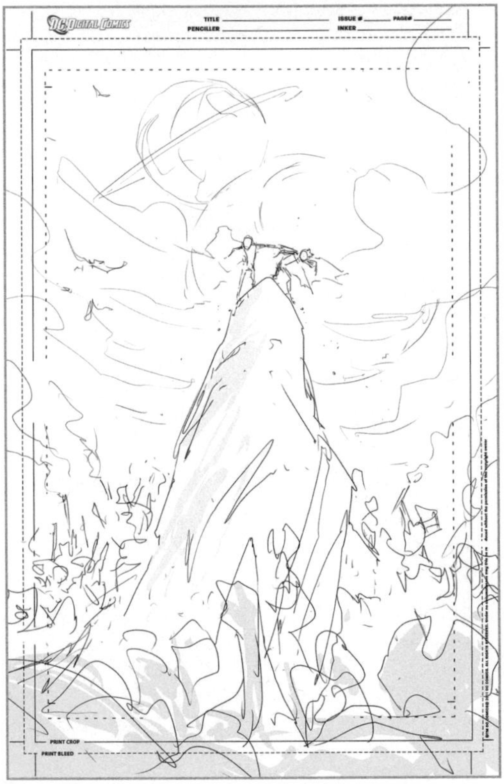
DC DIGITAL COMICS
TITLE
PENCILLER
ISSUE #
PAGE#
INKER
PRINT CROP
PRINT BLEED

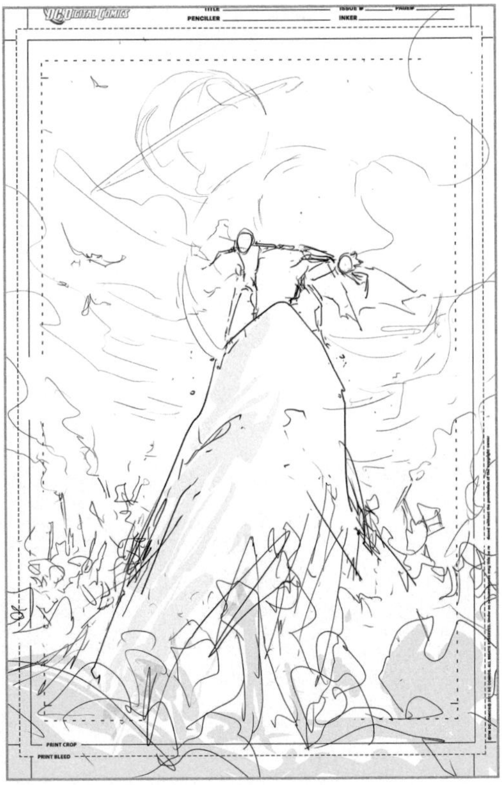
DC DIGITAL COMICS
TITLE
PENCILLER
ISSUE #
PAGE#
INKER
PRINT CROP
PRINT BLEED

SUPER SONS #10 COVER SKETCHES
BY JORGE JIMENEZ

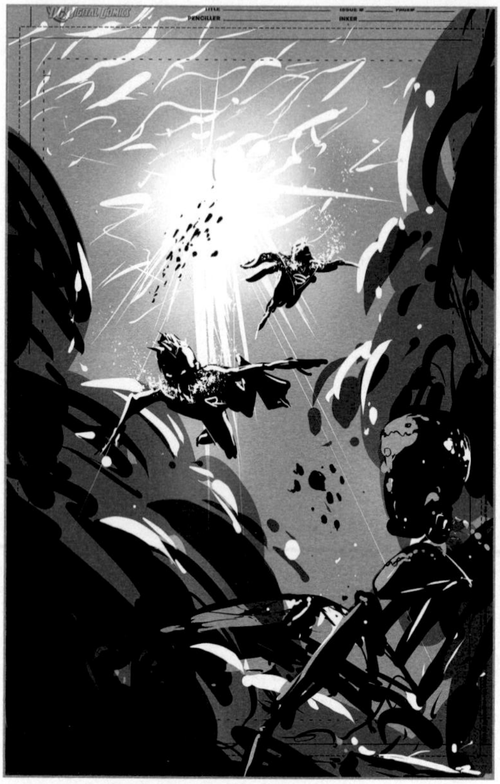

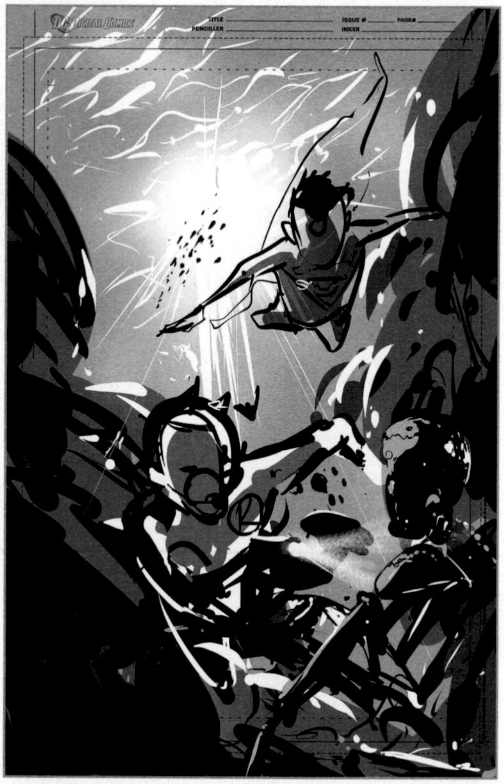

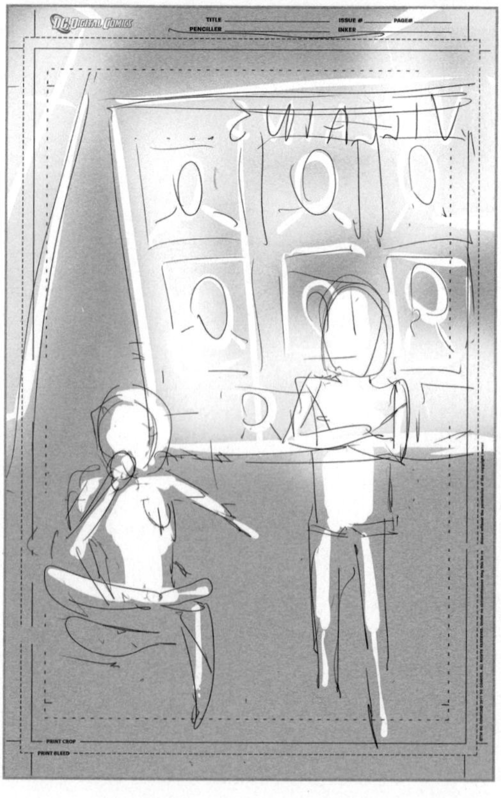

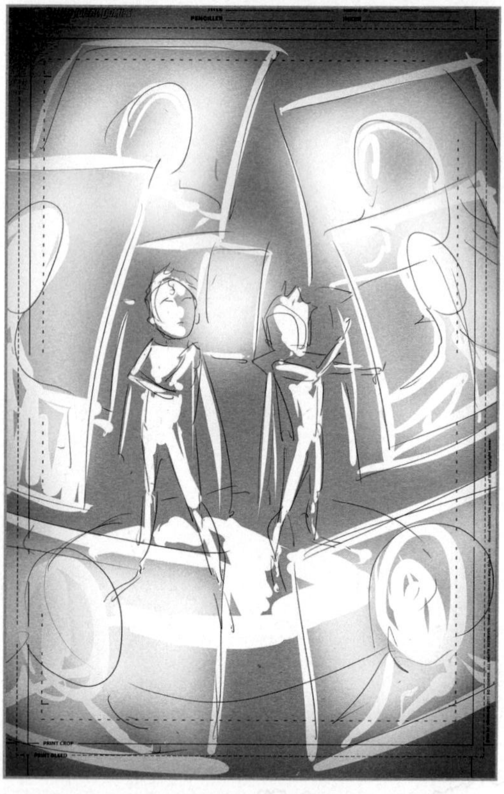

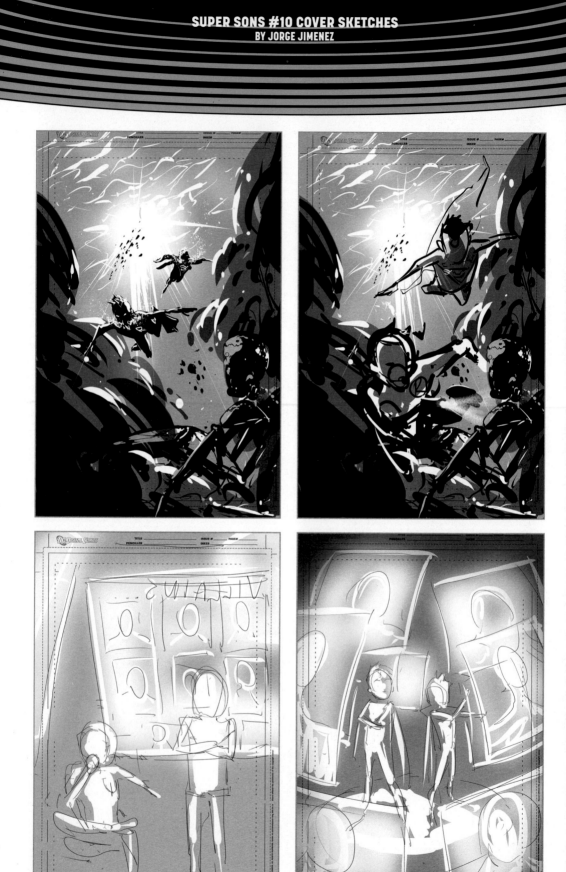